ANTI-PIKETTY

Capital for the 21st Century

ANTI-PIKETTY

Capital for the 21st Century

EDITED BY

JEAN-PHILIPPE DELSOL,

NICOLAS LECAUSSIN, AND

EMMANUEL MARTIN

CATO INSTITUTE
WASHINGTON, D.C.

eBook ISBN: 978-1-944424-26-8
Print ISBN: 978-1-944424-25-1

Library of Congress Cataloging-in-Publication Data available.

Originally published in France © 2015 by Libréchange, 16, rue Pastorelli, 06000 Nice.
ISBN: 979-10-93166-06-3
Original articles in French translated by Emmanuel Martin.

Cover design: Jon Meyers.

Printed in the United States of America.

Cato Institute
1000 Massachusetts Ave., N.W.
Washington, D.C. 20001
www.cato.org

Contents

List of Figures and Tables

Foreword

Tom G. Palmer

Thomas Piketty has written a big book. A very big book. I know because I read it. I read it because so many people had cited it to me, and after asking them I found that not one of them had read it, so I thought I should do them the favor of trudging through it to find out what it said. It didn't help, though; even after I had read it, I still couldn't find anyone citing it as evidence of the horrors of capitalism who had read it or was even able to state what Piketty's main thesis was, other than that inequality of something is bad and that that bad inequality is sure to get worse unless we do something to stop it. I do hope the book looks good on their coffee tables, though. And at least I had an opportunity to see a skillful rhetorician of socialism at work.

Few people will actually read the book and, honestly, I would not wish that burden on many. (Ok, maybe some.) Fortunately, three scholars—Jean-Philippe Delsol, Nicolas Lecaussin, and Emmanuel Martin, who hail from the country where the book seems to have gotten the most tepid reception—have assembled a group of scholars to explain Piketty's ideas fairly and to do him and us the favor of thinking seriously about them. They've provided an important service. Their excellent collection, *Anti-Piketty*, also gave me the opportunity to put to good use my own copy of *Capital in the 21st Century*, by checking the most important quotes and tables and their contexts. They check out. And as a bonus, to do so, I carried all 685 pages of *Capital in the 21st Century* on the road to visit my family in rural northeast Thailand near the border with Laos, which provided an excellent venue to think about inequality in a global context and to witness the results of plummeting global inequality of income, wealth, and consumption.

The delightful thing about *Capital in the 21st Century* (and the book does contain some delights, literary and otherwise) is that there is so much to criticize. I'm not a statistician, but I enjoyed trying to follow the leaps of logic (and especially the leaps over gigantic gaps in data, which Piketty sometimes helpfully fills in without informing us that he just made the numbers up). If you like card tricks, you should enjoy the treatments in Part 2 of *Anti-Piketty*, in which a great deal of sleight-of-hand is revealed. Reading those chapters was as enjoyable as watching a professional magician show how someone else had tricked you.

In the process of criticizing Piketty's big book, *Anti-Piketty* provides the reader with a readable and fresh introduction to important topics in economics, history, and statistics. This is a book for reading, and not merely for displaying on the coffee table.

I honestly enjoyed *Capital in the 21st Century*. I started enjoying the book shortly after opening it—on page 6 (Piketty 2014), to be precise, when Professor Piketty described "the mechanism of supply and demand":

> If the supply of any good is insufficient, and its price is too high, then demand for that good should decrease, which should lead to a decline in its price.

Confusing a shift in the demand curve with movement *along* the demand curve was an interesting start to a treatise on economics. It reminded me of my freshman microeconomics course, in which the professor drilled us over and over again on the importance of not confusing the two. But that was just the enticement to read further, for what followed was a *tour de force* of very weak economics and sophistical argumentation. (I was worried that the statement reflected so poorly on Piketty's grasp of fundamental economics that I checked the French, just in case the translator had garbled Piketty's text. In fact, the French was even less coherent, so the translator apparently did M. Piketty a favor by trying to introduce some clarity: "Certes, il existe en principe un mécanisme économique fort simple permettant d'équilibrer le processus: le jeu de l'offre et de la demande. Si un bien est en offre insuffisante et si son prix est trop élevé, alors la demande pour ce bien doit baisser, ce qui permettra de calmer le jeu." [Piketty 2013, 23])

Since the authors in *Anti-Piketty* do such a fine job of dealing with Piketty's sometimes head-scratchingly strange moves, I'll just note one of my favorites, namely, his argument for excluding from the capital stock almost all the capital I have, which is my modest human capital, for the accumulation of which I invested years of schooling, foregone income, tuition fees, and more. Piketty claims that there are "many reasons for excluding human capital from our definition of capital," but the only one he advances is that "human capital cannot be owned by another person or traded on a market (not permanently, at any rate)" (Piketty 2014, 46). That's an interesting stipulation. Human capital is something in which people invest heavily (look at all the time and money invested in schooling, training, and the like; I didn't go to school all those years just for the fun of it) and it yields a measurable income stream. So why does Piketty exclude it from his definition of capital? Well, because if you think that human capital is important to include in the capital stock, you must be a very, very wicked person because you are an advocate of slavery! According to Piketty, "Attributing a monetary value to the stock of human capital makes sense only in societies where it is actually possible to own other individuals fully and entirely—societies that at first sight have definitively ceased to exist" (Piketty 2014, 63). And there you have it! Any numbers that might undermine Piketty's narrative about an allegedly inexorably growing share of national income going to "capital"—and including human capital would effectively knock his case off the coffee table—can be dismissed because trying to measure human capital is tantamount to advocating slavery. All those economic statisticians who try to decide whether to use the cost-based approach or the lifetime income-based approach to measuring human capital, which would threaten Piketty's entire thesis, are really just trying to reinstitute chattel slavery. Touché! Take that, bad people!

This book could have been so much longer, rather like *Capital in the 21st Century* itself. There are plenty of other writings that the editors might have included, including Deirdre McCloskey's body slam (cited in *Anti-Piketty*), Carlos Góes's study (Góes 2016) of the "drivers of income inequality" (which concluded that "there is little more than some apparent correlations the reader can eyeball in charts containing very aggregated multi-decennial averages"), and others. Of course, the readers can find those easily enough online. Readers could even read Piketty's own walk-back of his argument in the *American Economic Review*, which provides a charming rebuttal to his own work.

In *Capital in the 21st Century*, Piketty caught the attention of all those who looked at the first page with an eye-popping assertion:

> When the rate of return on capital exceeds the rate of growth of output and income, as it did in the nineteenth century and seems quite likely to do again in the twenty-first, capitalism automatically generates arbitrary and unsustainable inequalities that radically undermine the meritocratic values on which democratic societies are based (Piketty 2014, 1).

That inequality is the heart of Piketty's whole book and the reason so many people bought so many copies and read so few pages. In Piketty's breathless words,

> The fundamental inequality, which I will write as $r > g$ (where r stands for the average annual rate of return on

> capital, including profits, dividends, interest, rents, and other income from capital, expressed as a percentage of its total value, and g stands for the rate of growth of the economy, that is, the annual increase in income or output), will play a crucial role in this book. In a sense, it sums up the overall logic of my conclusions (Piketty 2014, 25).

Wow!

Within a year, that claim was, shall we say, modified.

> I do not view $r > g$ as the only or even the primary tool for considering changes in income and wealth in the twentieth century, or for forecasting the path of inequality in the twenty-first century. Institutional changes and political shocks—which to a large extent can be viewed as endogenous to the inequality and development process itself—played a major role in the past, and it will probably be the same in the future (Piketty 2015, 48).

Well.

That walk-back from the thesis of "capital" inevitably dominating labor was accompanied by a pivot to the rather less thrillingly grand topic of the determinants of "labor income inequality in recent decades." In a rather short time, Thomas Piketty's hefty *Capital in the 21st Century* shrank in his own hands into a substantially more modest, albeit still interesting, research thesis.

Although Piketty walked back his main thesis, the number of readers *aware* of that (*a*) is likely to be greatly exceeded by the number of those who *remember* (*r*) that a big, big book proved that inequality of something is bad and that that bad inequality is sure to get worse unless we do something to stop it, or, in short, that $r > a$. And that just won't do, which is yet another reason that I hope *Anti-Piketty* gets a very wide reading.

The thesis of *Capital in the 21st Century* has been quietly withdrawn by the author, but the topic of inequality remains an important one. I spend much of my time in countries with weak rule of law and lots of state interventionism and, consequently, with both low average incomes and huge gaps between the powerful and the rest of the population. In those countries, it's often the case that those with the greatest wealth acquired it, not by creating value for others, but by getting special favors from their friends in the state apparatus, by taking bread from the poor in the form of subsidies, and generally by being scoundrels. It's called cronyism, or, for Professor Piketty, le capitalisme de copinage. And I've devoted decades of my life to replacing it by le libre marché, also known as le système d'échange libre. I work with those who focus their attention on the inequalities that matter, such as unequal access to the judicial system, unequal treatment by the state, and inequality of rights generally. Focusing on the inequalities that matter turns out to be the best way to address the other inequalities, as well. So let's not give up on the theme of inequality just because of the failures of one book.

Tom G. Palmer
Ubon Ratchathani, Thailand

Tom G. Palmer is a senior fellow at the Cato Institute. He holds the George M. Yeager Chair for Advancing Liberty at and is executive vice president of the Atlas Network, a global network of classical liberal think tanks.

Góes, Carlos. 2016. "Testing Piketty's Hypothesis on the Drivers of Income Inequality: Evidence from Panel VARs with Heterogeneous Dynamics." IMF Working Paper WP/16/160.

McCloskey, Deirdre. 2014. "Measured, Unmeasured, Mismeasured, and Unjustified Pessimism: A Review Essay of Thomas Piketty's *Capital in the 21st Century.*" *Erasmus Journal for Philosophy and Economics* 7 (2): 73–115.

Piketty, Thomas. 2013. *Le Capital au XXIe Siècle.* Paris: Éditions du Seuil.

———. 2014. *Capital in the 21st Century.* Cambridge, MA: Belknap Press.

———. 2015. "About *Capital in the Twenty-First Century.*" *American Economic Review* 105 (5): 48–53.

Introduction

Jean-Philippe Delsol and Emmanuel Martin

Should one write a book opposing the ideas of another? It would be preferable, and more positive, to set out one's own vision of society and the economy and let history deliver its verdict on Thomas Piketty's *Capital in the 21st Century*, a book that made the news and opened a broad debate. However, even if we think that the book became, largely, a sort of fad (as demonstrated by a reading rate inversely proportional to its sales),[1] it did garner numerous criticisms. We thought it essential to permit readers who are interested to access those criticisms—which were growing, but in a dispersed fashion. It seemed necessary not to let Piketty's ideology prosper without opposing it with academic critiques that undo his thesis. Otherwise, his thesis might continue to benefit from a scientific aura to which, as we will show, it should not aspire. The power of ideas should never be overlooked. Words are weapons and can cause plenty of damage. It was thus crucial not to let Piketty's "bad" words grow like weeds.

Piketty received favorable accolades from a left in need of new references, enabling the left to persist in its errors since communism collapsed and socialism failed everywhere. His book offered the left something it had been waiting for—a new scientific materialism after the ideas of Karl Marx went bankrupt. However, Piketty shares the same quirk—a one-dimensional model—which is always dangerous because it is partial and biased. History cannot be squeezed into just one formula or one idea, even if the idea is genius. Society is infinitely complex; it is continuously creative and escapes all categories in which ideologues want to imprison it. Similarly, economics cannot be entirely explained by algebra.

Economics remains a social science, made up of stories and histories and unexpected developments, as well as of rules—useful and yet never certain because man is always capable of surprises.

Thomas Piketty accumulated data to construct the theory he wanted to write. When the statistics were missing, he invented them. He redid Marx—something to which his title launches a mischievous wink. But from Marx he should have remembered that "history always repeats itself: the first time as tragedy, the second time as farce" (Marx [1885] 1954, 10). Let us hope that his work becomes little more than a passing farce, quickly forgotten, rather than a new tragedy along the lines of those that communism inflicted on the world, from the gulags to the laogai. Under the pretext of academic analysis, Piketty advances his belief that we need to equalize men, to even out wealth, so that everyone lives as "equals," regardless of whether doing so will make us all poorer. We would undoubtedly become poorer, as experience has shown. But ideologues like Piketty do not care: they want to construct a perfect world and are ready to destroy the real world to follow their dream.

Piketty had already hoped for a tax revolution in a book that undoubtedly influenced the French presidential campaign of 2012 (Landais, Piketty, and Saez 2011). He proposed to tax all income at 60 percent at the first euro for people earning above €100,000 a month. In *Capitalism in the 21st Century*, he gives a wealth of data and concludes that we must tax the rich until they are not rich anymore. It looks like an obsession.

Thomas Piketty's Theory

What is Piketty's theory? It is that of the return of a catastrophic 19th-century capitalism à la Balzac or Dickens, characterized by glaring inequality and the upsurge of a rich dynastic minority living off its capital, whose growth knows a rhythm far superior to that of the growth of the economy. This is the now famous formula: $r > g$ (the fundamental inequality), in which r represents the return on capital and g the rate of economic growth. The formula implies a cumulative spiral, enriching owners of capital in the medium and long term and giving them an increasingly disproportionate share of national income, at the expense of labor.

The figures and curves Piketty presents show the opposite trend in the 20th century as inequality declined. However, that was only a brief, happy interlude amid the long increase of inequality in the capitalist system. The interlude was essentially due to two world wars and to communist regimes that destroyed or collectivized much of the capital stock, thus slowing the mad rush of returns. According to Piketty, since the 1970s, the share of capital in national income has come back and risen. In addition, given that economic growth would henceforth be more modest, the gap between the return on capital and the rate of global economic growth would increase, foreshadowing an ominous 21st century.

All of that would be dangerous not only in terms of inequality, which is widening with the return of a society of heirs and rentiers, but also for democracy, which is at risk of turning into a plutocracy; the economic power of the extremely rich means they could easily control politics. According to Piketty, mechanisms should be put in place that mimic the *effect* of the world wars and destructive totalitarianism but, of course, in a peaceful and democratic manner. He means, essentially, tax mechanisms. They consist of, on the one hand, a steep increase in income taxes on the very rich, with a marginal top rate culminating at 80 percent and, on the other hand, a global wealth tax, up to 5 percent or 10 percent (although the latter, as the author admits, may seem utopian).

A Book "Based on Facts"?

Piketty's thesis is intended to be indisputable. It claims to rest on a gigantic gathering of statistics on incomes and wealth: the "facts" cannot lie; thus the book cannot be wrong. Piketty wants to distance himself from the abstractions of contemporary economics. Indeed, the discipline is generally mathematically formalized, which renders it very dry but often also too remote from reality. His theory is simply stated. It can be summed up as a "fundamental" inequality (between *r*, the return on capital, and *g*, the rate of economic growth). Piketty tells us this inequality perfectly sticks to history, and his book has curves and graphs to confirm it.

The simplicity of the central thesis of the book constitutes a powerful sales point. The "U curve," which describes the return of rentier capitalism, can be understood by the average citizen who never took a course in economics. That simplicity—some would call it "simplistic"—represents an essential strength for the message to be understood, defended, shared, and spread. It is a fundamental virtue to break into the marketplace of ideas. Simplicity in itself is a form of aesthetics, which can take on an almost religious dimension: fundamental inequality is the original sin of capitalism. But we know that simplicity is also the weapon of populists who hammer away at slogans by way of explanation.

Simplicity is also found in the grand (preferably apocalyptic) predictions of the book: inequality will explode, generating a "potentially terrifying" situation in which "the past devours the future" (Piketty 2014, 571). Such predictions are nothing new, really. Merchants of doom have always thrived. However, were Thomas Malthus, David Ricardo, and Marx right? Despite the failed predictions of these men, the public seems to love the grand historicist theories with their visceral pessimism. Of course, we are living in times of pessimism, and the book follows the trend.

Denouncing the rich—who supposedly enrich themselves on the backs of workers—combines a subtle mix: a response to envy on the one hand and a need to do good when faced with injustice and frustration on the other hand. This strategy always works better if the actual context is that of a never-ending crisis, generating a variety of frustrations. Thus, even if the crisis is due in large part to public policies that encouraged subprime mortgages and created an artificial boom through below-market interest rates and to clumsy interventionism, the general public sees only the guilt of the finance world. Finance equals rich. Such a shortcut is easy, and resentment easily feeds on it.

Alluding to Marx in the title of the book with the word "capital" and offering an alternative version of the thesis of the reproduction of the elites a half century after Pierre Bourdieu gives a "class struggle 3.0" dimension to the work. This concept sells well, primarily because there is a revolutionary background to it—even if here Piketty's proposition is to avoid a violent revolution. What he proposes in reality is "Revolution in the 21st Century."

A "Useful" Theory?

The concept also works because our politics seem to have fallen long ago into an astonishing intellectual vacuum. The democratic competition for votes has narrowed the possible spectrum of positions of the major parties. Politics is almost no longer made along *grand principles* but only according to shortsighted electioneering. Abstention levels in many countries are not, from this point of view, surprising. Politics no longer responds to our "doctrinal need," as economist Daniel Villey once described it, a need that makes us always look for "overarching systems" to understand the world (Villey 1967). Piketty fills this void, badly but better than the rest. He has not truly founded a doctrine because his analysis is actually fragmented. But his thesis is altogether radical, while remaining under the cozy umbrella of democracy, helping to bring a kind of "principle" to the thinking of the left and to assist in its doctrinal "reconstruction." Some on the left find this refreshing, or at least reassuring. As sociologist Raymond Boudon would say, Thomas Piketty proposes a "useful" theory (Boudon 2004, 158).

Moreover, Piketty's economics book also claims to be a scholarly work. It includes references to history and to literature to illustrate the main point. It incorporates authors of our (rebellious?)

adolescence such as Honoré de Balzac or Jane Austen. The intention of not developing a treatise of pure economics adds to the didactic side of the work. Such a treatise would have been off-putting; instead he has written a storybook, which takes the reader by the hand through various demonstrations.

Although the book feeds the debate on inequality, its radical tax prescriptions would be hard to impose in the United States. Even socialist France has come to understand the negative real-world effects that such theories can generate: François Hollande's 75 percent tax, which was strongly inspired by Piketty, had to be discreetly but quickly scrapped. The convergence between labor and capital taxation, defended by Hollande for a time, also proved negative and had to be put aside by the French government. The French socialist government eventually had to turn to the supply side, realizing that without capital, there is no employment. Times are changing: the French government now "loves businesses."

Why This Book?

In the meantime, Piketty's book unleashed critics. In France, some negative reviews emerged as soon as the book was released. For example, historian Nicolas Baverez saw in the book what he labeled a "sub-prefecture Marxism" (Baverez 2013). Now, given time to digest the book, many critics have developed on both its theoretical background and empirical work. The size of the international marketplace of ideas has helped. Jean-Philippe Delsol of the Institute for Research in Economic and Fiscal Issues (IREF) was one of the first to offer a scathing critique of the apocalyptic prediction of rising cumulative inequalities. In May 2014, Chris Giles of the *Financial Times* attacked Piketty's supposedly undeniable statistics (Giles 2014). Everything else followed. The seeds of doubt were sewn. At the start of 2015, facing a hailstorm of criticism, even Thomas Piketty seemed to backpedal from his positions! But does the general public know?

Thus, it was important to unite in one volume the essential criticisms of Thomas Piketty's book *Capital in the 21st Century*. Given that book's global success, and especially given the proposed policies, it seemed necessary to inform the public of any defects found in the book's theory and statistics. This volume gathers together the major criticisms of not only the vision, the empirical and historical work, and the theory, but also the political recommendations of Thomas Piketty.

Indeed, the work of Thomas Piketty fits into a very particular vision, which is the subject of the first part of this volume. This vision concentrates first of all on income and wealth inequality, ignoring the reduced inequalities elsewhere. The latter include the case of the great enrichment of the large majority, which was made possible by capitalist development over two centuries and, notably, recently in developing countries. Jean-Philippe Delsol recalls the enrichment process of the masses that reduced inequality worldwide, releasing billions of people from poverty. One of the characteristics of this grand enrichment is an unprecedented decrease in inequality in access to consumption. But Piketty maintains "the class struggle software" of his great inspirer. His pessimistic vision of the economy is largely a zero-sum game: what is gained by Peter is lost by Paul, the rich oppose the poor, and social mobility plays little if any part. Likewise Piketty omits the reduction of other inequalities in access to education or longevity, the reduction of which, as demonstrated by Nicholas Eberstadt, has been crucial.

All of this helps explain Piketty's view of the rich, whom Piketty occasionally almost considers as thieves. Entrepreneurs? Risk-takers? Even if they can sometimes play those roles, in Piketty's eyes they quickly become rentiers that society needs to curb lest they turn into plutocrats. However, as Juan Ramón Rallo shows, the ranking of the Forbes 400 shows a surprising mobility. Henri Lepage then focuses on Piketty's view of managers. In fact, Piketty ignores social mobility and the porous nature of deciles. As Nicolas Lecaussin recalls it, the rich are essentially entrepreneurs who take risks: they create wealth, they don't take it. Lecaussin thus attempts to capture Piketty's anti-rich obsession: would it come from the "class interest" of a civil servant paid by taxpayers' money?

One solution to better allocate capital would be to facilitate access to capital for the poor, but oddly enough we can see that this is not an option for Piketty. This is the point for which Michael Tanner criticizes Piketty. Should the less affluent not have access to capital, in order to preserve the Marxist socioeconomic categories of the class struggle? Juan Ramón Rallo sees a fundamental theoretical contradiction in that view. Yet the most recent history of emerging countries seems to offer a scathing lie to the ultimately not-so-pro-poor vision of Piketty. This is what Álvaro Vargas Llosa recalls: the accumulation of capital, which permits development, is in fact good for the poor.

The reader will discover how the statistics, expected to be Piketty's indisputable contribution, are in reality doubtful. That is the purpose of the second part of this volume. A general rule is that the quality of statistics depends on the precautions taken to collect them. Statistics are never "raw" in the sense that some degree of selection has been made during their collection. Depending on those choices, the content of the data can vary widely. This precise problem appears throughout the work of Thomas Piketty. He measures the inequality of wealth by choosing tax returns as a main source, but doesn't take into account the evolution of tax rules, which affects these same declarations. This constitutes an important gap, which Martin Feldstein denounces. The same goes for measuring income: Piketty, for example, doesn't take into account income redistribution or the evolution of the size of households. Richard Burkhauser shows this to be problematic. Henri Lepage notes that Piketty's integration of housing in the definition of capital also will be problematic. Further, Jean-Philippe Delsol notes that the same kind of problem arises if we want to evaluate the return on capital: one ought better take the correct measurement, especially when making comparisons, not switch from one reference point to another. Thus, the neutrality of the statistics is to be taken with a pinch of salt.

Beyond the selection of certain sources of data over others, the question is raised of possible tinkering between and within the series. Several researchers have found that Piketty's empirical work is often arranged to provide proof to the idea that he absolutely wants to promote. Chris Giles summarizes the discoveries of the *Financial Times* on this issue. Malin Sahlén and Salim Furth analyze the Swedish case. Phillip W. Magness and Robert P. Murphy provide evidence of a practice that is extremely problematic from a scientific point of view: they discover that the practice not only affects the statistics but also the historical interpretations in Piketty's *Capital.*

In the third part of this book, Piketty's theory, conceptual foundations, and recommendations are closely scrutinized and strongly undermined. First, like Marx, Piketty's theoretical and predictive framework is founded in a very narrow determinism that does not take into account the crucial role of institutional context to grasp the social and economic evolution. Daron Acemoglu and James A. Robinson make this point. Then they deliver a fatal blow to *Capital in the 21st Century*'s supposed strength: its thesis is not empirically valid. Also, Piketty practically ignores the teachings of microeconomics. His concepts of wealth or capital and performance, notably in a context of risk, are, as Donald J. Boudreaux and Randall Holcombe analyze them, based on a major misunderstanding. And Piketty's theory leaves aside a major source of inequality: government itself, as Jeffrey Miron shows. Moreover, the fundamental inequality, $r > g$, which constitutes the heart of Piketty's theory, is given a hyperbolic role to create the divergence mechanism. This is what Hans-Werner Sinn denounces. Henri Lepage recalls how Piketty's theory is founded on an auxiliary hypothesis that proves to be very controversial. Finally, as shown by Jean-Philippe Delsol, the theory leads to totally unrealistic conclusions regarding wealth concentration in France.

Piketty hopes for tax reform. But are his recommendations desirable? What would be the effects of his confiscatory tax policies? Are there not alternative tax reforms? James A. Dorn calls for egalitarians to focus first on equality in terms of rule of law, whereas the policies of Piketty are more in line with destroying the rule of law. Jean-Philippe Delsol and Nicolas Lecaussin explain why an alternative tax policy should not penalize enrichment and suggest the framework of the true "tax revolution" that France and other countries should put in place.

Let's emphasize the point again: Piketty's obsession with the accumulation of capital leads him to an apparent incomprehension of the role of capital in development. The constitution of capital has pulled billions of people out of poverty. Should we slow down its process because a few get richer faster than the others—as if they were enriched by impoverishing the majority? Those are not the lessons we learned from recent history. Piketty's program would therefore be equally dangerous for development in poor countries and economic growth in rich countries. It would be a major blow to the foundations of prosperity.

The whole vision of Thomas Piketty is problematic. Although the author denies being a Marxist or an anti-capitalist, the system that he proposes aims to install a global system with a police suprastate. Under the guise of democracy, his program dangerously threatens civil liberties. It announces a tax dictatorship, the signs of which we are already witnessing in several countries. In the tradition of John Maynard Keynes, Piketty's obsession with the use of cumulative oppressive power of the rentiers—who should be "euthanized" in the name of the general interest—would lead to the erosion of savings. History has taught us that the road to hell is paved with good intentions.

In this volume, the editors have tried to gather contributions from a diverse spectrum of the intellectual scene, from thorough think tank analysis to scientific articles. The reader will come across prestigious authors. We have also included a mix of

American, French, and foreign authors: the reaction to the work of Thomas Piketty is truly international. Finally, we have tried to combine scientific quality and accessibility; a few passages contain more technical analysis, but readers can thumb through those without prejudice to their general understanding. We hope that readers will appreciate the arguments here and better understand the fundamental criticisms that Thomas Piketty's work *Capital in the 21st Century* cannot escape.

References

Baverez, Nicolas. 2013. "Piketty, un marxisme de sous-préfecture." *Le Point*, September 26.

Boudon, Raymond. 2004. *Pourquoi les intellectuels n'aiment pas le libéralisme.* Paris: Odile Jacob.

Giles, Chris. 2014. "Piketty Findings Undercut by Errors." *Financial Times*, May 23.

Landais, Camille, Thomas Piketty, and Emmanuel Saez. 2011. *Pour une révolution fiscale* [For a Tax Revolution]. Paris: Seuil.

Marx, Karl. (1885) 1954. *The Eighteenth Brumaire of Napoleon Bonaparte.* Moscow: Progress Publishers, translated from the German, 3rd revised ed.

McCloskey, Deirdre. 2014. "Measured, Unmeasured, Mismeasured, and Unjustified Pessimism: A Review Essay of Thomas Piketty's *Capital in the 21st Century*." *Erasmus Journal for Philosophy and Economics* 7 (2): 73–115.

Piketty, Thomas. 2014. *Capital in the 21st Century*. Cambridge, MA: Belknap Press.

Villey, Daniel. 1967. *À la recherche d'une doctrine économique.* Paris: Éditions Guénin.

Part 1. An Apocalyptic Vision

The empirical and theoretical work of an author is inevitably marked with a vision. It is important to discuss that vision to form a complete critique of the author's work and thereafter to better understand those empirical and theoretical choices.

As with Karl Marx, the vision that permeates the work of Thomas Piketty is decidedly pessimistic about capitalism. Class struggle is always in the background: society is in conflict, and what A gains is lost by B. In such a society, the rich are "the wicked" side of the story. The idea that the poor can enrich themselves through capital accumulation—the tool of domination of the rich—is nearly taboo in Piketty's world. The fact that the poor are already enriched by the market economy obviously doesn't fit in with the rest of the vision.

Part 1 of this volume therefore offers a critique of Thomas Piketty's vision—a vision in which reductions in various inequalities are hidden, a vision which is tainted by an anti-rich bias, a vision which does not serve the poor.

Section 1. No Declining Inequality?

Thomas Piketty pictures a world caught in an unstoppable spiral of enrichment of a minority, at immense cost to the majority. While the 1 percent of rentiers accumulates fortune in a snowball effect, what becomes of the 99 percent? In reality, are the 99 percent becoming poorer? Are they so badly off?

This section looks at the phenomenon—unprecedented in history—of the enrichment of the masses, notably in the form of extended life expectancy and access to consumption and education. It attempts to offer a realistic vision about the evolution of types of inequality, which is a lot less pessimistic than Piketty's.

1. The Great Process of Equalization of Conditions

Jean-Philippe Delsol

Thomas Piketty's book *Capital in the 21st Century* (2014) is an undeniable commercial success. A large part of this success is undoubtedly due to the Marxist affiliation claimed in the title "Capital." Twenty-five years after the fall of the Berlin wall, one might have thought that the Marxist heritage would be stored in the cupboard of the history of ideas. But the recent financial and debt crisis generated legitimate frustrations, and intellectuals who propose explanations and answers have a ready market.

Anti-capitalist ideas have been especially well received. The American and European crises have largely been presented to the public as crises of *capitalism* although they were, to a large degree, crises generated by *interventionism* of public policy (monetary, budgetary, housing, and land policies) in the market process (Norberg 2009; Salin 2010). Regardless, the ideological ground was ready for Piketty, thanks to the "Occupy Wall Street" movement—the rebellion by the Greek people with grand speeches against "finance without a face," as François Hollande once put it (2012).

The Great Enrichment of the Masses

Of course, inequality in a market economy is a legitimate concern that cannot simply be swept under the rug. However, focusing on inequality should not mean dismissing other fundamental issues. People who focus on inequality often seem to forget a historical fact: market economies have allowed a great many people to get rich and to get out of poverty. This effect is unprecedented in history. The American historian and economist Deirdre McCloskey calls it "the Great Enrichment" (2014, 76).

Our view of human history is often biased by a historical effect of position, a kind of 21st-century glasses, undoubtedly amplified by the persistent myth of a precapitalist golden age, populated by cheerful people, eating their fill and living free, healthy, and long lives. In reality, the daily life of an average person before the advent of capitalism was much crueler than even the images evoked by Balzac of the 19th-century industrial age, which have haunted our conscience since adolescence.

To be clear, yesterday's world was no less harsh on poor people, and they were no less numerous. Rome, at the end of the Empire, supported 120,000 indigents. There was massive poverty in the eastern part of the Roman world in the sixth century. During the Middle Ages, the poverty level fluctuated but was generally much worse than today. In Burgundy, France, "in Dijon in 1397 the miserable represented 83 percent; in 1431 and 1433, they were still 58 and 54 percent, and 27 and 34 percent of beggars" (Mollat 1992, 283). The church and the monks took active care of the poor at the time.

In time, the liberal revolution and the industrial revolution lifted a greater number of people out of poverty. The living and working conditions of the "proletariat" at the start of the industrial capitalist era were without doubt abominable by today's standards. But in their historical context, those conditions were not abnormal, and they actually attracted many impoverished people—as shocking as that may sound today. We must therefore realize what the capitalist revolution has allowed. It has ignited a process of liberation, contrary to what the Marxist or Neo-Marxist vision would have us believe.

The Reduction in Consumption Inequality

The speed at which the market economy allows sections of humanity to get out of poverty should make us marvel. Again, without minimizing the question of inequality in income or wealth, this process of liberation and enrichment has clearly reflected a decline in consumption inequality. Steven Horwitz reminds us: "For most of human history, the difference between the rich and the poor was a difference in the kinds of things they had access to. Rich people had stuff that poor people didn't" (2015, 22). The gap in consumption between the rich and poor has recently decreased like nothing before thanks to the unprecedented rise in exchanges and innovations. Consumption inequality in food and basic services has never been as low.

Of course, only the rich can drive in Ferraris, but that does not prevent the poor from driving. As Jonah Goldberg (2014) puts it, "There's a significant difference between not being able to feed your family and not being able to feed your family as well as a wealthier man might." A poor American has the same access to basic foods as Bill Gates. The idea of not being able to eat meat more than once a week or once a month, common for the vast majority of people a century ago, has become foreign to us (at least in the countries that have chosen the path to development). It takes fewer hours of work to pay for similar goods than a generation ago.[1] Poor people today have access to foods that, two centuries ago, even kings could not procure; they can cure a toothache cheaply when even the richest in former times remained in agony in such a case, despite their wealth. The number of new products has exploded,[2] and their quality has increased,[3] rendering more and better services, especially for the poorest.

The same goes for the reduction of inequalities in longevity, life expectancy, access to education (Eberstadt 2016), or access to leisure. We can therefore criticize the analysis of Thomas Piketty for focusing on the increasing wealth of the 1 percent and forgetting a bit too quickly about the increasing wealth of the 99 percent (Strain 2014; Winship 2014).

The Reduction in Inequality on a Global Level

As with any process, change will not happen by waving a magic wand. The fate of assembly-line workers working 12 hours a day in developing countries like Cambodia concerns us, just as Korean workers' conditions concerned our parents a generation ago. Now Korea is a developed country and working conditions have improved. This progress illustrates a point that is somewhat obscured in Piketty's book: focusing on inequality within particular countries can make us forget that inequality is gradually decreasing worldwide, across countries. Indeed, the phenomenon of liberation of the greatest number by the capitalist revolution is being reproduced on a global scale. Between 1990 and 2010, the income and wealth gap increased, as both Piketty and Pope Francis complain in unison. But at the same time, world poverty was retreating.

In 1990, 47 percent of the world population lived on less than a dollar a day. Twenty years later, 22 percent still shared that terrible lot, surviving on less than $1.25 per day (the equivalent of $1.00 in 1990). Viewed more positively, 700 million people were lifted out of extreme poverty. A study conducted for the Organisation for Economic Co-operation and Development shows that the number of Latin Americans living on less than $4.00 a day decreased from over 40 percent in 2000 to less than 30 percent in 2010 (OECD/UN-ECLAC/CAF 2013). In Latin America today, the poor are equal in number to the middle class, whereas they were two and a half times as many just a decade ago.

The Economy: A Zero-Sum Game?

The principal lesson is that the market economy is *not* a zero-sum game (Shuchman 2014). Piketty, however, proposes a vision in which whatever the capitalist gains, the worker loses: the enrichment of one implies the impoverishment of the other; a bigger piece of cake for Jack means a smaller piece for John. His vision stems from a fundamentally static view of socioeconomic development. The enrichment of the wealthiest actually goes hand in hand with that of the poorest (Saab 2014[4]). The very concept of development rests in the idea of the snowball effect, which profits everyone (albeit at different rates): the size of the cake gets bigger.

Note that Piketty's "natural" explanation of inequality reduction involves war and economic crises. Obviously, and fortunately, Piketty does not advocate war or economic depression; he proposes radical taxation. However, his objective is the same, which is shocking in its cynicism and absurdity. Effectively, the result of Piketty's proposal would be, if not the destruction of capital, at least the "decumulation" of capital (Reisman 2014) with all of its consequences, such as potentially stifling growth and development and preventing the decline in poverty. Ensuring that the wealthiest get poorer simply reduces the size of the "cake"! Is not economics about, instead, promoting the reduction in poverty (indirectly, through the accumulation of capital)? Piketty seems to be seduced not only by the vision of the economy as a zero-sum game, but also by economic policy as a negative-sum game.[5]

Class-Struggle Theory Recycled in a World without Human Capital

The view of the economy as a zero-sum game fits perfectly with the theory of class struggle. Piketty denies being a Marxist, though, and claims that he likes the market economy: "I love market forces" (Piketty and Roberts 2014). He says his own experience with communism during a trip to Romania in the 1980s vaccinated him against hard-line Marxism. However, it is difficult not to see in Piketty's work a rehashing of the old theme of class struggle—a softened, 21st-century version. The simplistic employee/capitalist cleavage, however, does not fly for two reasons.

First, the "great enrichment" has allowed the working masses to effectively become capitalists by making wealth for themselves through their savings. The wealth of the poor has increased—with no comparison to what it was a century ago. Thus, workers are becoming capitalists: for example, many workers are employees who open retirement savings accounts. That is, they can do so if their government does not prohibit it, on the advice of experts fond of Piketty's theories. For Piketty does not approve of the practice: according to him, although the accumulation of capital is quasiautomatic and without risk for the rich, curiously it is too risky for the poor, as Rallo (2016a) and Tanner (2016) explain.

Second, one of the powerful causes of inequality reduction is the accumulation of human capital (Strain 2014). This investment, which the poor as well as the less poor can effectively make to become more productive and thus climb the income ladder, is the foundation of social mobility and the great disruptor of class boundaries. Human capital is undoubtedly the most profitable form of capital (Butler 2014). The differences in accumulation of human capital in large part explain the differences in remuneration. We cannot overlook the analysis of human capital if we are to understand the sources of growth and reductions in extreme poverty and many inequalities (McCloskey 2014; Meltzer 2014).

Although Piketty's book is supposed to be about the analysis of capital, he puts aside human capital, arguing that human capital is not transferable. However, his analysis is already founded on confusion between capital (i.e., productive, financial, property capital) and transferable wealth or inheritance. Moreover, the fruits of the accumulation of human capital *are* in large part transferrable. It is thus difficult not to believe the author's choice was aimed at intensifying the bias of the book.

The Immobile Society?

Here is another sign of Piketty's extremely static view of social changes: Piketty does not understand—or pretends not to understand—real mobility. He reckons that wage mobility has been weak (Piketty 2014, 299), while admitting the appearance of a middle class that has replaced the rentiers. Indeed, he notes that "the decrease in the upper decile's share of national wealth in the twentieth century benefited the middle 40 percent of the population exclusively, while the share of the poorest 50 percent hardly increased at all" (Piketty 2014, 342). Thus, today, the middle class[6] owns about a third of the national wealth.

The stratification in deciles from the poorest to the wealthiest ignores the central fact that deciles are porous. Piketty does not analyze the transfer from one to the other as social mobility occurs in both directions. Yet, this social mobility is an important factor, especially in advanced societies and in particular in the United States.[7]

Movement between deciles depends in part on age, as young people are generally poorer but capable of climbing the economic ladder given time. This observation also holds between generations.[8] Stephen Moore cites the work of economist Ron Askin, who has shown that two-thirds of Americans today enjoy higher incomes than did their parents at their age (Moore 2012, 50). Moore adds that a Federal Reserve Bank of Dallas study covering the period 1975–1991 shows that 98 percent of poor households in 1975 were no longer poor in 1991 (Moore 2012, 48).

Inequality: A Threat to Democracy?

One of Piketty's main arguments against inequality is that it constitutes a threat to democracy: too high inequality generates a risk of revolution, and chaos could follow. However, a general rule is that people are more interested in bettering their own lot (if they are permitted to) than in depriving the wealthiest. Thus, employment and growth matter most. Even during the recent crisis and its aftermath, many elections brought to power parties that were not particularly egalitarian, which seems to reflect the concerns of the majority (Barone 2014).

Is democracy doomed to turn into a plutocracy? Events in the United States can sometimes lead us to believe that is the case, for example with the Bush and Clinton families. Yet, let's observe that the two families are in opposing camps, and the camp dear to Piketty is well represented here (Epstein 2014). In fact, wealthy donors appear all along the political spectrum: should George

Soros be prohibited from supporting the Democrats? In addition, not all the people in power are rich: Barack Obama and John Boehner both come from modest environments (Goldberg 2014).

Furthermore, if we are really faced with a government of the rich, why did that government put in place generous redistribution systems (Bourne 2014)? Why, indeed, would the government shoot itself in the foot? Finally, is the link between a fall in inequality and democracy that evident? If so, why did the "egalitarian" interwar period in Piketty's analysis produce fascism and communism (Dubay and Furth 2014)?

Inequality and Noninclusive Institutions

Clearly, a problem of inequality does exist. Wealth and income gaps are indeed intolerable when they result from perverse, mafia-like, or collectivist political regimes. As noted by Jia Zhangke, movie director of *A Touch of Sin*, the worst problem in China today is not that it has a class system, but that there is no way to move from one class to another. The rich join forces with those in power by corrupting them, which lets the rich control resources and obtain political clout in their turn. This collusion of power and wealth is what makes people angry.

When government is not propping up dying companies or establishing useless and costly privileges, only those who create products and services bought freely by consumers will prosper. It is elsewhere, in collectivized societies, where the bureaucracy has taken hold of wealth, that the people who merely stamp permits—whose incongruous authorization is needed and paid for—accumulate wealth. Wealth also accumulates in satellite states, supported by governments that funnel billions collected through local authorities—as vain as they are servile.

Here is the crucial point about inequality: if political institutions create privileges and special favors—some sort of economic apartheid (De Soto 2011)—by granting monopolies or protections, then inequality results from the redistribution in favor of the wealthiest and best connected: that is cronyism or crony capitalism (McCloskey 2014; Lepage 2016). Cronyism is the problem in many countries, notably those of the Arab spring. A genuine study of inequality should devote itself in depth to the origins of noninclusive institutions (Acemoglu and Robinson 2016). Inequality in terms of access to the rule of law (Dorn 2016) or to good government (Lips 2014) should therefore be at the top of the list of subjects to analyze in a work claiming to be the foremost study on inequality.

Liberty and Equal Conditions

Where people are free to develop and change position or social class, where people can climb the income and wealth ladder, inequality is easier to bear. Sometimes inequality is even borne well because it enables people to observe what they are capable of through their own efforts, tenacity, and work—as has been stated most scientifically by Michel Forsé and others (2013) in their work on the "passion of equality" in France.

History shows that in free societies where the rule of law is respected, wealth gaps do not increase infinitely, but contribute to greater growth for the benefit of all. In places where competition works in a transparent and spontaneous way, companies will only develop under the pressure of market forces and within the limits of the prices offered by competitors. For example, in France, the mobile phone company Free recently entered the market and dramatically pushed down the prices of all its rivals and their profits, to the benefit of consumers.

Where financial markets are complex and adaptive, rentiers quickly disappear. Even investing in government bonds is dangerous today, and being a successful investor requires attention and perspicacity.

The Dangers of Perfectionism and "Angelism"

The market is not responsible for bad human behavior. On the contrary, it is the system that best directs human action in the best manner, however imperfectly. To paraphrase Winston Churchill's statement about democracy, the market economy is doubtless the worst system, except for all the others. As imperfect as it is and despite all the risks entailed, the market economy rests on individual responsibility and respect for the dignity of human beings, capable of finding their own way, regardless of where they start.

Too much assistance leads to a new form of slavery, soft yet tyrannical, and to the loss of any self-worth. The wealthiest and brightest must realize that they hold greater responsibilities toward their fellow men in a free society. In this respect, the free market is also the lesser evil because it allows those who have succeeded to bear their share of human imperfection (through charity or the development of new companies), by acknowledging that some are less fortunate and incapable of getting out of poverty. "The belief in democracy presupposes belief in things higher than democracy" (Eduard Heimann quoted in Hayek 2013, 348). This concept also applies to the free market.

None of these arguments denies the wealth gap or how it is evolving. In this respect, Piketty's data are useful and interesting. But he has politicized the issue, and it has become a vehicle for an egalitarian obsession that has nothing to do with economics. Granted, too-large gaps in incomes and wealth may destabilize society and create tensions. Yes, the wealth of some may be unbearable, conceited, and arrogant. But the question is less about whether such gaps are morally justified, even if this may be relevant, than about reflecting on the impact of such gaps and their influence on economic and social conditions.

The Apocalypse of "Saint Thomas"

Yes, Piketty is right to think that too-wide or unjustified gaps engender misunderstandings, uproars, and social strife. But when wealth is produced through hard work, innovation, or services offered on a free market, and when accumulated capital can hardly survive those who produce it or keep it in the general interest, wealth is less likely to spark a revolution.

Unfortunately, like Marxist authors, Piketty endeavors to transform his discourse into a scientific demonstration. He wants not only to convince, but also to nail down his own truth, supposedly grounded in the mathematical formula that he presents. Granted, he states that "one should be wary of any economic determinism in regard to inequalities" (Piketty 2014, 20). But he uses statistics—in fact a mere "graphic inference"—to announce the expected wealth distribution in the 21st century, as if there were little or no risk of making mistakes. He claims that the divide between rich and poor will inevitably widen, even though he admits the opposite took place during the 20th century.

Piketty extrapolates trends, as did Thomas Robert Malthus in the 18th century or the Club of Rome in the 1970s to predict that the world would die of starvation. He questions Simon Kuznets's inequality bell curve, sketching trends that ignore human action. On the one hand, he notes that "Marx totally neglected the possibility of durable technological progress and steadily increasing productivity" (Piketty 2014, 10) in his theory that an infinite capital accumulation will kill off capitalism. But on the other hand, he reproduces a theory of endless growth of the rich's wealth. In brief, he is selling the apocalypse.

References

Acemoglu, Daron, and James A. Robinson. 2016. "The Rise and Decline of the General Laws of Capitalism" in this volume, Chapter 16.

Barone, Michael. 2014. "Nobody Is Pushing Thomas Piketty's Policies to Combat Economic Inequality." *Washington Examiner*, November 24. http://www.washingtonexaminer.com/nobody-is-pushing-thomas-pikettys-policies-to-combat-economic-inequality/article/2556478.

Bourne, Ryan. 2014. "Why Piketty's Socialist Manifesto Doesn't Stack Up," *City A.M.* (London), May 6. http://www.cityam.com/article/1399345590/why-piketty-s-socialist-manifesto-doesn-t-stack.

Butler, Eamonn. 2014. "Twelve Problems with Piketty's Capital." Adam Smith Institute, May 12. http://www.adamsmith.org/blog/uncategorized/twelve-problems-with-pikettys-capital/.

De Soto, Hernando. 2011. "Egypt's Economic Apartheid," *Wall Street Journal*, February 3. http://www.wsj.com/articles/SB10001424052748704358704576118683913032882.

Dorn, James. 2016. "Piketty's Plan for Equality Would Reduce Personal Freedom and Undermine Growth" in this volume, Chapter 22.

Dubay, Curtis, and Salim Furth. 2014. "Understanding Thomas Piketty and His Critics." The Heritage Foundation Backgrounder no. 2954 on Economy, September 12.

Eberstadt, Nicholas. 2016. "Longevity, Education, and the Huge New Worldwide Increases in Equality" in this volume, Chapter 2.

Epstein, Richard. 2014. "The Piketty Fallacy." The Libertarian, Hoover Institution, May 5. http://www.hoover.org/research/piketty-fallacy.

Forsé, Michel, Olivier Galland, Caroline Guibet Lafaye, and Maxime Parodi. 2013. *L'Égalité, une Passion Française?* Paris: Armand Colin.

Goldberg, Jonah. 2014. "Mr. Piketty's Big Book of Marxiness." *Commentary*, July 1. https://www.commentarymagazine.com/articles/mr-pikettys-big-book-of-marxiness/.

Hayek, F.A. 2013. *Law, Legislation and Liberty.* 3 vols. London and New York: Routledge.

Hollande, François. 2012. Speech at Le Bourget during the 2012 presidential campaign, January 22.

Horwitz, Steven. 2015. "Inequality, Mobility, and Being Poor in America." Draft for publication in *Social Philosophy and Policy*, Spring, http://papers.ssrn.com/sol3/papers.cfm?abstract_id=2559403.

Lepage, Henri. 2016. "Piketty on Management and Wealth" in this volume, Chapter 4.

Lips, Brad. 2014. "Defeating Piketty's Charge." Working paper, Atlas Network, November. https://www.atlasnetwork.org/assets/uploads/misc/Defeating_Piketty's_Charge_Nov25_2014.pdf.

McCloskey, Deirdre. 2014. "Measured, Unmeasured, Mismeasured, and Unjustified Pessimism: A Review Essay of Thomas Piketty's *Capital in the 21st Century.*" *Erasmus Journal for Philosophy and Economics* 7 (2): 73–115.

Meltzer, Alan. 2014. "The United States of Envy." Defining Ideas, Hoover Institution, April 17. http://www.hoover.org/research/united-states-envy.

Mollat, Michel. 1992. *Les Pauvres au Moyen-Age*. Brussels: Editions Complexe.

Moore, Stephen. 2012. *Who Is the Fairest of Them All*. New York: Encounter Books.

Norberg, Johan. 2009. *Financial Fiasco: How America's Infatuation with Home Ownership and Easy Money Created the Financial Crisis*. Washington, D.C.: Cato Institute.

Organisation for Economic Co-operation and Development (OECD), United Nations Economic Commission for Latin America and the Caribbean (UN-ECLAC), and the Development Bank of Latin America (CAF). 2013. *Latin American Economic Outlook 2014*. Paris: OECD Publishing.

Piketty, Thomas. 2014. *Capital in the 21st Century*. Cambridge, MA: Belknap Press.

Piketty, Thomas, and Russ Roberts. 2014. "Thomas Piketty on Inequality and Capital in the 21st Century." EconTalk Podcast, Library of Economics and Liberty, September 22. http://www.econtalk.org/archives/2014/09/thomas_piketty.html.

Rallo, Juan Ramón. 2016a. "Where Are the 'Super Rich' of 1987?" in this volume, Chapter 3.

______. 2016b. "Thomas Piketty's Great Contradiction" in this volume, Chapter 7.

Reisman, George. 2014. *Piketty's Capital: Wrong Theory, Destructive Program*. Laguna Hills, CA: TJS Books.

Saab, Kevin. 2014. "Piketty: Quand la Démagogie Fait Recette." *Contrepoints*, June 3, http://www.contrepoints.org/2014/06/03/166946-piketty-la-demagogie-fait-recette.

Salin, Pascal. 2010. *Revenir au Capitalisme pour Éviter les Crises*. Paris: Odile Jacob.

Shuchman, Daniel. 2014. "Thomas Piketty Revives Marx for the 21st Century." *Wall Street Journal*, April 21. http://www.wsj.com/articles/SB10001424052702303825604579515452952131592.

Strain, Michael. 2014. "Stop Worrying about the 1 Percent. Their Money Can't Help the Middle Class." *Washington Post*, July 16. https://www.washingtonpost.com/posteverything/wp/2014/07/16/stop-worrying-about-the-one-percent-their-money-cant-help-the-middle-class/.

Tanner, Michael. 2016. "Piketty Gets It Wrong" in this volume, Chapter 6.

Winship, Scott. 2014. "Whither the Bottom 99 Percent, Thomas Piketty?" *Forbes*, April 18. http://www.forbes.com/sites/scottwinship/2014/04/17/whither-the-bottom-90-percent-thomas-piketty/.

2. Longevity, Education, and the Huge New Worldwide Increases in Equality

Nicholas Eberstadt

Is the human condition becoming more unequal?[1] A chorus of authoritative voices today insists that the answer is yes, unquestionably so. Inequality, the voices say, is sharply on the upswing in America, as everyone is supposed to know. It is also on the rise throughout other affluent democracies, they inform. We further hear that growing worldwide inequality is all but foreordained by the global triumph of capitalism: in 2014's runaway international bestseller *Capital in the 21st Century*, Thomas Piketty even has a formula to prove it.

The trouble with today's received wisdom about growing inequality, though, is that it focuses almost exclusively on the matter of *economic* inequality, and usually more narrowly still on only *income* inequality. Although this distinction may sound unobjectionable, it is actually quite problematic in two key respects.

For one thing, our true ability to measure economic inequality remains far less precise than is generally understood. Even in data-rich America, for example, statistics on the nation's wealth distribution are at best rudimentary. Estimates of economic inequality differ dramatically depending on whether one looks at personal income or instead examines personal consumption, which seems to be distributed much more evenly.

Yet more important, economic inequality is hardly the only form of inequality bearing directly on human well-being and life chances—and trends in income inequality are not necessarily representative of the other basic changes that so powerfully shape modern living standards.

If we widen our gaze just a bit, it should be almost immediately apparent that a number of remarkable worldwide trends that are not only improving the human condition overall, but also making that condition markedly *less* unequal. Paramount among those trends are the ongoing global revolutions in longevity and education. Such curiously overlooked trends are worth understanding and, indeed, celebrating.

Consider first the modern revolution in length of life and what it has meant for equality in the distribution of lifespans in some well-studied countries. (The historical estimates adduced here come from the *Human Mortality Database*, a pioneering project by demographers from the University of California, Berkeley, in the United States and the Max Planck Institute for Demographic Research in Germany.)

Take the case of Sweden, where good vital records go back several centuries. In 1751, Sweden's overall life expectancy at birth was barely 38 years. Yes, that's right: Sweden's life expectancy back then was lower than the very lowest life expectancies for the poorest countries in the world today. But an average life expectancy at birth of 38 years did not mean that Swedes typically lived to be about 38 and then passed away. Rather, this was an arithmetic average for a population within which survival prospects were wildly, brutally disparate.

Back then, roughly a fifth of all Swedes died in their first year of life. In addition to this savage toll from infant mortality, another tenth of the Swedish population perished in early childhood: by age 5, only 70 Swedes were still alive from every 100 born. But about half of the children who made it to age 5 lived on to age 60 and beyond. In fact, aside from early childhood, more of those early modern–era Swedes died in their 74th year of life than at any other age (See Figure 2.1).

Such extraordinary dispersion of lifespans within a population could only mean that its distribution of survival was

Figure 2.1

CHANGES IN LIFESPAN INEQUALITY WITH IMPROVING HEALTH: TOTAL, SWEDEN 1751 VS. 2014 (AGE AT DEATH FROM EVERY 100,000 PERSONS BORN)

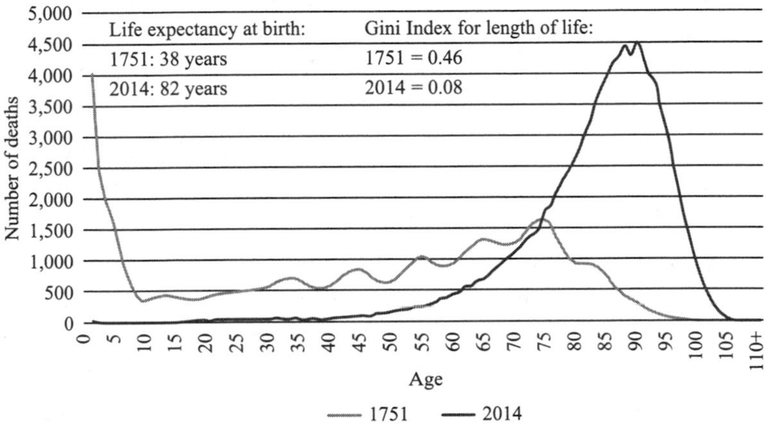

NOTE: The number of deaths per 100,000 infants ages 0–1 was 19,722 in 1751, and 218 in 2014.

SOURCE: Human Mortality Database. Sweden, Total (1x1) Life tables, available at http://www.mortality.org/cgi-bin/hmd/country.php?cntr=SWE&level=1. Accessed April 18, 2016.

correspondingly unequal. When measuring disparities in the distribution of income, economists nowadays conventionally use the "Gini coefficient," an index that runs from 0 (for conditions of perfect equality) to 1.0 (representing perfect inequality, where a single person possesses everything). If we use that metric to assess inequality in Sweden's lifespans in 1751, we get a Gini index of 0.46.

What does that mean exactly? Think of how extremely lopsided income distribution is right now in a Latin American country such as Mexico. According to the World Bank, the Gini index for income in Mexico in 2010 was 0.47. By those estimates, length of life in 18th-century Sweden was distributed just about as unequally as incomes are in Mexico today.

Now, flash forward to 2014, the most recent year for which Swedish data are available from the *Human Mortality Database*. In 2014, Sweden's life expectancy at birth was over 82 years—more than twice as high as in the 1750s. This great accomplishment entailed a total transformation in patterns of age at death. The risk of dying in infancy in Sweden today is about 100 times lower than in 1751—and the risk of dying in early childhood is much more than 100-fold lower. Ninety percent of Swedes can now expect to survive to age 65. Fully half of current-day Swedes die between the ages of 82 and 95—and more contemporary Swedes live to age 89 than to any other particular age.

This tremendous compression in range for age at death speaks to a radical equalization in the distribution of Swedish lifespans. Over the past several centuries, the estimated Gini index for Sweden's inequality in age at death has plummeted by more than four-fifths, to just 0.08 today. For Sweden's men and women, lifespans have never been so long—or so equally distributed—as they are now.

What holds for Sweden holds for the rest of the world as well. In the early 1870s, for example, Italy was a desperately unhealthy country, with a life expectancy of less than 30 years and odds of death before age 5 of nearly 45 percent. With an estimated Gini index for age at death of 0.56, its distribution of lifespans was even more harshly unequal than preindustrial Sweden's. By 2012, as in Sweden, Italy's life expectancy at birth had risen to above 82 years, and modern Italy's Gini index for the distribution of national lifespans is just as low as modern Sweden's. As life expectancy improves, so does equality with respect to length of life.

We see the same dynamic at play in the United States (see Figure 2.2). According to the *Human Mortality Database*, U.S. life expectancy has risen progressively since the Great Depression, increasing from about 61 years in 1933 to about 79 as of 2013. Over those same decades, America's Gini index for lifespan inequality was cut in half—from 0.22 to 0.11. Irrespective of all the ethnic,

Figure 2.2

GINI INDEX FOR LIFESPAN INEQUALITY VS. LIFE EXPECTANCY AT BIRTH: UNITED STATES, 1933–2013

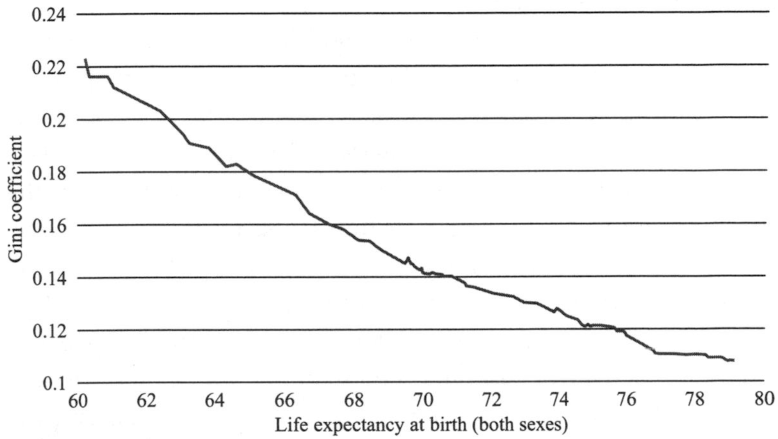

SOURCE: Calculations based on author's calculations derived from data available at Human Mortality Database. United States, Total (1x1) Life tables, available at http://www.mortality.org/. Accessed April 18, 2016.

income, and other enumerated gaps that characterize our society, Americans of all backgrounds have never before enjoyed such equality in length of life as we know today.[2]

Vital statistics are intrinsically easier to collect (and check for errors) than are income data. But unlike with global income distribution, it is possible to proxy global trends in lifespan inequality over the past century with reasonable confidence. In part, this is because summing lifespans lived out in different countries is a wholly straightforward proposition, unlike, say, the summing of barbershop wages from Canada and Vietnam. Further, despite certain "signature" differences in local mortality patterns (which fascinate demographers), the broad pattern for every national population ever observed is essentially the same: the higher the life expectancy at birth, the lower the inequality in age at death. And the correspondence between rising life expectancy and falling lifespan inequality for all populations yet observed happens to be very tight—not perfect, but just about as close to it as correlations in the social sciences involving really large numbers of human beings permit.

Leading demographers have suggested that our planetary life expectancy at birth in 1900 would have been, very approximately, around 30 years (in other words, pretty near the awful level recorded for Italy for the early 1870s). By 2000, much less conjectural estimates have placed world life expectancy in the mid-60s, in effect doubling over the course of the 20th century. Today global life expectancy at birth is placed above 70 years by the World Health Organization and the United Nations Population Division, and at just under 70 years by the U.S. Census Bureau. (Thanks to the ongoing revolution in global longevity, Bangladesh, the Gaza Strip, and Paraguay are among the places that have now exceeded the 70-year threshold for life expectancy.)

Given the regular and highly predictable correspondence between life expectancy and the Gini index for age at death, we can be essentially certain that the worldwide explosion in life expectancy over the past century has been accompanied by a monumental narrowing of worldwide differences in length of life. Given the enduring and overarching relationship between life expectancy and inequality in longevity, it seems safe to say that inequalities in age at death for our species fell by something like two-thirds over the course of the 20th century—and those inequalities have dropped even further since the dawn of the new millennium.

To go by our admittedly approximate estimates for the former and World Bank income distribution numbers for the latter, global lifespans in 1900 were even more unequally distributed than is income nowadays in a sub-Saharan kleptocracy such as Nigeria. In the 21st century, by contrast, no country's income distribution looks to be anywhere near as egalitarian as the planet's current distribution of lifespans for all its peoples.

On its face, this revolution in survival constitutes an epochal advance in the human condition and implies other benefits as well. The radical decline in worldwide risk of death from diseases of poverty—communicable and infectious illnesses exacerbated by malnutrition, lack of medical care, or both—speaks for itself. A broader, fundamental improvement in worldwide "health equality" seems to have accompanied the revolution in lifespan equality, even if we do not yet have the data to prove it.

If this global blessing could be "priced in" to worldwide macroeconomic accounts—through a willingness-to-pay adjustment for longer and more equal lifespans, or expected value of additional consumption, or some other factor—economic inequality trends around the globe would look strikingly different. But such adjustments cannot be entered into those ledgers.

Perversely, the existing national accounts calculus weighs entirely in the opposite direction. As the eminent economist Peter T. Bauer was fond of noting, the birth of a calf raises per capita gross domestic product (GDP), and the death of a child has the same effect (Bauer 2000, 30–31). If the modern revolution in life chances has been "poor friendly," as we have every reason to believe, it has ironically contributed to the measured "economic inequality" that so many now decry.

As for education, the story of its spread and distribution in the modern era reads much like the worldwide longevity explosion—but here the revolutionary transformations may have been even faster. In the early postwar era (1950), roughly half of the world's adults—and the overwhelming majority of men and women from low-income regions—had never been exposed to any schooling. By 2010, despite the intervening worldwide population growth and the disproportionately rapid growth in poorer regions, completely unschooled men and women ages 15 and older accounted for just one-seventh of the world's adult population, and for about one in six adults from developing areas.

Those estimates come from Harvard's Robert Barro and Korea University's Jong-Hwa Lee, who have painstakingly reconstructed trends in educational attainment for 146 countries on the basis of local census returns and survey results (Barro and Lee 2013). According to the Barro-Lee dataset, mean years of schooling for the world's adult population rose from just 3 years in 1950 to about 8 years in 2010. Although the level remained lowest in the developing regions, it more than tripled—from 2 years to 7 years—over those same decades. For more developed countries, the level remains much higher than in the poor world, averaging more than 11 mean years of schooling per adult in 2010.

As we know, the world is still beset by enormous and highly consequential disparities in educational attainment. Less appreciated may be the degree to which such global inequalities have been reduced in the postwar era. Using the Barro-Lee numbers, three Moroccan economists demonstrated that global inequalities in educational attainment (as measured by the crude but nonetheless telling proxy of years of schooling) plunged between 1950 and 2010 (Wail, Hanchane, and Kamal 2011). For the world as a whole, by their reckoning, the Gini index for adult mean years of schooling was cut roughly in half between 1950 and 2010. Every region on earth has evidently witnessed progressive reductions in such inequality (see Figure 2.3).

Such global inequalities in educational attainment are estimated to be lowest for today's youth population. For males and females ages 15–24, years of schooling are more evenly distributed than is income in any country on the map today. On the current trajectory, global inequalities in the distribution of schooling can be expected to fall still further with each succeeding generation.

To be sure, not all years of schooling are the same. Educational quality can differ sharply within countries as well as between them. (The same might be said of years of life as well.) Moreover, Justin Sandefur and Amanda Glassman of the Center for Global Development have detected discrepancies in data for some sub-Saharan countries that lead them to conclude local authorities may be

Figure 2.3

GINI INDEX OF EDUCATION BY REGION AND GENDER

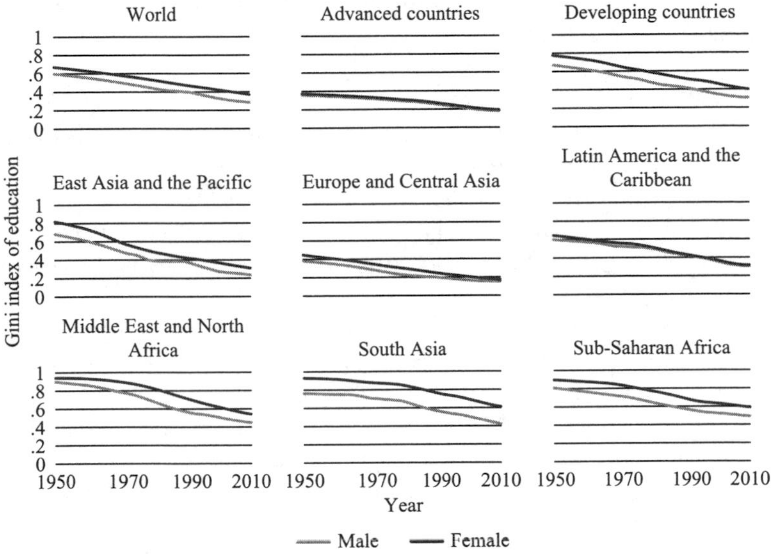

SOURCE: Wail, Hanchane, and Kamal. 2011. Figure A.2.

padding educational enrollment data (Sandefur and Glassman 2014). In America, according to estimates by Daniel Bennett (2011) of Florida State University, the decline in educational inequality as measured through mean years of schooling may have stalled since the early 1990s. Those and all other qualifications notwithstanding, however, we can still accept the global post–World War II education explosion for what it is: a revolutionary improvement and equalization of the human prospect.

Whatever may be said about economic inequalities in our epoch, material forces are quite obviously *not* working relentlessly and universally to increase differences in living standards across humanity today. From the standpoint of length of life and years of education, indeed, the human condition is incontestably more equal today than it has ever been before. And unlike with personal income, planners and collectivists cannot redistribute lifespans and educational attainment from one individual to another or from certain people to the state—yet another reason, perhaps, to cheer these triumphs.

References

Arias, Elizabeth. 2016. "Changes in Life Expectancy by Race and Hispanic Origin in the United States, 2013-2014." *NCHS Data Brief 244*. http://www.cdc.gov/nchs/products/databriefs/db244.htm.

Barro, Robert J., and Jong-Wha Lee. 2013. "A New Data Set of Educational Attainment in the World, 1950–2010." *Journal of Development Economics* 104 (C): 184–98.

Bauer, Peter T. 2000. *From Subsistence to Exchange and Other Essays*. Princeton, N.J.: Princeton University Press.

Bennett, Daniel L. 2011. *Educational Inequality in the United States: Methodology and Historical Estimation of Education Gini Coefficients*. Washington, D.C.: Center for College Affordability and Productivity.

Case, Anne, and Angus Deaton. 2015. "Rising Morbidity and Mortality in Midlife among White Non-Hispanic Americans in the 21st Century." *Proceedings of the National Academy of Sciences of the United States of America* 112 (49):15078–83.

Chetty, Raj, Michael Stepner, Sarah Abraham, Shelby Lin, Benjamin Scuderi, Nicholas Turner, Augustin Bergeron, and David Cutler. 2016. "The Association between Income and Life Expectancy in the United States, 2001–2014." doi:10.1001/jama.2016.4226.

Human Mortality Database. Max Planck Institute for Demographic Research and University of California, Berkeley. http://www.mortality.org.

Piketty, Thomas. 2014. *Capital in the 21st Century*. Cambridge, MA: Belknap Press.

Sandefur, Justin, and Amanda Glassman. 2014. "The Political Economy of Bad Data: Evidence from African Survey and Administrative Statistics." Center for Global Development Working Paper no. 373.

Wail, Benaabdelaali, Said Hanchane, and Abdelhak Kamal. 2011. *A New Data Set of Educational Inequality in the World, 1950–2010: Gini Index of Education by Age Group*. Rochester, NY: Social Science Research Network. http://papers.ssrn.com/sol3/papers.cfm?abstract_id=1895496.

World Bank. "Gini Index (World Bank Estimate)." *Data*. http://data.worldbank.org/indicator/SI.POV.GINI.

Section 2. An Anti-Rich Bias

Reading the work of Thomas Piketty, one is struck by his obsession with the rich whom he sees as "rentiers." Although his work claims to rest on a heightened scientific level, based on grand economic demonstrations and a collection of advanced statistical data, it struggles to mask the ideological bias that animates its author. That bias is an integral part of Piketty's static vision, in terms of the quasi class struggle, addressed in the first section.

This section poses questions that challenge Piketty's somewhat simplistic thesis. Is the evolution of the rich, notably in the famous *Forbes* ranking, actually going in the direction Piketty predicts? Do the rich not create wealth, jobs, and innovations that benefit everyone? How can we explain the ideological bias underlying Piketty's work?

3. Where Are the "Super Rich" of 1987?

Juan Ramón Rallo

Many people have a static view of wealth.[1] They make the error of believing that if one person becomes rich, that person and any heirs will always be rich, and each succeeding generation will get even wealthier—forever. The economist Thomas Piketty tries to demonstrate in his deliciously misguided book, *Capital in the 21st Century*, that there is a tendency within capitalism to set capital return above the growth rate of the economy; the capitalist class, thereby, accumulates an ever increasing portion of national income, thus aggravating social inequality. Worse yet, Piketty seems to think that the richest individuals within the capitalist class have greater opportunities to get a higher rate of return than capitalists of more modest means. Thus, the natural tendency of capitalism permits the super rich (and their heirs) to seize increasing portions of the total wealth.

On the Correct Use of the Forbes 400

To demonstrate his point, Piketty reviews the list of billionaires drawn up annually by *Forbes*. If we aggregate the wealth of the hundred-millionth section of the adult population in 1987 (the 30 wealthiest people in the world) and compare that number to the wealth of the hundred-millionth section of the adult population in 2010 (the 45 wealthiest people in the world), we conclude that this tier of the world's wealth grew at a real average rate of 6.8 percent (taking into account inflation): that percentage amounts to three times the annual growth of the world economy of 2.1 percent.

Therefore, according to Piketty, the super rich are ever more wealthy, not because they deserve it thanks to their good management as entrepreneurs, but simply because they have accumulated enormous wealth, which is capable of reproducing itself—in a kind of autopilot mode. As Piketty writes, "One of the most striking lessons of the *Forbes* rankings is that, past a certain threshold, all large fortunes, whether inherited or entrepreneurial in origin, grow at extremely high rates, regardless of whether the owner of the fortune works or not" (Piketty 2014, 439).

However, Piketty's argument is based on an inadmissible logical leap: indeed, although the wealth of the richest *stratum* of society rose at an average annual rate of return of 6.8 percent between 1987 and 2010, that does not mean that the rich people of 1987 are the same as those in 2010. For example, individual A, the richest person in the world in 1987 with $20 billion, could be completely ruined in 2010; at that moment, another person, individual B, would become the richest person in the world with $40 billion. From that example, can we conclude that the preservation and increase of wealth is a simple and automatic process that requires no personal attention from the owner? Evidently not.

Fortunately, we do not need to delve into complicated theoretical assumptions about the growth of the wealth by the super rich between 1987 and today because we can simply study what has happened to the super rich of 1987. Has their wealth since increased at a rate of 6.8 percent annually, as stated by Piketty? Has it remained the same? Or has it diminished—have those super rich been replaced by other creators of wealth?

The 10 Richest People in the World in 1987

In 1987, *Forbes* started to put together its list of billionaires. Nearly three decades later, it would be surprising to find virtually anyone from 1987 on the most recent list. The primary reason is not that a number of those individuals are dead, but that virtually all have seen their assets run out in an important way.

Let us start with the richest man in the world in 1987: the Japanese Yoshiaki Tsutsumi, with an estimated fortune of $20 billion. The last time he appeared on the *Forbes* list was 2006; by then, his wealth had melted down to $1.2 billion, which—taking into account inflation—was equivalent to $678 million. Since 2006, his fortune has continued to fall, and he is no longer on the *Forbes* list. But by referring to the last known value ($678 million in terms of purchasing power similar to that of 1987), we face the fact that his wealth dropped by 96 percent since 1987. According to Piketty, it should have multiplied by six.

Let's continue with another Japanese, Taikichiro Mori, the second richest man in the world in 1987. At that time he had amassed a fortune of $15 billion, which made him the richest man in the world in 1991, surpassing Tsutsumi. Taikichiro Mori died in 1993 and bequeathed his fortune to his two sons: Minouri Mori and Akira Mori. Today the combined inheritance of his sons is worth $6.3 billion, equivalent to $3.075 billion in 1987 dollars—a collapse of 80 percent of their wealth.

I have not been able to find the figures for the current fortunes of the men (or their heirs) in third and fourth place on the 1987 list, Shigeru Kobayashi and Haruhiko Yoshimoto, with fortunes of $7.5 billion and $7 billion, respectively. But they mostly invested in the Japanese housing sector in 1987, and there is no trace of them (or their families) on the Internet, which suggests that they have not fared better than Tsutsumi and Mori.

Fifth place on the 1987 list was occupied by Salim Ahmed Bin Mahfouz, a professional stockbroker and creator of the largest bank in Saudi Arabia (National Commercial Bank of Saudi Arabia). At that time, he enjoyed a fortune of $6.2 billion. In 2009, his heir, Khalin bin Mahfouz, died with a fortune of $3.2 billion, equal to $1.7 million in 1987—a decrease of 72.5 percent.

In sixth place, we find the brothers Hans and Gad Rausing, owners of the Swedish multinational Tetra Pak: together their wealth totaled $6 billion. Currently, Hans Rausing, age 92, owns assets of $12 billion dollars (and sits in 92nd position amongst the richest in the world); Gad Rausing died in 2000, at which point he had accumulated a fortune of $13 billion. In total, the brothers' wealth rose from $6 billion to $25 billion. Accounting for inflation, however, we find that the growth was much lower: from $6 billion to $12.2 billion. That change equals an annual rate of return of 2.7 percent—far less than the 6.8 percent suggested by Piketty.

In seventh place were three brothers: the Reichmanns, owners of Olympia and York, one of the largest property developers in the world. Their wealth was also estimated to be $6 billion in 1987, but five years later they were the protagonists of one of the most famous bankruptcies in history, which reduced their wealth to $100 million. One of the brothers has been reborn from the ashes, and today his wealth is estimated to be $2 billion, equal to $975 million in 1987—a loss of 84 percent.

Eighth place was occupied by a Japanese, Yohachiro Iwasaki, with a fortune of $5.6 billion. His heir, Fukuzo Iwasaki, died in 2012 with assets of $5.7 billion, equal to $2.8 million in 1987 dollars: a 50 percent decrease in assets.

A better fate was reserved for 1987's ninth richest man in the world, the Canadian Kenneth Roy Thomson, owner of the Thomson Corporation (today part of the Thomson Reuters group). At that time he owned $5.4 billion worth of assets. By the time he died in 2006, he had managed to increase his fortune to $17.9 billion, equal to $9.3 billion in 1987. Thus, Thomson's annual rate of return was 2.9 percent: again, far from the 6.8 percent "guaranteed" by Piketty.

In last place we find Keizo Saji, with assets of $4 billion. Saji died in 1999 with a fortune of $6.7 billion, which, accounting for inflation during that period, adds up to $4.6 billion. That's an average rate of return of 1.1 percent.

Conserving Capital Is Very Difficult

Contrary to what many people imagine and what Thomas Piketty claims to show, it is not easy to conserve assets in a market economy. Assets are at the mercy of changing consumer preferences, the emergence of new competitors, and the possible overvaluation (and ultimate collapse) of asset prices. It is simply wrong to say that there is a threshold at which capital accumulation takes place at an almost automatic pace.

The greater an individual's personal wealth, the more difficult it is to keep it "profitable." Opportunities to reinvest all of one's capital at high rates of return are rare unless one moves to markets where one normally has no competitive advantage. The same reasons that governments are poor money managers (i.e., the Hayekian "knowledge problem") explain why billionaires sometimes remain without ideas and faculties to manage their wealth—to the point that they may be unable to reinvent themselves and end up seeing their assets decimated. The popular wisdom on the subject is worth more than the rantings of a few short-sighted economists: "from shirtsleeves to shirtsleeves in three generations." Today, not even three generations are needed: three decades are sufficient to lose almost everything.

Today the names Tsutsumi, Mori, Reichmann, Iwasaki, and Saji are almost unimportant. Likewise, in 1987 many of the richest people in the world today—Bill Gates, Amancio Ortega, Larry Ellison, Jeff Bezos, Larry Page, Sergey Brin, and Mark Zuckerberg—were unknown: working in a garage, studying at school, or playing in a preschool. It remains to be seen how many of them will still be on the *Forbes* list in three decades and which other great creators of wealth will enter it.

Reference

Piketty, Thomas. 2014. *Capital in the 21st Century*. Cambridge, MA: Belknap Press.

4. Piketty on Management and Wealth

Henri Lepage

A note of caution should apply to Thomas Piketty's (2014) statements about the rise, in the Western world, of a new generation of super-executives and the bankruptcy of the traditional capitalist model of corporate governance.[1] He defends the thesis that present-day inequality is owed primarily to the disproportionate explosion in high wages among senior managers and attributes the phenomenon to the structural deterioration of control mechanisms within very large companies. Senior management, in his view, has acquired power over managing directors and the shareholders who sit on salary committees. But does Piketty's theory correspond to the facts? Piketty has been so focused on reviewing tax data that he seems not to have bothered to subject his theory to an analysis of the data, which researchers have recently updated from other sources.

Pundits, journalists, and politicians are convinced that there has been a stratospheric surge in the remuneration paid to chief executive officers (CEOs) by the largest corporations. Furthermore, they believe that this surge corresponds to the reality of a business world in which the gap between those earning the highest salaries and everyone else is growing exponentially. They do not seem to be aware that even if top-level salaries did increase dramatically during the 1990s, the average compensation of the CEO of an S&P 500 company nevertheless declined by 46 percent between 2000 and 2010 (see figure 1 and figure 2 in Kaplan [2012]).[2] Nor do they seem aware that during the same period, the median value of remuneration for those individuals has risen by 8 percent since 2000, but fallen by 7 percent compared with 2001 (see figure 1 in Kaplan [2012]). The convergence of the mean and median values implies that, since 2000, boards of directors have been much less likely to pay their CEOs ever-more-exorbitant windfall compensation.

A similar follow-up study was performed on a sample of 1,000 CEOs of smaller companies that are not part of the S&P 500. It shows comparable changes in patterns of remuneration or, certainly, no obvious disparity. In both cases, the average CEO's salary—which in the larger companies is still 200 times the average annual income of an American household—returned, in 2010, to 1998 levels. Note that these figures apply to a new generation of CEOs, whose tenures at the top have significantly decreased (from eight years to six years, on average, if mergers and acquisitions are included) over this period. According to the economist Steven Kaplan, this reflects an increase in the risks of pursuing a top managerial career; it does not really correspond to the putative emergence of mega-managers who name their own salaries and control the very people who assign and define the terms of their jobs. Finally, a comparison of the average income of CEOs in the S&P 500 with the average income of taxpayers in the top 0.1 percent of the income hierarchy, measured by declared tax revenue—a comparison Piketty makes in his book—shows that this ratio, too, has very much declined since its peak in 2001. It has stabilized at levels corresponding to those of the mid-1990s (see figure 2 in Kaplan [2012]).

In other words, the gain in the incomes of S&P 500 CEOs vis-à-vis other professions in the same income cohort hardly amounts to a trend that could be described as exponential drift, as Piketty would have it. And to put this observation in a longer-term perspective, note that the ratio in 2007 was about the same as it was in the late 1930s. To be sure, in the 1930s, John Kenneth Galbraith was already worried about a rise in managerial power compared with that of shareholders, but that concern was certainly not yet a real issue (Kaplan 2012).

These observations are not sufficient to forever obviate Piketty's thesis. No one doubts that this topic is destined to nourish professional debate for many years to come. But the observations do suggest that traditional factors—the market and competition, professional competence and efficiency (otherwise known as talent), and the technological changes that increasingly promote the efficient management of ever larger and more complex organizations—are mostly driving the rise in senior managers' compensation, even in the largest companies. These observations thus *do* contradict Piketty's assertion that from now on, economists should treat the neoclassical concept of marginal productivity as an obsolete research tool, at least when attempting to explain the remuneration of senior managers. Certainly, the observations here lend no support to the notion that we are witnessing the collapse of the traditional model of corporate governance. In reality, economies and markets do not function in the stylized and simplistic fashion they do in Piketty's book, which reflects throughout his resolutely macroeconomic and deterministic approach.

Indisputably, the wages earned by a handful of the best-paid managers in the largest companies are astronomical in absolute terms. In 2010, three American CEOs in the S&P 500 earned more than $50 million per year apiece, compared with an average top salary for S&P 500 CEOs of about $10 million a year. That disparity is a legitimate source of ethical and political concern. But Piketty's proposals would result in an effective marginal tax rate of about 330 percent in the United States (Homburg 2014). Throwing ourselves willy-nilly into the great utopia of such a confiscatory global tax regime would not solve the problem of modern society's extreme distaste for inequality.

A modest improvement, perhaps, would be to begin by focusing on the nexus of national laws, regulations, and tax schemes. In our democratic societies, those factors keep generating a rising and endless search for virtually indestructible legal privileges—through collusion; mutual dependence; and chronic rent-seeking among politicians, bureaucrats, corporations, and civil society organizations (such as trade unions and nongovernmental organizations). But this concept is never mentioned, not even as an afterthought, in a volume comprising almost 700 pages. Piketty's failure to mention public choice theory and its relevance to the question of inequality is surely not the least of the defects in a book that styles itself as encyclopedic in its scholarship.

References

Homburg, Stefan. 2014. "Critical Remarks on Piketty's *Capital in the 21st Century*." Discussion Paper no. 530, Institute of Public Economics, Leibniz University of Hannover, Germany, May.

Kaplan, Steven Neil. 2012. "Executive Compensation and Corporate Governance in the U.S.: Perceptions, Facts and Challenges." Chicago Booth Research Paper no. 12-42, Fama-Miller Working Paper, University of Chicago Booth School of Business; National Bureau of Economic Research (NBER), August 22.

Piketty, Thomas. 2014. *Capital in the 21st Century*. Cambridge, MA: Belknap Press.

5. The Sociology of Piketty's Anti-Rich Stance

Nicolas Lecaussin

The Richest in the World Are Entrepreneurs

Instead of being scandalized, like Thomas Piketty (2014), by the enormous fortunes of the wealthiest people in the world, undoubtedly it would be wiser to observe the three-quarters of them who are entrepreneurs, and not "rentiers." They have created jobs, raised purchasing power, and reduced the number of poor.

In December 2013 the ranking of the wealthiest in the world compiled by the Bloomberg company ("Bloomberg Billionaires") triggered a media reaction on the theme of aggravating inequalities between the richest and the poorest. Observers emphasized the extravagance of the wealth of the 300 richest individuals, estimated to be at $3.7 million. In the same vein, a 2015 Oxfam report on inequality provided data on the richest in the world, including the origin of their wealth; but that report was misleading (Oxfam 2015).

A careful reading of the Bloomberg ranking gives very instructive information on the sociology of the richest individuals in the world: they are mainly entrepreneurs ("self-made men"). Of the 200 wealthiest individuals (i.e., multibillionaires: as of this writing, the 200th has an estimated fortune of $6.38 billion), 140 are entrepreneurs. They built their fortunes on the businesses they created or expanded. Of the 50 largest fortunes worldwide, 40 are entrepreneurs; of the 10 wealthiest, 9 are entrepreneurs. And contrary to what the authors of the Oxfam report argue, of the

80 richest people, only 5 have made their wealth in the finance industry.

The origins of the billionaires' fortunes are diverse. Only 23 of the 200 represent finance fortunes, and only 10 of them are from energy or property; 12 made their fortune in media and 4 in telecommunications; 26 represent new technologies; and 34 made diverse investments (commerce, services, etc.). We have moved far from the early 20th century when many fortunes were made in oil and mining (only 10 of 200 today).

According to "Bloomberg Billionaires," of the 200 wealthiest individuals, 67 are American (in the top 10, 7 are American). Among these American billionaires, 50 are entrepreneurs. "In 2010, self-employed business owners account for an astonishing 70 percent of the wealth of the top 0.1 percent" in America (Sanandaji 2014). The 200 wealthiest people also include 9 French, of whom 4 are entrepreneurs. Germany counts 14 billionaires in the top 200, of whom 8 are entrepreneurs. Not a single billionaire is from the United Kingdom, and Switzerland—the country of choice for the wealthiest—is represented by only 2.

Contrary to clichés, the wealthiest in the world are mainly individuals who create businesses, jobs, and wealth for all.

Wealth That Comes and Goes

For Piketty, world wealth tends to concentrate (the 1 percent of the wealthiest). To remedy that concentration (and fight against inequality), he suggests implementing a worldwide tax on the capital of the wealthiest. Yet, Piketty ignores that even among the wealthiest, mobility is high.

Of the Americans who were in the top 1 percent of the wealthiest people in the world in 1987, only 24 percent were still in that group in 2007, 20 years later (Bernstein and Swan 2008). And only 37 percent were in the top 5 percent of the wealthiest. Almost every year, the individuals in the ranking change and, on average, only two out of five are still present in the 1 percent after 10 years.

The primary source of their fortunes is business creation—and business creation is risky. American entrepreneur Elizabeth Holmes, founder of blood-testing start-up Theranos, is a good example of a rising star quickly downgraded to failure status.

Bill Gates Is Right: Thomas Piketty Forgot Something about the Rich

In a post published on his blog, Bill Gates writes, "Imagine three types of wealthy people. One guy is putting his capital into building his business. Then there's a woman who's giving most of her wealth to charity. A third person is mostly consuming, spending a lot of money on things like a yacht and plane. While it's true that the wealth of all three people is contributing to inequality, I would argue that the first two are delivering more value to society than the third. I wish Piketty had made this distinction" (Gates 2014).

Piketty's statistics show that the wealthiest 1 percent of Americans in 2012 held less than 19.2 percent of the total wealth compared with 18.3 percent in 2007. According to him, the percentage has doubled since 1980. But he forgets to specify that the form of wealth has changed enormously in the past 30 years. The share of income coming from entrepreneurial activity has increased, and the share of wealth from "rents" has declined steadily over the same period. Gates is right to fear that the new tax Piketty proposes would hit new entrepreneurs. The French economist should have tried to understand the rich first.

Take Gayle Cook. The wealth of this entrepreneurial woman and her late husband came from their idea to build "wire guides, needles, and catheters"—in the spare room of their apartment back in the 1960s. The Cook(s) created value for all with their top quality medical devices. Take the late Steve Jobs: I am typing on a MacBook, the thing that has made my life so much easier and made me so much more productive. In France, the entrepreneur Xavier Niel disrupted competition—against the president's will—and made prices decline in the mobile network industry. That effort immensely benefited consumers. Think about Pierre Omidyar, the father of eBay, the platform that allows us to exchange second-hand stuff so much more easily. Or take Peter Thiel, who created PayPal, another system that makes our lives a lot easier. The list could go on and on. These people are billionaires, but they are wealthy because they have created value for mankind.

Rich entrepreneurs create value, of course, but they also create jobs. A French team used the Survey of Consumer Finances and found that "of the 117 million U.S. jobs identified in 2013, 68.5 million or 58 percent were employed in businesses directly managed by the entrepreneurs who had created these businesses—not inherited or even bought. Of those 68 million, 31.6 million are attributable to entrepreneurs whose income rank them in the 1 percent" (Emploi 2017, 2015).

The Philanthropy of the Rich, Another Engine of Progress

Let us return to another point raised in the Gates blog post: philanthropy. This aspect of wealth is often mocked in France, a country where the mainstream thought conceives of solidarity as organized by government, not by a free and responsible civil society. Why is that? The French Revolution's suspicion about intermediate bodies undoubtedly dies hard.[1] French republican ideology is fundamentally based on state control and is, in this regard, somewhat "socialist." Education is also responsible for conveying a culture of dependence and state solidarity. Incentives to solidarity—interindividual and nonpoliticized—are also quite weak in comparison with other countries, in terms of tax deductions, for example. Thus, almost the entire population of France likely sees philanthropy (which is part of what the French would call voluntary solidarity) as a nice idea but a tiny drop of water compared with state-organized solidarity. Piketty himself could evoke such a position (Piketty and Roberts 2014).

A drop of water could, however, transform into a river. The philanthropic behavior of French entrepreneurs, for example, is a start. The last French "philanthropic barometer" showed that "73 percent of business owners and leading executives are personally benefactors. Fifty-six percent of entrepreneurs partake in giving money, with an average of €900, and 54 percent lead supporting actions in projects of general interest (counseling, fund raising, lobbying...). These commitments, which increase with age and income, concern about 300,000 entrepreneurs for a global budget of 200 million euros per year" (ADMICAL 2015). A drop of water? Maybe for France.

A 2012 study on philanthropy of the rich gives an idea of the potential if we consider American philanthropy (Bank of America and Center on Philanthropy 2012). The study focuses on households earning more than $200,000 per year or those with a net inheritance of more than $1 million in 2011. Of those households, 95 percent gave money. The average amount given was close to $53,000 per household, which is 8.7 percent of income. The education sector received the biggest amount of donations (79 percent). The primary motivation was to "give back to the community." This image is far from that of the selfish rich that Piketty conveys.

To reinforce his depiction of the rich as people with questionable ethics, Piketty refers to the *Titanic* story, which he perceives as illustrating, beyond class differences, the arrogance of the rich. Piketty has clearly not grasped that the detestable Cal Hockley, in the movie version of *Titanic*, who Piketty uses as a kind of scarecrow, was in fact a fictional character from director James Cameron's imagination. The horrible capitalist who committed suicide in the film, during the 1929 stock market crash, obviously takes the perfect role in Piketty's story (Goldberg 2014). In fact, many wealthy individuals were particularly virtuous when the ship sank. In his review of Piketty's work, the analyst Jonah Goldberg (2014) questions Piketty's clichés.[2] Goldberg notes, "This *Titanic* business on its own is trivial, but it demonstrates how Piketty sees the super rich as an undifferentiated agglomeration—a single static class bent on protecting its own collective self-interests."

A Self-Serving Declaration of Faith?

As this volume demonstrates, Piketty has constructed his tax policy on a fragile theory and highly debatable statistics. He adds the argument that wealth inequality is dangerous for democracy because it can stir up revolution—because the masses envy the rich. Could it be that his theory, empirical work, and pro-democracy justification are simply a way to "scientifically" dress up good old egalitarianism? Note that, contrary to what he would have us believe, Piketty's position is not necessarily that of the masses; it is that of an intellectual claiming to interpret and speak for the masses.

Let us go a step further. Piketty easily indulges in criticism based on arguments that his targets—especially his fellow economists with whom he disagrees—have a special interest in defending their views. It is tempting to do the same in return. Goldberg (2014), for example, points out that Piketty is not a radical Marxist: after all, he is part of the ruling class. As a former adviser to presidential candidate Ségolène Royal and a columnist for the newspaper *Libération*, he belongs to a leftist class that is not exactly proletarian.

> There is a reason the most passionate foes of income inequality tend to be very affluent but not super rich, intellectuals like Paul Krugman and other journalists eager to set the threshold for confiscatory tax rates just beyond their own income levels. But this sort of class war—the chattering classes versus the upper classes—is only part of the equation. Power plays a huge part as well. A full-throated endorsement of classic leftist radicalism would set a torch to Piketty's own tower of privilege. The State, guided by experts, informed by data, must be empowered to decide how the Rawlsian difference principle is applied to society. Piketty's assurance that inequality "inevitably" leads to violence amounts to an implied threat: "Let us distribute resources as we think best, or the masses will

> bring the fire next time." Once again the vanguard of the proletariat takes the most surprising form: bureaucrats (the true "rentiers" of the 21st century!). A revealing sub-argument running throughout *Capital* is that we need to tax rich people in ever more, new, and creative ways just so we can get better data about rich people! To borrow a phrase from James Scott, author of *Seeing Like a State*, Piketty is obsessed with making society more "legible." The first step in empowering technocrats is giving them the information they need to do their job (Goldberg 2014).

Is this image exaggerated? Nothing proves a priori that Piketty is in the position of the intellectual who produces his analyses because they serve his own interests—a position that he himself criticizes with regard to other economists. However, we find that his vision, whatever its intrinsic motivation, does serve his interests—those of a civil servant living on taxpayers' money and advocating higher taxes for the rich among them. Goldberg's analysis is thus food for thought.

An Ethics of Envy?

Thus, we arrive at the sociology of intellectuals and their hatred not only toward the rich but also toward the system that produces the rich: capitalism. Here, the case is a little difficult because Piketty is supposed to be an economist, not a "simple" intellectual.[3] But, despite his title and his connection to the prestigious Paris School of Economics, he seems not to agree with some of the basic analyses of his discipline: indeed, Piketty's *Capital* is not very concerned about microeconomics and incentive theory. Even his work's macroeconomic theory is contestable. In many ways, *Capital* is a political book, as even its author acknowledges.[4] In that sense, we can place Piketty in the category of "intellectuals."

Joseph Schumpeter, in *Capitalism, Socialism and Democracy*, proposed an explanation for intellectuals' hostility toward capitalism. His idea is that capitalism, allowing a dazzling increase in incomes, doesn't sow the seeds of its fundamental contradiction but of its contradictors. "Capitalism inevitably and by virtue of the very logic of its civilization creates, educates and subsidizes a vested interest in social unrest" (Schumpeter [1942] 2003, 146). Furthermore:

> One of the most important features of the later stages of capitalist civilization is the vigorous expansion of the educational apparatus and particularly of the facilities for higher education. This development was and is no less inevitable than the development of the largest-scale industrial unit, but, unlike the latter, it has been and is being fostered by public opinion and public authority so as to go much further than it would have done under its own steam (Schumpeter [1942] 2003, 152).[5]

Ludwig von Mises also subscribes to this sociological analysis in which intellectuals "loathe capitalism because it has assigned to this other man the position that they themselves would like to have" (Mises [1956] 2008, 16). Robert Nozick (1998) goes even further: The education system, based on centralized and meritocratic logic, is very different from a market economy. The latter is by nature decentralized; in a market economy, merit depends above all on the ability to provide services. Intellectuals, however, who are generally good students, find themselves a bit lost when they leave their favorite mode—school—which gave them confidence and status. In effect, none of that sort of "acquired status" exists in the market; they thus readily perceive the latter as unjust since it does not recognize them at—what they think is—their "fair value." Hence, intellectuals form an aversion to capitalism and its apparent chaos.

Cognitive Biases

We have seen arguments of "class interest" turned against Piketty. Without going too far into determinism, we must remember that

Piketty is a public servant, who, almost by definition, does not truly understand business—as is apparently true of many economists in France. A serious question is the following: how can one write about capital returns and propose radical policies without having taken the slightest risk in life? What true understanding—that is to say, actual experience, not learned from manuals—can one have on the accumulation of capital if one has not set up a business, suffered failures, survived a sometimes unjust business climate, and fought for markets? Such thinkers can easily be too theoretical—in other words, far from reality.

The analyses of the French sociologist Raymond Boudon are useful here. Boudon devoted a large part of his sociological work to the study of the world of ideas, not only ideology (Boudon 1986) but also scientific theories (Boudon 1990). To capture the persistence of anti-liberal views among intellectuals, Boudon distances himself from the idea of producers' interests as a main explanation and focuses instead on cognition. He shows the difficulty, even for an intellectual or a scientist, in getting rid of a mode of thought or what he calls an "a priori" and how it may persist despite one's efforts toward unbiased thinking. In 2004, Boudon could declare the following:

> These views...have gradually crept into social sciences in the 19th and 20th centuries. They have survived the end of ideology and particularly the collapse of regimes aligning themselves with Marxism, first because, as I have tried to show, Marxism is only one of their sources of inspiration among many others; second, because *we* may well renounce a doctrine and yet continue to use without even realizing the explanatory patterns it has placed on the market. This is why it is not uncommon today to observe that intellectuals who renounce Marxism—often in good faith—continue to view the world through Marxist patterns (2004a).

Piketty's "Useful" Theories

Boudon does not minimize socioeconomic factors in his explanation of the anti-liberal—and undoubtedly, by extension, anti-rich—vision of intellectuals: if intellectuals' anti-liberal ideas are not, according to him, based on self-interest, the success of those theories is, by contrast, strengthened by a "market," or rather a demand on the market of ideas. Boudon thus takes on Vilfredo Pareto on the theme of the "useful theory": a theory that proves useful for some applications (i.e., a theory that responds to a demand) may achieve some success. Therefore, the selection of ideas does not operate on the side of production but on the side of the market of ideas.

Boudon illustrates his remarks by recalling how theories on North–South inequalities emerged in the 1960s, notably the idea of the vicious circle of poverty. That idea postulates that poor countries do not have savings and so cannot invest and initiate development. Thus, the North intervenes to help the South. The theory proved useful for many people in that it reinforced not only the ideology but also the irresponsibility of the leaders in the South and a sense of postcolonial guilt in the North.[6] The parallel with Piketty is striking: in its efforts to restart the American economy, the Obama administration in the United States has had to focus on an alternative political theme that sells: inequality. The arrival of Piketty's "useful" book in the United States was timely, and the author was received by Treasury Secretary Jack Lew.

There are undoubtedly advantages to useful theories on both sides of the Atlantic. As numerous U.S. commentators noted, the reading of Piketty's *Capital* does not leave any doubt that the United States represents the "bête noire" (e.g., Boudreaux 2016). Piketty seems to "scientifically" add grist to the mill of a French anti-American tradition and, as a ricochet effect, of anti-liberalism. As Jean-François Revel noted, "the primary purpose of anti-Americanism [is] to blacken liberalism in its supreme incarnation" (2002, 31).

Let us follow Revel further. His important work on the survival of the socialist utopia provides another line of thought around the idea of the useful theory (Revel 2000). Piketty's work not only reinforces our belief that liberalism is the "real culprit of the 20th century," but that it will be the real culprit of the 21st century as well. In this sense, Piketty's book is a weapon of the "grande parade" (*parade* in French means at the same time "parade," "charade," and "parry"), which has prevented the questioning of socialist ideas since the fall of the Berlin Wall. The maneuver is subtle because, though he uses the title *Capital*, Piketty promises to distance himself from Karl Marx—while in reality he proposes a new form of socialism. His remarks in favor of free enterprise should not mask this point: his "corrective" policies would destroy capital. Even if Piketty does not defend economic central planning, his propositions rely on an advanced form of economic control.

The true reasons for the anti-rich obsession of Piketty (and his supporters) are undoubtedly hard to determine. Sociology has its limits. Nevertheless, his acquaintance with the socialist party in France and his radical positions, some of which are, in his own view, "usefully utopian," make Piketty an engaged intellectual before a rigorous scientist. The fragility of the statistics and theoretical constructions on which he bases his conclusions of public policy would make any scientist cautious and skeptical. And though he has more recently softened his remarks, it is difficult not to consider that his analysis is tainted by an ideological bias: a visceral anti-rich bias.

References

ADMICAL. 2015. *Baromètre du Mécénat des Entrepreneurs*, http://www.admical.org/contenu/barometre-du-mecenat-des-entrepreneurs.

Bank of America and the Center on Philanthropy at Indiana University. 2012. *The 2012 Bank of America Study of High Net Worth Philanthropy*. https://philanthropy.iupui.edu/files/research/2012_bank_of_america_study_of_high_net_worth_philanthropy.pdf.

Bernstein, Peter W., and Annalyn Swan. 2008. *All the Money in the World: How the Forbes 400 Make—and Spend—Their Fortunes.* New York: Vintage.

Bloomberg L.P. "Bloomberg Billionaires." http://www.bloomberg.com/billionaires/2016-02-19/cya.

Boudon, Raymond. 1986. *L'idéologie, ou l'Origine des Idées Reçues*. Paris: Fayard.

———. 1990. *L'Art de se Persuader des Idées Douteuses, Fragiles ou Fausses.* Paris: Fayard.

———. 2004a. "Pourquoi les Intellectuels N'Aiment-Ils Pas le Libéralisme?" Presentation at the Institut Turgot in 2004, transcript made available by *Contrepoints* in 2011. http://www.contrepoints.org/2011/08/19/41363-pourquoi-les-intellectuels-n'aiment-pas-le-liberalisme.

———. 2004b. "Pourquoi les Intellectuels N'Aiment Pas le Libéralisme." *Commentaire* 104, Hiver (2003–2004): 773–83.

Boudreaux, Donald J. 2016. "Get Real: A Review of Thomas Piketty's *Capital in the 21st Century*" in this volume, Chapter 17.

Emploi 2017. 2015. "Les Américains riches sont ceux qui ont créé l'*Emploi*." http://www.emploi-2017.org/les-americains-riches-sont-ceux-qui-ont-cree-l-emploi,a0539.html.

Gates, Bill. 2014. "Why Inequality Matters." *GatesNotes* (blog), October 13. http://www.gatesnotes.com/Books/Why-Inequality-Matters-Capital-in-21st-Century-Review.

Goldberg, Jonah. 2014. "Mr. Piketty's Big Book of Marxiness." *Commentary*, July 1. https://www.commentarymagazine.com/articles/mr-pikettys-big-book-of-marxiness/.

Hayek, F. A. [1949] 1990. *The Intellectuals and Socialism.* Arlington, VA: George Mason University, Institute for Humane Studies. First published by the *University of Chicago Law Review.*

Mises, Ludwig von. [1956] 2008. *The Anti-Capitalistic Mentality*. Auburn, AL: Ludwig von Mises Institute.

Nozick, Robert. 1998. "Why Do Intellectuals Oppose Capitalism?" Cato Policy Report, vol. 20, no. 1.

Oxfam. 2015. "Wealth: Having It All and Wanting More." Oxfam Issue Briefing, January. https://www.oxfam.org/sites/www.oxfam.org/files/file_attachments/ib-wealth-having-all-wanting-more-190115-en.pdf.

Piketty, Thomas. 2014. *Capital in the 21st Century*. Cambridge, MA: Belknap Press.

Piketty, Thomas, and Russ Roberts. 2014. "Thomas Piketty on Inequality and Capital in the 21st Century." EconTalk Podcast, Library of Economics and Liberty, September 22. http://www.econtalk.org/archives/2014/09/thomas_piketty.html.

Revel, Jean-François. 2000. *La Grande Parade. Essai sur la Survie de l'Utopie Socialiste*. Paris: Plon. Translated by Jean-François Revel. 2009. *Last Exit to Utopia: The Survival of Socialism in a Post-Soviet Era*. New York: Encounter Books.

———. 2002. *L'Obsession Anti-Américaine. Son Fonctionnement, ses Causes, ses Inconséquences*. Paris: Plon. Translated by Jean-François Revel. 2003. *Anti-Americanism*. New York: Encounter Books.

Sanandaji, Tino. 2014. "Piketty's Missing Entrepreneurs." *National Review*, November 13. http://www.nationalreview.com/article/392596/pikettys-missing-entrepreneurs-tino-sanandaji.

Schumpeter, Joseph. [1942] 2003. *Capitalism, Socialism and Democracy*. London and New York: Routledge. First published by Harper & Brothers.

Section 3. No Capital for the Poor?

Thomas Piketty based his reasoning on the strong assumption that capital accumulation by the rich is safe and relatively simple—in short, almost automatic. That would undoubtedly be good news for the poor in rich countries and worldwide, because they would also benefit from the windfall. Should Piketty therefore not defend better access for the poor to the capitalist accumulation process?

6. Piketty Gets It Wrong

Michael Tanner

For those who believe in the redistribution of wealth, the hero of the hour is Thomas Piketty, the French economist whose book *Capital in the 21st Century* provides a serious critique of inequality in modern capitalist economies and warns that market economies "are potentially threatening to democratic societies and to the values of social justice on which they are based" (Piketty 2014, 571).[1] To remedy that inequality, he argues for a globally imposed wealth tax and a U.S. tax rate of 80 percent on incomes over $500,000 per year.

The left has been rapturous. Piketty's book has been cited multiple times by the *New York Times*, more than any other book in recent memory. Paul Krugman hails it as "the most important economics book of the year" (Krugman 2014). Martin Wolf, writing in the *Financial Times*, lauds it as "an extraordinarily important book" (Wolf 2014). *Capital in the 21st Century* is well researched and contains much useful information and some important insights. But it is not without flaws. Some of the problems are technical—Piketty tends to underestimate the elasticity of returns on capital—but more are deeply philosophical. Piketty takes the evilness of inequality as a given, ignoring the broader question of whether the same conditions that lead to growing wealth at the top of the pyramid also improve material well-being for those at the bottom. In other words, does it matter if some people become super rich as long as we reduce poverty along the way? Which matters more, equality or prosperity?

To cite just one example, Piketty devotes considerable effort to criticizing the rise of inequality in China over the past three decades as it has adopted market-oriented policies. But he largely glosses over the way those policies have lifted millions and millions of people out of poverty.

Piketty's proposed "solutions" are equally problematic. He seems to believe that "confiscatory taxes" (his term) can be imposed without changing incentives or discouraging innovation and wealth creation. Piketty's solutions would undoubtedly yield a more equal society, but also a remarkably poorer society.

Still, Piketty makes some important points. In particular, he notes correctly that returns on capital nearly always exceed the return on labor. With capital held by a relatively narrow group, therefore, rising inequality is inevitable. Moreover, with the wealthy able to pass capital on to their heirs, that inequality will be perpetuated and even extended over generations.

One wonders why, then, Piketty's fans ignore the obvious answer to this problem. Instead of attacking capital and capitalism, why not expand the number of people who participate in the benefits of having capital? In other words, let's make more capitalists.

Yet, the left is unremittingly hostile to exactly those policies that would give workers more access to capital.

Take, for example, 401(k) plans, which allow some 52 million American workers to own stocks and bonds as part of their retirement portfolios. Teresa Ghilarducci, director of the Schwartz Center for Economic Policy Analysis at the New School in New York, has argued before Congress that 401(k) plans should be abolished and replaced by an expanded social-insurance system. Rep. Jim McDermott (D-WA), who sits on the tax-writing Ways and Means Committee, has pronounced himself "intrigued" by Ghilarducci's ideas. And retiring congressman George Miller (D-CA) has called for eliminating or reducing the tax break for 401(k) contributions. The Obama administration has also sought to limit tax breaks for 401(k)s, although primarily for wealthier participants. In a speech calling for the expansion of Social Security, Sen. Elizabeth Warren (D-MA) criticized private retirement accounts like 401(k) plans "that leave the retiree at the mercy of a market that rises and falls and, sometimes, at the mercy of dangerous investment products" (Warren 2013).

No policy proposed in recent years would have done more to expand capital ownership than allowing younger workers to invest a portion of their Social Security taxes through personal accounts. One of the unsung benefits of such Social Security reform is that it would enable even the lowest-paid American worker to benefit from capital investment. Indeed, since the wealthy presumably already invest as much as they wish to, lower-income workers would be the primary beneficiaries of this new investment opportunity.

In Chile, workers, through their pension accounts, own assets equal to approximately 60 percent of the country's gross domestic product. As José Piñera, the architect of Chile's successful pension reform, points out, personal accounts "transform every worker into an owner of capital" (Piñera 1999).

Moreover, my Cato colleague Jagadeesh Gokhale has demonstrated that, because personal accounts would be inheritable, privatizing Social Security would significantly reduce inequality across generations (see, for example, Gokhale et al. [2001]).

It is this "democratization of capital" that attracted honest liberals like Daniel Patrick Moynihan to the idea. Yet, Democrats in Congress today would sooner sell their firstborn to the Koch brothers than even consider the idea.

In the end, there are two ways to address inequality. You can bring the top down, or you can lift the bottom up. Free-market capitalism gives us a chance to do the latter. And if there is a problem today, it is more likely a result of too little capitalism, not too much.

That's something that Piketty's fans should think about.

References

Gokhale, Jagadeesh et al. 2001. "Simulating the Transmission of Wealth Inequality via Bequests." *Journal of Public Economics* 79 (1): 93–128.

Krugman, Paul. 2014. "Wealth Over Work," *New York Times*, March 23. http://www.nytimes.com/2014/03/24/opinion/krugman-wealth-over-work.html?_r=0.

Piketty, Thomas. 2014. *Capital in the 21st Century*. Cambridge, MA: Belknap Press.

Piñera, José. 1999. "Bismarck vs. Piñera: The Innovators Who Changed Global Investing." *Global Custodian Special Report*, Fall.

Warren, Elizabeth. 2013. "The Retirement Crisis." Speech before the U.S. Senate, November 18. http://www.warren.senate.gov/files/documents/Speech%20on%20the%20Retirement%20Crisis%20-%20Senator%20Warren.pdf.

Wolf, Martin. 2014. "Review of *Capital in the 21st Century*, by Thomas Piketty." *Financial Times*, April 15. http://www.ft.com/intl/cms/s/2/0c6e9302-c3e2-11e3-a8e0-00144feabdc0.html.

7. Thomas Piketty's Great Contradiction

Juan Ramón Rallo

In his book *Capital in the 21st Century* (2014), Thomas Piketty concludes that the rate of return on capital is superior to the growth of the overall economy (his famous $r > g$ inequality).[1] As the economist Tyler Cowen (2014) has noted, if Piketty's conclusions are true, then the most reasonable economic policy proposition would not be a global tax on wealth (as Piketty proposes) but instead the privatization of public pensions. And if any underlying trend increases capital proportionately compared with the rest of the economy, why politically suppress that trend (with a wealth tax) instead of allowing all of society to benefit through pension privatization?

Cowen accuses Piketty of omitting the slightest reference to public pension privatization as an alternative to his ambitious tax on wealth. But in fact, Piketty does briefly evaluate the possibility of privatizing pensions and, in my view, his opinions on the subject are a lot tastier and revealing than any omission.

Thomas Piketty on Pension Privatization

According to Piketty, the transition toward private-funded pension systems—by which workers could benefit from the disproportionate appreciation of capital—is not a good idea for the following reason:

> In comparing the merits of the two pension systems, one must bear in mind that the return on capital is in practice extremely volatile. It would be quite risky to invest all

> retirement contributions in global financial markets. The fact that $r > g$ on average does not mean that it is true for each individual investment. For a person of sufficient means who can wait ten or twenty years before taking her profits, the return on capital is indeed quite attractive. But when it comes to paying for the basic necessities of an entire generation, it would be quite irrational to bet everything on a roll of the dice (Piketty 2014, 488–89).

That is to say, according to Piketty, pensions cannot be privatized because the rate of capital return is too volatile and uncertain, taken individually.

Let us recall the general proposition of the French economist: according to him, capitalism tends to offer capital returns superior to the overall growth of the economy, which makes capitalists become proportionally richer and allocates to them larger shares of society's income. As Piketty himself summarizes it: "The entrepreneur inevitably tends to become a rentier, more and more dominant over those who own nothing but their labor. Once constituted, capital reproduces itself faster than output increases. The past devours the future" (Piketty 2014, 571). Or worse: "Regardless of whether the wealth a person holds at age fifty or sixty is inherited or earned, the fact remains that beyond a certain threshold, capital tends to reproduce itself and accumulates exponentially. The logic of $r > g$ implies that the entrepreneur always tends to turn into a rentier" (Piketty 2014, 395).

Piketty's Contradiction

There is an obvious and profound contradiction in Piketty's arguments. On the one hand, he proclaims that capital reproduces itself in an automatic manner, which contributes to its uncontrollable accumulation between fewer and fewer hands; on the other hand, he argues that capital self-reproduces only in average terms, being highly volatile and uncertain as an individual mechanism of wealth accumulation. In fact, I presented this same argument in

Section 2 of this volume, to critique Piketty's view that the incredibly wealthy become ever richer: not only do we find that individuals who were multimillionaires at the end of the 1980s are no longer multimillionaires today, but many among them have since lost more than 80 percent of their fortune (Rallo 2016).

Furthermore, if we want to articulate in one way or another Piketty's two affirmations stated in the previous paragraph, common sense tells us that we should take the opposite position from the French economist's view. With few exceptions, the wealth of the super rich is concentrated in a few companies (Bill Gates in Microsoft, Amancio Ortega in Inditex, Larry Ellison in Oracle, the Koch brothers in Koch Industries, the Walton family in Wal-Mart, etc.). That concentration means those fortunes are subject to volatility and potentially very high uncertainty: if one of those companies disappeared, the corresponding fortune of the extremely wealthy individual would soon collapse. In contrast, private pensions could be invested in a large and diversified portfolio with thousands of businesses, so the middle class would be exposed to the volatility of the global market and not that of one company in a specific sector. The average return from the stock market of the past century is about 5.5 percent per year. In the long term—the period in which we invest for retirement—the stock market offers a fairly stable and low risk return: it's the opposite of investing in individual companies.

Unless Piketty wants to suggest that the companies of the incredibly wealthy are inherently more conservative than the rest of the economy, his assertion—that the wealthier individuals become, the more their wealth automatically capitalizes—loses its meaning. If Piketty supposes that the investments of the rich are very low risk, then his argument that the rich get extraordinary returns—above the rest of the market—doesn't make sense.

More profitability with less risk? If this was the case, there could be only two explanations: (1) businesses of the extremely wealthy enjoy government privileges, or (2) the businesses of the extremely wealthy create more value for consumers than all the other companies because they are always two steps ahead of the competition. In the first case, it would be reasonable for Piketty to demand the suppression of harmful government support; in the second case, Piketty should applaud the excellent management of shareholders in spite of competitive pressure. However, recognizing the second explanation would directly clash with one of the central theses of Piketty's book: capital accumulation is an automatic process, independent of the merits of the investor at managing capital (the reason for which it may be subject to a wealth tax).

Ultimately, as Tyler Cowen said, if we accept the essential message of Piketty's book, then public pensions should be privatized. The French economist is only able to dodge this logical conclusion by falling into a deep internal contradiction that challenges the philosophical perspective in which he analyses economic data. Basically, capital management and accumulation are part of a very complex process of adaptation to a dynamic and changing environment; in that environment, risks and difficulties can be minimized only by an extraordinary knowledge of the economic sector in which one invests—an option available only to talented successful investors—or through a broad diversification of assets—an option available to average savers. Savings and smart business investment: here are the two great strengths that explain the enrichment of a society respectful of property rights and contracts.

References

Cowen, Tyler. 2014. "The Policy Proposals Thomas Piketty Forgot to Mention." *Marginal Revolution* 22, April. http://marginalrevolution.com/marginalrevolution/2014/04/the-policy-proposals-thomas-piketty-forgot-to-mention.html.

Piketty, Thomas. 2014. *Capital in the 21st Century*. Cambridge, MA: Belknap Press.

Rallo, Juan Ramón. 2016. "Where Are the 'Super Rich' of 1987?" in this volume, Chapter 3.

8. Piketty and Emerging Markets

Álvaro Vargas Llosa

Much has been said to refute Thomas Piketty's important book, *Capital in the 21st Century* (2014), from the perspective of developed countries, but not from the standpoint of emerging markets.[1] He contends that the rate of return of capital, roughly twice the rate of growth of the economy, leads to increasing inequality. That view, however, is not consistent with what has happened in the developing world. His notion—that the economy is destined for a modest rate of growth and that capitalists' share of aggregate income will increase at the expense of workers—runs against the evidence from up-and-coming economies.

Before addressing the question of emerging markets, I would note some broader points. Various Austrian School economists have exposed significant flaws in Piketty's understanding of the value of capital and its relation to the return on capital. Randall Holcombe (2016) states that the French economist gets it backwards when he makes the return on capital dependent on the starting value of capital. It is by discounting the expected return generated by capital goods in the minds of entrepreneurs who combine them productively that an estimate of the value of capital can be reached. Because the discount factor depends of the rate of interest, the same capital goods can have very different values depending on the environment. And the aggregate value of capital doesn't tell us how many ventures failed.

Spanish economist Juan Ramón Rallo (2014), for his part, has shown that the rate of return of capital is not the same as the rate of growth of the income generated by capital. It is perfectly possible for the rate of return to be greater than the rate of growth of the economy, and for the ratio between capital and income to be fairly constant throughout the ages. Piketty himself demonstrates that point—but he draws the wrong conclusion from his data.

None of those arguments disproves the fact that inequality has grown in certain periods. Piketty shows that the years leading up to the Great Depression and the Great Recession were two such periods. But given that the rate of interest was manipulated by government in both cases, the inequality derived from the increased value of capital was a byproduct not of perverse free markets, but of monetary interventionism.

Those flaws help us understand why Piketty has not paid enough attention to what the emerging world tells us in relation to capital and income.

Three decades ago, half the world population was living on less than $1.25 a day; today only one-fifth finds itself in that condition (Olinto and Uematsu 2013). About 12 percent of the population of Latin America and the Caribbean were extremely poor at the end of the 1990s; the percentage is half of that today. The key is in the rise of the so-called middle classes. Thanks to Latin America's increasing (though still modest) role in the world economy, the number of people who fill the space between the rich and the poor has grown impressively—according to some estimates, by as much as 50 percent in the new millennium (Ferreira et al. 2013).

Part of that improvement is due to economic growth and part is an effect of income redistribution. We don't need the many studies that largely credit the former to conclude that investments seeking a return have been crucial. The countries that invested less and redistributed more, such as Venezuela, are the ones where the middle classes have been hurt the most in recent years. In Chile, Peru, and Colombia, where the rate of private investment has reached 20 to 25 percent as a percentage of gross domestic product (Peruvian Ministry of Finance 2016), the middle classes have expanded. Only 14 percent of Chileans are poor (Chilean Ministry of Social Development 2015), and the percentage of poor Peruvians has dropped almost by half since 2001 (Mining Press 2015). The capital invested produced value, which generated jobs and better incomes for millions, which led to an expansion of the middle classes. And what did those people do? They got their hands on capital, of course, to create even more value.

According to Piketty, about half of the total value of capital is linked to housing in developed countries. People in emerging countries have also sought to own property—and not just houses. In many countries, they own stock through private pension accounts. Their assets have generated income, part of which has been reinvested and the rest consumed. When they reinvested capital, Latin Americans did not stop to think, What fraction of the national income am I going to lay my hands on, and how is my rate of return going to compare with the rate of growth of the economy? Instead they risked their wealth in all sorts of ventures, expecting to earn more than the cost of capital. The spurt of new businesses opened by the children of poor rural immigrants on the outskirts of Latin America's main cities is the proof.

The value of the capital they own depends on the expected future returns discounted by the prevailing long-term interest rate. What is clear is that, where there were once a few fat cats and a mass of poor people, there is now the product of social mobility—just as in the developed world after (relatively) free markets were allowed to do their job over the past couple of centuries.

References

Chilean Ministry of Social Development. 2015. "Informe de Desarrollo Social 2015." http://www.ministeriodesarrollosocial.gob.cl/pdf/upload/IDS2.pdf.

Ferreira, Francisco H. G., Julian Messina, Jamele Rigolini, Luis-Felipe Lopez-Calva, Maria Ana Lugo, and Renos Vakis. 2013. *Economic*

Mobility and the Rise of the Latin American Middle Class. Washington, D.C.: The World Bank.

Holcombe, Randall. 2016. "Capital, Returns, and Risk: A Critique of Thomas Piketty's *Capital in the 21st Century*" in this volume, Chapter 18.

Mining Press. 2015. "BCR: Pobreza en Perú se redujo a la mitad. Qué dicen el FMI e INEI." http://www.miningpress.com/nota/280604/bcr-pobreza-en-peru-se-redujo-a-la-mitad-que-dicen-el-fmi-e-inei.

Olinto, Pedro, and Hiroki Uematsu. 2013. "The State of the Poor: Where Are the Poor and Where Are They Poorest?" Draft, Poverty Reduction and Equity Department, The World Bank. http://www.worldbank.org/content/dam/Worldbank/document/State_of_the_poor_paper_April17.pdf.

Peruvian Ministry of Finance. 2016. "Investor Presentation: Peru." https://www.mef.gob.pe/contenidos/english/presentations/Peru_Investor_Presentation_20160218.pdf.

Piketty, Thomas. 2014. *Capital in the 21st Century.* Cambridge, MA: Belknap Press.

Rallo, Juan Ramón. 2014. "Leyendo a Piketty: La Auténtica Relación entre Capital y Renta," http://juanramonrallo.com/2014/06/leyendo-a-piketty-la-autentica-relacion-entre-capital-y-renta/.

Part 2. Criticizing the Empirical Strength of *Capital in the 21st Century*

"We have data which prove that…." This type of phrase is usually the punchline to authority in economic debates. The opposition can only keep silent: "They have the *data*…." When faced with theoreticians presented as too abstract, having data seems to allow one to rise above the fray. That implies theory is necessarily detached from reality. The evolution of economic science in the 20th century has indeed imposed levels of theoretical abstraction—or rather *types* of abstraction, imported from physics—which are problematic in their application in social sciences. Work that relies on data appears refreshing.

However, empirical work is not without a degree of abstraction. The word *data* is somewhat misleading: although its Latin origin means "something given," the numbers in question are more likely "picked" than simply "given." A mechanism of selection is inevitably at work: the collection of data is not impartial, and the resulting statistics can be tainted with a certain vision. Furthermore, data processing is another opportunity to practice "smoothing" and "averaging" that can strengthen even further the trends that the researcher would like to demonstrate.

The "art of measurement" of a social scientist can thus be very subtle, with fairly broad room for maneuver in methodological choices. The data can quite easily be made to "speak" in a desired manner. Thomas Piketty is accused of such maneuvering in his empirical analysis of inequality—especially since the book claims that its high empirical content is its major strength.

Section 4. On Capital and Incomes: Questionable Data, Regrettable Omissions

A major challenge in social sciences is that of linking data to concepts. The first problem obviously emerges when the concept itself is fuzzy. How can we evaluate capital? How can we evaluate average household income? What is the right definition and the right way to measure those terms? Do certain measures not imply bias? Can the use of the same official figure through time be a good way to depict the evolution of a phenomenon? In the end, is empirical analysis that simple—in fact, can it not be simplistic? From those different points of view, Thomas Piketty's analysis is not exempt from defects. In both the choice of the content of his concepts and the selection of key figures, the methodological choices of the French economist are easily vulnerable to criticism.

9. Piketty's Numbers Don't Add Up

Martin Feldstein

Thomas Piketty has recently attracted widespread attention for his claim that capitalism will now lead inexorably to an increasing inequality of income and wealth unless there are radical changes in taxation.[1] Although his book, *Capital in the 21st Century* (Piketty 2014), has been praised by those who advocate income redistribution, his thesis rests on a false theory of how wealth evolves in a market economy, a flawed interpretation of U.S. income-tax data, and a misunderstanding of the current nature of household wealth.

Piketty's theoretical analysis starts with the correct notion that the rate of return on capital—the extra income that results from investing an additional dollar in plant and equipment—exceeds the rate of growth of the economy. He then jumps to the false conclusion that the difference between the rate of return and the rate of growth leads through time to an ever-increasing inequality of wealth and of income unless the process is interrupted by depression, war, or confiscatory taxation. He advocates a top tax rate above 80 percent on very high salaries, combined with a global tax that increases with the amount of wealth to 2 percent or more.

His conclusion about ever-increasing inequality could be correct if people lived forever. But they don't. Individuals save during their working years and spend most of their accumulated assets during retirement. They pass on some of their wealth to the next generation. But the cumulative effect of such bequests is diluted by the combination of existing estate taxes and the number of children and grandchildren who share the bequests.

The result is that total wealth grows over time roughly in proportion to total income. The Federal Reserve flow-of-funds data show that, since 1960, real total household wealth in the United States has grown at 3.2 percent a year, while the real total personal income calculated by the Department of Commerce grew at 3.3 percent.

The second problem with Piketty's conclusions about increasing inequality is his use of income-tax returns without recognizing the importance of the changes that have occurred in tax rules. Internal Revenue Service data, he notes, show that the income reported on tax returns by the top 10 percent of taxpayers was relatively constant as a share of national income from the end of World War II to 1980, but the ratio has risen significantly since then. Yet the income reported on tax returns is not the same as individuals' real total income. The changes in tax rules since 1980 create a false impression of rising inequality.

In 1981 the top tax rate on interest, dividends, and other investment income was reduced to 50 percent from 70 percent, nearly doubling the after-tax share that owners of taxable capital income could keep. That rate reduction thus provided a strong incentive to shift assets from low-yielding, tax-exempt investments like municipal bonds to higher yielding taxable investments. The tax data therefore signaled an increase in measured income inequality even though there was no change in real inequality.

The Tax Reform Act of 1986 lowered the top rate on all income to 28 percent from 50 percent. That change reinforced the incentive to raise the taxable yield on portfolio investments. It also increased other forms of taxable income by encouraging more work, by causing more income to be paid as taxable salaries rather than as fringe benefits and deferred compensation, and by reducing the use of deductions and exclusions.

The 1986 tax reform also repealed the General Utilities doctrine, a provision that had encouraged high-income individuals to run their business and professional activities as Subchapter C corporations, which were taxed at a lower rate than their personal income. The corporate income of professionals and small businesses did not appear in the income-tax data that Piketty studied.

The repeal of the General Utilities doctrine and the decline in the top personal tax rate to less than the corporate rate caused high-income taxpayers to shift their business income out of taxable corporations and onto their personal tax returns. Some of that transformation was achieved by paying themselves interest, rent, or salaries from their corporations. Alternatively, their entire corporation could be converted to a Subchapter S corporation whose profits are included with other personal taxable income.

These changes in taxpayer behavior substantially increased the amount of income included on the returns of high-income individuals. This creates the false impression of a sharp rise in the incomes of high-income taxpayers even though there was only a change in the legal form of that income. This transformation occurred gradually over many years as taxpayers changed their behavior and their accounting practices to reflect the new rules. The business income of Subchapter S corporations alone rose from $500 billion in 1986 to $1.8 trillion by 1992.

Piketty's practice of comparing the incomes of top earners with total national income has another flaw. National income excludes the value of government transfer payments including Social Security, health care benefits, and food stamps that are a large and growing part of the personal incomes of low- and middle-income households. Comparing the incomes of the top 10 percent of the population with the total personal incomes of the rest of the population would show a much smaller rise in the relative size of incomes at the top.

Finally, Piketty's use of estate-tax data to explore what he sees as the increasing inequality of wealth is problematic. In part, the problem is due to changes in estate and gift-tax rules, but more fundamentally Piketty fails to recognize that bequeathable assets are only a small part of the wealth that most individuals have for their retirement years. That wealth includes the present actuarial value of Social Security and retiree health care benefits, and the income that will flow from employer-provided pensions. If those sources were taken into account, the measured concentration of wealth would be much less than Piketty's numbers imply.

The problem with the distribution of income in this country is not that some people earn high incomes because of skill, training, or luck. The problem is the persistence of poverty. To reduce that persistent poverty we need stronger economic growth and a different approach to education and training, not the confiscatory taxes on income and wealth that Piketty recommends.

Reference

Piketty, Thomas. 2014. *Capital in the 21st Century*. Cambridge, MA: Belknap Press.

10. The Rich, and Everyone Else, Get Richer

Richard V. Burkhauser

Consensus has it that the rich are getting richer, the poor are getting poorer, and the middle class is barely staying afloat—essentially, that the slice of the economic pie enjoyed by the rich is getting larger at the expense of everyone else.[1]

Research papers I've completed with Philip Armour of the Pardee RAND Graduate School, Kosali Simon of Indiana University, and Jeff Larimore of the Federal Reserve Board show that this "fixed pie" view of the economy is mistaken (Armour et al. 2013, 2014; Burkhauser and Larrimore 2014, and Burkhauser et al. 2012). Growth in after-tax household income was substantial across the entire income distribution spectrum in the 30 years before the Great Recession hit at the end of 2007.

Rather than being applauded for providing valuable goods and services, helping to create jobs, and paying their "fair share," top-income Americans have been turned into villains in an income-inequality story line that urges raising their taxes. The foundation for this tale starts with the well-known research of French economist Thomas Piketty and University of California, Berkeley, professor Emmanuel Saez, which shows that the percentage of taxable market income (e.g., wages, interest, dividends) going to Americans in the top tax brackets is at its highest level since at least 1917. (See especially Piketty 2014 and Piketty and Saez 2003, 2008.)

The point is true, but it's also misleading. Piketty and Saez answer the technical question of how taxable income earned by tax units (i.e., a single filer or a married couple filing jointly, unadjusted for the number of dependents) has changed over time. But that answer has vastly different real-world implications from the answer to this question: How has the access of American households to after-tax resources changed over time?

Consider these points: government-provided Social Security benefits and the Earned Income Tax Credit flow in much greater proportion to lower-income Americans than those in upper-income quintiles; and our income tax system takes progressively more from higher-income households. Fringe benefits and non-wage compensation (employer-provided health insurance, for example) have also become a much larger portion of workers' compensation, as have the value of Medicare and Medicaid health insurance for the aging and the poor.

Because Piketty and Saez's numbers focus on only taxable market income, they miss those additional sources of income and the progressive effects of our tax system on after-tax resources. And, by focusing their analysis on individual tax filing units, unadjusted for the number of persons residing within them, they miss changes in the composition of American households (i.e., an increasing number of households are made up of unmarried single tax filers who share their income).

Such seemingly minor differences in measurement turn out to yield dramatically different changes in the after-tax resources available to all Americans. Consider Figure 10.1. The light gray bars depict changes over time (1979–2007) in the measure of income used by Piketty and Saez, which I call "conventional wisdom." The dark gray bars show that method is a very poor measure of what has actually happened to the after-tax resources available to Americans across the income distribution spectrum during that period. If we take into account unmeasured shifts in household size and the tax units within them, the taxes and transfers of government, and the increasing importance of employer-provided health insurance, then a vastly different picture of growth emerges than the conventional wisdom suggests.

Figure 10.1

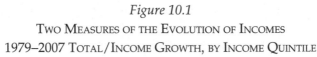

Two Measures of the Evolution of Incomes
1979–2007 Total/Income Growth, by Income Quintile

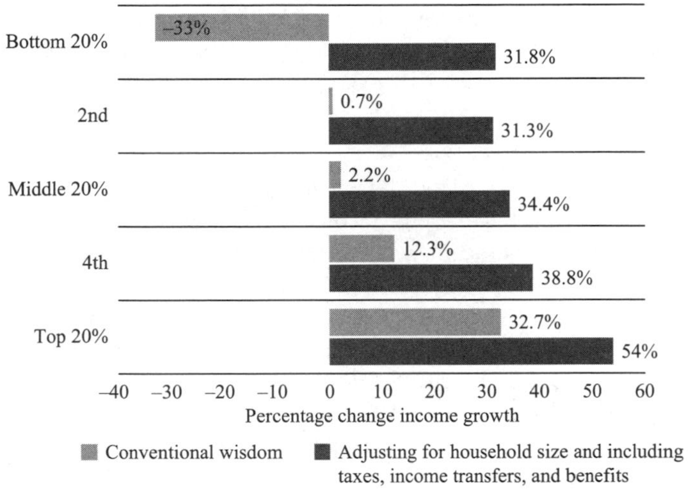

Source: Armour et al. 2014.

The rich did get richer over this period; but so did the middle class, so did the working class, and so did the poorest. Instead of seeing their income shrink by 33 percent, the bottom quintile experienced household after-tax income growth of nearly 32 percent. And, far from stagnating, the middle quintile's after-tax income grew by more than a third. In short, the growth in the productivity of Americans in the top tier of tax units (as shown in the light gray bars in Figure 10.1) increased the size of the economic pie sufficiently to fund the major gains across the distribution of after-tax income (shown in the dark gray bars).

Why is that finding important? That research shows that the period between 1979 and 2007, during which top marginal tax rates were substantially reduced, was generally good for all Americans. Yes, the rich got richer, but so did everyone else. Similarly, the Great Recession had a negative impact on the poor and the middle class, but it also hit those in the top income brackets.

Rather than scapegoating top income groups and further delaying recovery with counterproductive increases in top marginal tax rates, Washington policymakers should focus on policies that encourage the private market investment and innovation that powers economic growth and enlarges an economic pie that can be shared by all.

References

Armour, Philip, Richard V. Burkhauser, and Jeff Larrimore. 2013. "Deconstructing Income and Income Inequality Measures: A Cross-Walk from Market Income to Comprehensive Income." *American Economic Review* 103 (3) (May): 173–177.

———. 2014. "Levels and Trends in U.S. Income and Its Distribution: A Crosswalk from Market Income towards a Comprehensive Haig-Simons Income Approach." *Southern Economic Journal* 81 (2): 271–93.

Burkhauser, Richard V., and Jeff Larrimore. 2014. "The Top One Percent." *Journal of Economic Perspectives* 28 (1): 245–47.

Burkhauser, Richard V., Jeff Larrimore, and Kosali Simon. 2012. "A Second Opinion on the Economic Health of the American Middle Class and Why It Matters in Gauging the Impact of Government Policy." *National Tax Journal* 65 (March): 7–32.

Piketty, Thomas. 2014. *Capital in the 21st Century*. Cambridge, MA: Belknap Press.

Piketty, Thomas, and Emmanuel Saez. 2003. "Income Inequality in the United States, 1913–1998." *Quarterly Journal of Economics* 118 (1): 1–39.

———. 2008. "Income Inequality in the United States, 1913–1998 (tables and figures updated to 2006)." http://www.econ.berkeley.edu/~saez/TabFig2006.xls.

11. Is Housing Capital?

Henri Lepage

Thomas Piketty's argument in *Capital in the 21st Century* is essentially based on the idea of a return, in the late 20th century, of the Gilded Age's trend of the high concentration of capital in the very rich's hands.[1]

One of the book's critical graphs traces the evolution of the capital–income ratio in France, the United Kingdom, and Germany (Piketty 2014, 26, Figure 1.2). It shows the change in the total value of private assets (real estate, financial, and professional, net of debt), expressed in years of national income, from the 1870s to the 2010s. Since 1950, we have seen a huge increase in total asset holding, so much so that the numbers today appear to be approaching levels last witnessed before World War I. This high-amplitude U-shaped curve is central to Piketty's argument. But, there is cause for serious doubt about the probative value of the series.

In economics, we traditionally draw a distinction between *productive capital* (everything that contributes to physical production capacity) and *unproductive capital* (durable goods, primarily those intended for leisure or personal consumption). Yet in Piketty's world, *capital* encompasses everything: houses and other dwellings, arable land, tools, equipment, machinery, financial instruments such as stocks and bonds, patents, and even intellectual property. That definition can only lead to trouble. He includes housing in the global measure of capital, for example, but assesses its value by means of conventional national accounting techniques that report transaction values. Housing, however, is a special kind of good. It is both a consumer good and an investment in which returns are determined by rental prices (both *real*, when received by landlords, and *implicit*, in the form of homeowners' savings on rent they would otherwise be obliged to pay). Thus, it is changes in the ratio of rental prices to disposable income and, more specifically, changes in the ratio of capitalized lease prices to household disposable income that should be taken into account when calculating the capital–income ratios.

In principle, rents and real estate prices should grow in parallel, more or less, which, de facto, should not generate any major difference whether we refer to one (rents) or the other (real estate prices). But that is not what happened in the postwar period. Take France, for example. There has been remarkable stability in the ratio of rents to disposable incomes over the past few decades. Real estate prices, however, have surged by 60 percent in relation to household disposable income (Bonnet et al. 2014, 4, Figure 2). What this contrast tells us is that the spectacular rise in the value of housing assets—which appears, on Piketty's graphs, as the key to the rise of the capital–income ratio over the past 20 years—is a phenomenon related mainly to prices (Piketty 2014, 117, Figure 3.2). It is a property bubble that owes its origin to monetary policy (low interest rates, the creation of the single currency in Europe) and also to something we often forget: the massive rise of land planning schemes that exacerbates land shortages by depleting supply. What we have seen in the housing sector reflects this phenomenon more than it does the cumulative compounding of returns on capital. Although bubbles do have transfer effects, which exacerbate inequality, rising real estate prices do not augment the incomes of homeowners who are renting out their properties. Some people's gains are offset by other people's losses. These effects are quite different from those that Piketty analyzes and are not a cause of exponential divergence (Buiter 2008).

A team of researchers from the Paris Institute of Political Studies, known as Sciences Po, recalculated the housing component of the capital–income ratio in Piketty's argument, replacing numbers from national accounts with assessments based on the capitalized value of rents. Once they estimated the value of housing capital correctly, they found that the capital–income ratio is no higher today than it was in the 1950s (Bonnet et al. 2014). The researchers next applied the revised calculations to the other countries for which price and rents series are available: the United States, the United Kingdom, Canada, and Germany. They found that since 1970, "Aside from Germany, where this ratio appears to be lower than in other countries (Germans do not own as frequently as in other countries), the ratio of capital over income has remained stable in the other countries" (Bonnet et al. 2014, 5). Further research, conducted on data from the Organisation for Economic Cooperation and Development, confirms this diagnosis (Homburg 2014). Moreover, quite beyond technical issues of measurement, we should not forget that 56 percent of all housing stock in France, and as much as 70 percent in the United Kingdom, is owner occupied.

We are thus very far from late 19th century England, where only 36,000 members of the 20-million-strong population were homeowners. So, even assuming that Piketty's hypothesis about the statistics is correct—to wit, that we're in a new phase of accelerating income inequality as revealed by changes in the capital–income ratio—the situation is nothing like that of the Belle Époque, even though the book refers to it over and over. Once we understand that housing accounts for more than half of reported national capital relative to income, we see that the increase in total asset value since the 1970s, and especially since the 1990s, mostly reflects the relative enrichment of the middle class at the expense of those at the top and bottom of the income hierarchy.[2]

There is no explosive trend toward the concentration of wealth among a tiny caste of super rentiers. It thus becomes quite difficult to grant credit to Piketty's central thesis of a return of a serious and worrying dynamics of divergence.

References

Bonnet, Odran, Pierre-Henri Bono, Guillaume Chapelle, and Etienne Wasmer. 2014. "Does Housing Capital Contribute to Inequality? A Comment on Thomas Piketty's *Capital in the 21st Century*." Sciences Po Department of Economics Discussion Paper no. 2014-07. http://www.insee.fr/en/insee-statistique-publique/connaitre/colloques/acn/pdf15/ACN2014-Session5-4-texte-3.pdf.

Buiter, Willem. 2008. "Housing Wealth Isn't Wealth." *Economics: The Open-Access, Open-Assessment E-Journal* 4 (22): 1–29.

Homburg, Stefan. 2014. "Critical Remarks on Piketty's *Capital in the 21st Century*." Discussion Paper no. 530, Institute of Public Economics, Leibniz University of Hannover, Germany, May.

Piketty, Thomas. 2014. *Capital in the 21st Century*. Cambridge, MA: Belknap Press.

12. How to Inflate the Return of Capital

Jean-Philippe Delsol

Measuring capital is not easy. The question of how to do so lies at the heart of one of the most famous controversies in economic science. Measuring capital return is not an easy task either. And the way a particular concept is defined will in turn affect how it is measured. We must beware of "data" supposedly devoid of any theory or vision. In addition, any comparative measure needs a certain degree of coherence: one should not change the reference point depending on the "desired" results. From both these perspectives, unfortunately, Thomas Piketty's work is not exempt from defects.

Confusion in Numbers

Calculating the return of capital at a national level is no simple matter. Piketty defines capital as "the sum total of nonhuman assets that can be owned and exchanged on some market" (Piketty 2014, 46). Thus, he creates a deliberate confusion between capital (productive, financial, and real estate) and transferable assets.

The return on capital is calculated in relation to national income (gross domestic product − fixed capital consumption + net revenues from the rest of the world) as a share of privately held assets (households + nonprofit institutions serving households) net of debt. National income is supposed to be divided between labor and capital. The capital return is thus the ratio of the share of national income going to profits to private capital. This share is estimated from corporations' accounts in national accounting and not derived from all sectors.

Piketty's choices made for calculating return are debatable and lead to exaggerating the return on capital. To discuss wealth inequality among persons, we must focus on the household accounts in national accounting. According to the French National Institute of Statistics and Economic Studies (INSEE):

> Household resources consist mainly of the wages earned, income from property (interest, dividends, income from land, etc.), earnings from market production, and social benefits. The balance of the operating account of households owning sole proprietorships is called "mixed income" because it corresponds indistinctly to the remuneration for the work of the individual entrepreneur and to the remuneration of his productive capital.
>
> Similarly, when households are producers of goods and services for their own end use (excluding housing services), they have a "mixed income" in compensation for their work and tied-up capital. Furthermore, the balance of the operating account of households producing housing services is the gross operating margin, which corresponds solely to the remuneration of real estate capital (INSEE, 2016).

Calculating the gross income of households from assets therefore amounts to adding up the gross operating surplus and property income. The return on assets thus equals the gross income minus interest payments divided by the assets of households net of debt.

As an illustration, we calculated the household property rate of return from 1996 to 2012 according to the INSEE method, and then compared it with gross domestic product (GDP) growth rates, with the rate of return of national wealth net of debt, and with Piketty's results. Our result is far below Piketty's announced 5 percent. Since 1996, on average, the net nominal return of property of households is 0.4 percentage points above the growth rate in current prices (3.58 percent vs. 3.18 percent). This should not be surprising: the convergence between the rate of growth and return on capital is the very basis of the theory of balanced growth.

Moreover, all the return trends are decreasing over the period, which does not appear in Piketty's tables because he uses 10-year averages. In the period 2000–2010, the average rate according to his calculations is 4.3 percent, a figure that he maintains for predicting the rest of the 21st century (Piketty 2014, p. 354). This supposed "constant" is significant because it implies that the capital–output ratio also remains unchanged.

Measuring Growth: National Income or GDP— One Must Choose!

In his book as well as in his scientific paper "Capital Is Back" (Piketty and Zucman 2013), Piketty analyzes the development of the share of capital and its return in the national income of several countries. He specifies that national income includes incomes from land, real estate, and domestic goods as well as net incomes from abroad. This definition is certainly more accurate than GDP, but it is also different because it incorporates elements of both gross national product and GDP.

Further, in all the tables Piketty presents, the evolution of national income is expressed at current prices and not by volume or constant prices. This decision is not erroneous, per se, but its effect is to boost the growth rates of the national income and thus of all variables linked to it. Indeed, the growth rate of the United Kingdom national income was 6.32 percent in 2002 whereas its GDP growth was only 2.2 percent. Similarly, France experienced negative GDP growth in 2008, but its national income increased by 1.85 percent (see Figure 12.1).

National income at current prices thus experiences more important variations than the GDP growth rate in volume, as presented by statistics institutes such as Eurostat and by Piketty himself. However, Piketty calculates capital return based on

Figure 12.1

NATIONAL INCOME GROWTH VS. GDP GROWTH (FRANCE)

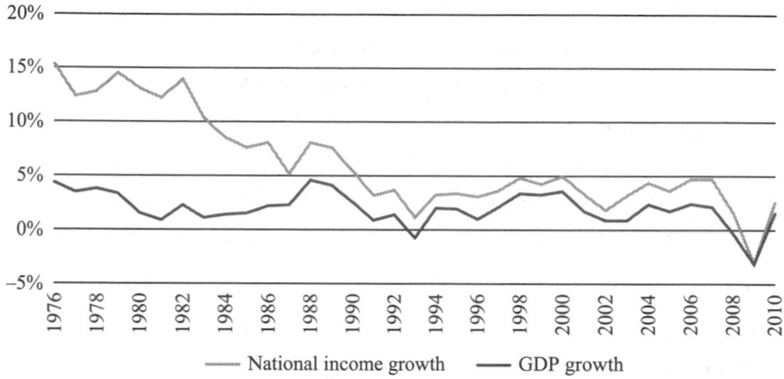

NOTE: See "Piketty Zucman Wealth Income Dataset," http://piketty.pse.ens.fr/files/capital21c/, for the following: For capital, Table A5 (Appendixtables.xls) and Graph G6.5. For national income, Tables A150. For capital income, Tables A48–A50. See also Graphs G3.1, G3.2, G4.1.

SOURCE: Tables from Piketty and Zucman (2013); "Piketty Zucman Wealth Income Dataset," http://piketty.pse.ens.fr/files/capital21c/; Eurostat "GDP main components" dataset, http://ec.europa.eu/eurostat/web/products-datasets/-/nama_gdp_k; Eurostat "Non-financial transaction" dataset, http://appsso.eurostat.ec.europa.eu/nui/show.do. Calculations by P&J Conseil for Institute for Research in Economic and Fiscal Issues.

national income at current prices. To do so, he estimates a country's national capital—a stock—as a percentage of the national income. He then evaluates capital incomes—a flow—as a percentage of national income and relates it to the national capital to calculate its return:

$$\textit{Return of Capital} = \frac{\textit{Rate of Return (\% of Nat. income)}}{\textit{National Capital (\% of Nat. income)}}$$

The outcome of such a calculation is that wealth, in terms of capital and its incomes, is also estimated at current prices, which implies exaggerated rates of return. That would not be a methodological problem if Piketty compared the return on capital (r) with the growth of national income (g). Unfortunately, when it comes to a definitive comparison of the two rates (r and g), he chooses GDP and not national income. Although he does not say so explicitly, that choice is evident in his statistical tables where we see that the national income in France grows at an average rate of 6.23 percent, whereas Piketty mentions an average growth of 2 percent for France. The 2 percent figure corresponds to GDP, not to national income.

Thus, Piketty compares two rates (r and g) that he defines using different methods (the former at current prices—therefore higher—and the latter in volume) and with different measures (the first taking into account foreign wealth, and the second only domestic wealth). According to the data Piketty provides, capital returns in the period 1975–2010 amounted to some 6 percent for France and the United Kingdom and 7 percent for Germany. Had he compared those figures to the growth rates of national income over the same period, he would have concluded that the return on capital (r) was below the growth rate (g) in France ($r = 5.95$ percent and $g = 6.27$ percent), almost equivalent in the United Kingdom ($r = 5.75$ percent and $g = 5.13$ percent), and far superior in Germany ($r = 7.62$ percent and $g = 3.3$ percent). Thus, Piketty would not have been able to draw any general conclusion.

However, by comparing the rates of return to GDP growth rates, Piketty observes that the latter are always lower: GDP increases by 2 percent, 2.4 percent, and 1.3 percent over the period 1975–2010 in France, the United Kingdom, and Germany, respectively. But as already mentioned, this observation is "mechanical" because the indexes and bases for calculations are different.

If Piketty excels in the art of "letting data speak," he has a very peculiar way to perform it, which is not only confusing but highly questionable.

References

INSEE (National Institute of Statistics and Economic Studies). 2016. "Households Resources." INSEE, Paris. http://www.insee.fr/en/methodes/default.asp?page=definitions/ressources-des-menages.htm.

Piketty, Thomas. 2014. *Capital in the 21st Century*. Cambridge, MA: Belknap Press.

Piketty, Thomas, and Gabriel Zucman. 2013. "Capital Is Back: Wealth-Income Ratios in Rich Countries, 1700–2010." *Quarterly Journal of Economics* 129 (3): 1155–210.

Section 5. Forging Statistics, Historical Inconsistencies

Section 4 described how the selection of a particular data type to measure concepts can be problematic. Those problems become serious ethical concerns when the selection *within a series* is made at the whim of the author. Indeed, in that case, it is hard not to foresee the political will "to make the data speak" in a desired direction. This aspect of Thomas Piketty's work is particularly suspect.

13. The *Financial Times* vs. Piketty

Chris Giles

Before the *Financial Times* exposed data errors and omissions found in *Capital in the 21st Century* in May 2014 (Giles 2014), the statistics in Thomas Piketty's best-selling economics book went unchallenged. The conclusions of his work, including his call for an international wealth tax, stirred controversy among academics, commentators, and policymakers. But even his critics generally praised the ambition and quality of the data presented in the text.

Reviewing the book, Lord Mervyn King, former governor of the Bank of England, said, "The principal weakness of the book is that the carefully assembled data do not live up to Piketty's rhetoric about the nature of capitalism" (King 2014). Piketty himself wrote, "Compared with previous works, one reason why this book stands out is that I have made an effort to collect as complete and consistent a set of historical sources as possible in order to study the dynamics of income and wealth distribution over the long run" (Piketty 2014, 19). The sense of diligence in Piketty's compilation of trends in wealth is bolstered by an online technical annex and spreadsheets containing the data, with sources.

Since the publication of the *Financial Times*' (FT) exposé, however, there has been something of a growth industry of researchers and academics querying whether Piketty was either accurate or truthful in stating that his numbers were beyond reproach (Giles 2014).

The FT revealed many unexplained data entries and errors in the figures underlying some of the book's key charts, few of which were adequately explained by Piketty after being challenged. Those unexplained entries and adjustments were sufficiently serious to undermine Piketty's claim that the share of wealth owned by the richest in society has been rising and "the reason why wealth today is not as unequally distributed as in the past is simply that not enough time has passed since 1945" (Piketty 2014, 372).

After referring back to the original data sources, the FT investigation found numerous mistakes in Piketty's work: simple fat-finger errors of transcription; suboptimal averaging techniques; multiple unexplained adjustments to the numbers; and data entries with no sourcing, unexplained use of different time periods, and inconsistent uses of source data. Together, the flawed data produce long historical trends on wealth inequality that appear more comprehensive than the source data allow, providing spurious support to Piketty's conclusion that the "central contradiction of capitalism" is the inexorable concentration of wealth among the richest individuals.

Once the data are cleaned and simplified, the European results do not show any systematic tendency toward rising wealth inequality after 1970. The U.S. source data are too inconsistent to draw a single long series. But when the individual sources are graphed, none of them supports the view that the wealth share of the top 1 percent has increased in the past few decades. There is, however, evidence of a rise in the top 10 percent wealth share since 1970.

The FT uncovered several types of defect. One example of an apparently straightforward transcription error in Piketty's spreadsheet is the Swedish entry for 1920. The economist appears to have incorrectly copied the data from the 1908 line in the original source. Some issues concern sourcing and definitional problems. Some numbers appear simply to be constructed out of thin air.

A second class of problems relates to unexplained alterations of the original source data. Piketty adjusts his own French data on wealth inequality at death to obtain inequality among the living. However, he used a larger adjustment scale for 1910 than for all the other years, without explaining why. In the data for the United Kingdom, instead of using his source for the wealth of the top 10 percent of the population during the 19th century, Piketty inexplicably adds 26 percentage points to the wealth share of the top 1 percent for 1870 and 28 percentage points for 1810.

A third problem is that when averaging different countries to estimate wealth in Europe, Piketty gives the same weight to Sweden as to France and the UK—even though it has only one-seventh of the population. Other inconsistencies pertain to the years chosen for comparison. For Sweden, Piketty uses data from 2004 to represent those from 2000, even though the source data itself includes an estimate for 2000.

Piketty's documents explaining his sources and methods suggest that he uses similar data from death duty records around the world. In fact, he interchanges those records and surveys of the living, which often give very different answers. Switching between the two sorts of data series, particularly for the United States, is important to his results.

Some of the biggest defects relate to the UK data, where his original sources consistently show very large declines of near 10 percentage points in wealth held by the rich in the highly inflationary 1970s. Conversely, Piketty shows the super rich held a greater share of wealth by 1980, and the top 10 percent saw their share fall only 1.5 percentage points. The official data series that Piketty says he used for the UK after 1980 shows little increase in inequality over the next 30 years, while his figures show a steep rise. So far, the official wealth data for the UK has not shown a rise in inequality when using any consistent data set over recent years.

These data errors and omissions do not mean that wealth inequality will not rise. The FT did not make any predictions. It did, however, uncover, investigate, and report that the deterministic charts in Piketty's book were based on flimsy foundations without sufficient recognition of that fact.

References

Giles, Chris. 2014. "Piketty Findings Undercut by Errors." *Financial Times*, May 23.

King, Mervyn. 2014. "Capital in the 21st Century by Thomas Piketty, Review." *Telegraph*, May 10. http://www.telegraph.co.uk/culture/books/bookreviews/10816161/Capital-in-the-Twenty-First-Century-by-Thomas-Piketty-review.html.

Piketty, Thomas. 2014. *Capital in the 21st Century*. Cambridge, MA: Belknap Press.

14. Piketty Is Misleading about the Swedish Case

Malin Sahlén and Salim Furth

When Thomas Piketty writes about the Swedish wealth distribution that "inequality in Sweden has increased significantly since 1980–1990 (and in 2010 was only just a bit smaller than in France)" (Piketty 2014a, 344), it is obviously very useful for Swedish debaters who want to see a reinstated estate tax or a tax on wealth or property.[1] Nevertheless, it is false. In fact, Piketty adjusted the available data, in a seemingly unfair way, to create a better story.

The figures provided by Thomas Piketty support the story he wants to show about Sweden and Europe (Sweden represents a disproportionate part of the European average, so what Piketty does with Swedish data is significant even for the international debate). The *Financial Times* has previously criticized Piketty's empirics, and we have now made a thorough comparison between the data over the last four decades that Piketty received from Swedish researchers Jesper Roine and Daniel Waldenström (2009) and Piketty's presentation of those data in his book. We find that Piketty uses Roine and Waldenström's data in a misleading way.

Roine and Waldenström published estimates of the concentration of wealth for 37 individual years from 1873 to 2006. Piketty explained in his response to the *Financial Times* that he used averages from his source data to smooth over short-term volatility and present only long-run trends. He explained, "[for] instance, '1870' is computed as the average for years '1873–1877',

'1910' as the average '1907–1908', and so on" (Piketty 2014b). This method is reasonable. However, Piketty did not stick to his own method.

Instead, for most decades he cherry-picked a single data point that best aligned with the story he wanted to tell, ignoring the rest of the data. In all, Piketty's 12 decadal data points are based on just 15 of Roine and Waldenström's data points. The majority of Roine and Waldenström's data, especially for recent years, was completely ignored.

Piketty's goal was to show wealth concentration rising as much as possible from the 1980s to the present. To do so, he used Roine and Waldenström's estimate of wealth concentration in 1985, which just so happens to be the most egalitarian year they measure. Piketty ignores data for 1983 and 1988. To represent the 1990s he chooses 1992. Anybody who lived through that era in Sweden knows that 1992 was not a typical year!

Worst of all, Piketty's data for the 2010s appear completely unrelated to their alleged source. Although Piketty's citation says that the 2010s are based on Roine and Waldenström's data for 2005 and 2006 (which is already a questionable choice, since those years should have been averaged along with the data from 2000–2004), his published estimate of wealth concentration in the 2010s is higher than Roine and Waldenström's estimates for any year after 2000! Perhaps Piketty used a different source; if so, it is his responsibility to correct the inaccurate citation.

So overall, he excludes the majority of the years in the data; he picks, seemingly arbitrarily, the years that fit the story he wants to show for Sweden; and he comes up with an estimate for 2010 that is unsupported by the source data.

In this dishonest way, Piketty can show a curve where wealth inequality since 1980 appears to have increased continuously and significantly. In reality, we saw a jump from the 1980s to the 1990s, but since then Sweden has become more equal—contrary to Piketty's story.

Figure 14.1

PIKETTY'S DATA DISCREPANCIES FOR SWEDEN

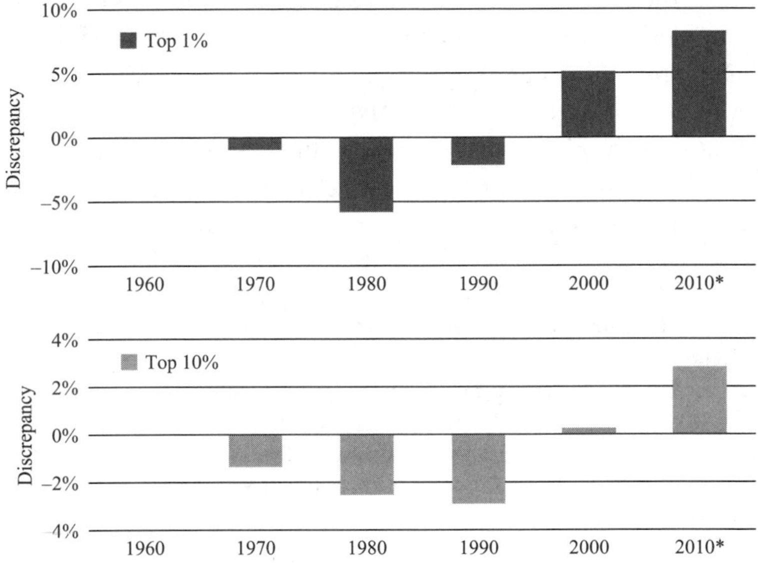

NOTE: * = 2010 estimates compare Piketty's estimates to data from 2005 and 2006.
SOURCES: Roine and Waldenström (2009) and Piketty (2014a).

For recent decades, Piketty used only 7 to 18 available data points. Figure 14.1 shows the discrepancy between Piketty's estimate and an estimate based on all available data points. Using all the data available, we find that Piketty systematically made wealth concentration appear lower than what it was in the 1980s and 1990s and higher than it was in the 2000s. The estimates labeled "2010*" compare Piketty's estimates to data from 2005 and 2006, which he claims are the source of his 2010 estimates. In our view, Roine and Waldenström do not provide enough data to accurately estimate wealth concentration in the 2010s.

What should be of greater interest in Sweden is that the distribution of wealth is now more equal than during most of the 20th century, and shows no signs of becoming much less egalitarian. That is positive in many ways, not the least since it means that more people now have possibilities to build savings. That itself allows for entrepreneurship, socioeconomic mobility, and more independence from government—things that Swedes could use more of. Sweden needs to continue the discussion about how even more people can build substantial savings—but it must be based on facts. Should Piketty's ideas gain a foothold in Sweden, however, we can expect a less factual discussion.

References

Piketty, Thomas. 2014a. *Capital in the 21st Century*. Cambridge, MA: Belknap Press.

———. 2014b. "Response to FT." Vox, May 30. http://www.voxeu.org/article/factual-response-ft-s-fact-checking.

Roine, Jesper, and Daniel Waldenström. 2009. "Wealth Concentration over the Path of Development: Sweden, 1873–2006." *Scandinavian Journal of Economics* 111 (1): 151–87.

15. Challenging the Empirical Contribution of Thomas Piketty's *Capital in the 21st Century*

Phillip W. Magness and Robert P. Murphy

Introduction

Thomas Piketty's *Capital in the 21st Century* begins with a bold claim (2014b). The ensuing work, he promises, is "based on much more extensive historical and comparative data than were available to previous researchers, data covering three centuries and more than twenty countries, as well as a new theoretical framework that affords a deeper understanding of the underlying mechanisms" of his subject matter (Piketty 2014b, 1). Though he qualifies his assertion with an acknowledgment of an imperfect and incomplete data set, that concession should not be mistaken for modesty. As Piketty repeatedly reminds his readers over the ensuing 700 pages, his unprecedented assemblage of data supposedly sets his work apart from the literature on wealth inequality that—he contends—frequently suffers from "an abundance of prejudice and a paucity of fact" (2014b, 2).

Piketty presents an unconventional theoretical argument rooted in hypothesized "laws of capitalism" and radical policy recommendations in the form of an 80 percent top marginal income tax rate and an *annual* 5 percent global wealth tax on the biggest fortunes (2014b, 512, 530). When paired with those factors, Piketty's claim to an empirically robust and data-heavy narrative has always been the strongest ecumenical feature of his work.[1] Empirics are also the root of much of the book's claimed novelty, as well as its self-stated purpose of "patiently searching for facts and patterns and calmly analyzing economic, social, and political mechanisms that might explain them" to better inform the public discourse about the causes and consequences of global wealth inequality (Piketty 2014b, 3).

Data—"as extensive as possible a set of historical data" as can be gathered—and, more specifically, the story in those data thus become the main evidentiary tool on which Piketty predicates his work (2014b, 16). Indeed, he goes on to extol his own "novel historical sources" and twice more lays claim to a patient, empirically driven search for "facts and patterns" within them before the conclusion of the first chapter (2014b, 20, 31–32). Although Piketty's product is part theoretical argument, part empirical exercise, and part policy recommendation, its unifying rationalization is an overarching historical narrative about the characteristics of human wealth accumulation, derived from and purportedly sustained in data.

Given these extensive claims, not to mention the heavy criticism directed toward certain other works in the wealth inequality genre, readers might be surprised to learn that Piketty's reported "three centuries" of empirics infrequently predate 1900 beyond a stray data point or two connected by a century's worth of linear interpolation. His claimed global analysis consistently examines only three countries—France, Great Britain, and the United States—with more than passing rigor, with only occasional forays into Sweden and Germany beyond that. Even many of his 20th-century figures, presumably constructed from better records and more readily available data sources, are often products of further interpolation and decennial averaging around multiyear and decade-long gaps. Taken alone, these circumstances might only attest to the inherent difficulties of amassing a large, continuous economic time series. A more serious problem emerges, though, when an author attempts to interpret highly specific historical events through data points that are substantially less thorough or conclusive than their initial presentation suggests.

Finally, the investigator may become downright alarmed when discovering the dubious foundation of some of Piketty's "novel" data sets, because Piketty's charts do not convey such weakness to the innocent reader. Furthermore, Piketty's narratives are occasionally peppered with wildly inaccurate historical "facts" that, coincidentally, seem to bolster his desired interpretation of the surrounding data. In that context, the various leaps and judgment calls that Piketty often makes in his historical reconstructions should raise alarm bells.

History: Misconstrued and Missing

At its most basic descriptive level, Piketty's presentation of major historical events at the center of his argument is laced with factual error. In addition to suggesting an inattentiveness to detail, a recurring problem of factual inaccuracy with historical events indicates that interpretive extrapolations from these errors, as well as more sophisticated data claims that appear throughout the book, may suffer from a basic fault in their underlying historical assumptions. Although we will not endeavor to pick apart his most extensive historical recounting—the 20th-century French economy—it is fair to note that he struggles, and struggles mightily at that, in many instances when he takes up the economic history of the United States. The book's favorable portrayal of Franklin Roosevelt's New Deal policy initiatives, which function as a seminal event in Piketty's 20th-century narrative as well as an important precedent for his prescription of confiscatory tax rates, is illustrative. Consider Piketty's descriptive retelling of Depression-era tax policy:

> The Great Depression of the 1930s struck the United States with extreme force, and many people blamed the economic and financial elites for having enriched themselves while leading the country to ruin.... Roosevelt came to power in 1933, when the crisis was already three years old and one-quarter of the country was unemployed.

> He immediately decided on a sharp increase in the top income tax rate, which had been decreased to 25 percent in the late 1920s and again under Hoover's disastrous presidency. The top rate rose to 63 percent in 1933 and then to 79 percent in 1937 (2014b, 506–7).

The problem with Piketty's historical narrative in this instance is one of basic fact. Simply put, his dates are all wrong. As readily accessible tax records illustrate, the top marginal income tax rate was actually brought down to 25 percent by the year 1925, which is not "the late 1920s" and which was well within the presidency of Calvin Coolidge (with Herbert Hoover taking office on March 4, 1929).[2] More troubling still for Piketty's narrative, it was under Hoover that the rate was raised to a decidedly punitive 63 percent under the Revenue Act of 1932. And just to round out Piketty's tax-error trifecta, the top rate increased under Franklin Roosevelt to 79 percent in 1936, not 1937 as Piketty claims.[3]

We see another example from this playbook—namely, inventing historical "facts" to support his narrative—a bit earlier in the book when Piketty informs his readers in a parenthetical remark, "Herbert Hoover, the U.S. president in 1929, thought that limping businesses had to be 'liquidated,' and until Franklin Roosevelt replaced Hoover in 1933, they were" (2014b, 472). The claim is simply not true. In his memoirs, Hoover quotes the (in)famous advice given to him by Treasury Secretary Andrew Mellon to "liquidate labor, liquidate stocks, liquidate the farmers, liquidate real estate" (1952, 30–31). But the rhetorical point of Hoover bringing up this advice was to assure his reader that he had *rejected* such tough love. Hoover was compassionate with his misguided subordinate, though, writing, "Secretary Mellon was not hard-hearted . . . . He felt there would be less suffering if his course were pursued. The real trouble with him was that he insisted that this was just an ordinary boom-slump." Piketty is not alone in attributing to Hoover the very view that Hoover explicitly renounced, but it is nonetheless one of many examples of demonstrably false statements in the book that conveniently align with Piketty's historical worldview.

The common theme of these factual errors is that Piketty uses them to augment certain historical political events and figures that align with his own modern prescriptions. In that sense, a specific narrative construction of the past—even though factually erroneous and misconstrued—may be seen to lend favor to desired policies in the present day.[4] We see a comparable episode when Piketty turns to more modern times and the U.S. federal minimum wage: "From 1980 to 1990, under the presidents Ronald Reagan and George H. W. Bush, the federal minimum wage remained stuck at $3.35, which led to a significant decrease in purchasing power when inflation is factored in. It then rose to $5.25 under Bill Clinton in the 1990s and was frozen at that level under George W. Bush before being increased several times by Barack Obama after 2008" (2014b, 309).

Here again, this "history" is utterly wrong, as readily available federal sources reveal.[5] Piketty's description is so at odds with actual history that it is easiest if we present the correct information in a table (see Table 15.1).

Table 15.1

U.S. FEDERAL MINIMUM WAGE, SELECT PERIODS

Date	Minimum Wage	President in Office
January 1, 1980	$3.10	Jimmy Carter
January 1, 1981	$3.35	Jimmy Carter
April 1, 1990	$3.80	George H. W. Bush
April 1, 1991	$4.25	George H. W. Bush
October 1, 1996	$4.75	Bill Clinton
September 1, 1997	$5.15	Bill Clinton
July 24, 2007	$5.85	George W. Bush
July 24, 2008	$6.55	George W. Bush
July 24, 2009	$7.25	Barack Obama

SOURCE: U.S. Department of Labor (2016).

Piketty's breezy discussion of minimum wage is *almost* correct—though unbelievably misleading—if one were to look at his treatment up through Clinton. (Even in that instance, he is wrong about 1980 vs. 1981; and the minimum wage under Clinton was $5.15, not $5.25.) But for him to claim that the minimum wage was frozen under George W. Bush until being raised under Obama is utter nonsense. If we wanted to be pedantic, we could bring up the fact that the July 24, 2009, increase that occurred under Obama was due to legislation signed by George W. Bush, but that would detract from the more basic point that Piketty cannot even get his years, dollar amounts, and presidential administrations right. There are many problems with Piketty's portrayal, given the ease with which a more conscientious researcher could have verified such basic information from U.S. Department of Labor tables. Indeed, Piketty's own data files indicate his awareness of that source.[6] Yet, Piketty's bizarre errors aren't completely without a pattern: they serve to paint ostensibly market-friendly Republican presidents as ogres and make liberal Democrats the heroes of the working class and purveyors of policies that Piketty embraces.

Keep these "easy" examples of Depression-era tax rates and minimum wages since 1980 in mind when we delve into harder areas of obscure data series on wealth distribution, where Piketty at many places asks the reader to trust him.

Before immersing ourselves in the wealth data, however, let's consider another error of omission in Piketty's figure 14.2 (2014b, 504), which is a comparative historical portrayal of the top estate-tax rate in the United States, Britain, and France. The chart shows the United States as a relative latecomer to the approvingly referenced practice of estate taxation, starting only after 1916. Piketty evinces no awareness that the United States actually began its modern experiments in estate taxation with the Spanish-American War Revenue Act of 1898.[7]

It is worth elaborating on this example because it typifies a recurring problem of shoddiness in Piketty's claims of historical "facts." At first glance, his figure 14.2 seems authoritative and authentic; the reader can see the different symbols representing the individual annual inheritance tax rates for each country. The issue is his careless omissions. What Piketty apparently did was research the origin of the *modern* federal inheritance tax in the United States, while simply assuming that the federal estate tax was nonexistent beforehand. The factual errors displayed in his chart thus reveal the absence of even cursory research. As an easily accessed Tax Foundation report notes, in contrast to Piketty's chart:

> The federal government resorted once again to transfer taxes in the 1860's when the Civil War and subsequent reconstruction forced Congress to look for additional federal revenue. A series of Acts passed in 1862, 1864, and 1866 created and refined the first federal inheritance tax. In 1870 Congress repealed this tax as demands for federal revenue eased. When the Spanish-American War flared up in 1898, Congress again relied on a transfer tax, this time an estate tax, to defray some of the costs of the conflict. This tax was repealed in 1902 (Fleenor 1994, 3–4).

The 1898 act's estate tax was even upheld in a Supreme Court ruling in 1900 (*Knowlton v. Moore*, 178 U.S. 41). Part of that dispute concerned the *progressivity* of the tax, making Piketty's oversight all the more surprising. But it does remain consistent with a historical narrative that casts the late 19th century as an "unenlightened" period of capitalism run amok.

Although a superficial credulity for partisan talking points seems evident in Piketty's rendering of the Depression, historical tax rates, and the minimum wage, there is also something more elementary at play in his recounting of historical events. Piketty's approach to the economic history of the United States shows telltale signs of a scholar who is deeply unfamiliar with the historical particulars of his subject matter and frequently errs in recounting them. Yet, he stakes strong interpretive claims upon his constructed "history" and chooses to enlist it for prescriptive purposes nonetheless.

Data Discrepancy or Data Discretion?

In the aforementioned cases, Piketty's facts are simply wrong or his data missing. As problematic as those failings may be, they are only the most easily detected of similar factual discrepancies and what appear to be wholly discretionary calls buried deep in his data files. And though Piketty has received praise for following the increasingly common practice of making his source data available to other scholars by posting them online, this act of courtesy should not be mistaken for a license to impute validity to their contents. Consider Piketty's figure 13.1 (2014b, 474), portraying historical tax revenue to national income ratios across a series of countries since 1870. The chart itself suffers from another tax history imprecision that is virtually undetectable by the investigator who relies solely on the information in the book; it becomes apparent only upon close scrutiny of its source files. Two images of Piketty's root data file for the United States and its formulas appear in Figure 15.1.

Note in particular that Piketty's figure for 1900 consists of a decennial average for that decade at 6 percent (expanded to 6.122 percent when rounding is removed). This figure comes from a U.S. Census Bureau–produced table of historical revenue data from 1902 to the present day. Although his figure 13.1 suggests a complete accounting to the casual reader, Piketty actually has no data source for the 32 years prior to 1902, extending his series backward to the reported starting point of 1870. His claimed numbers for those three decades appear not to have been obtained from any actual source, but rather through the alternating addition or subtraction of 0.5 percentage points projected backward from the 1900 average. He evidently filled the gap in his own data collection—needed to bring the U.S. time series into line with his

Figure 15.1

MANUFACTURED DATA POINTS IN PIKETTY'S ACCOUNTING OF HISTORICAL U.S. TAX REVENUE

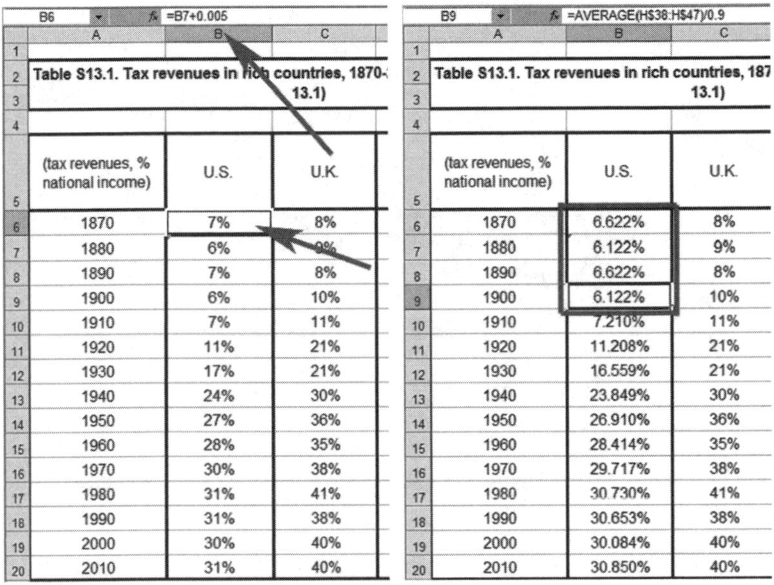

B6 =B7+0.005

	A	B	C
1			
2	Table S13.1. Tax revenues in rich countries, 1870-		
3			13.1)
4			
5	(tax revenues, % national income)	U.S.	U.K.
6	1870	7%	8%
7	1880	6%	9%
8	1890	7%	8%
9	1900	6%	10%
10	1910	7%	11%
11	1920	11%	21%
12	1930	17%	21%
13	1940	24%	30%
14	1950	27%	36%
15	1960	28%	35%
16	1970	30%	38%
17	1980	31%	41%
18	1990	31%	38%
19	2000	30%	40%
20	2010	31%	40%

B9 =AVERAGE(H$38:H$47)/0.9

	A	B	C
1			
2	Table S13.1. Tax revenues in rich countries, 187		
3			13.1)
4			
5	(tax revenues, % national income)	U.S.	U.K.
6	1870	6.622%	8%
7	1880	6.122%	9%
8	1890	6.622%	8%
9	1900	6.122%	10%
10	1910	7.210%	11%
11	1920	11.208%	21%
12	1930	16.559%	21%
13	1940	23.849%	30%
14	1950	26.910%	36%
15	1960	28.414%	35%
16	1970	29.717%	38%
17	1980	30.730%	41%
18	1990	30.653%	38%
19	2000	30.084%	40%
20	2010	30.850%	40%

SOURCE: Piketty (2014b), Data Appendix, Table S13.1, http://piketty.pse.ens.fr/en/capital21c2.

European records—by constructing it *ex nihilo*. Figure 15.2 shows Piketty's missing data points.

Clearly, such an invention of numbers, even on a relatively small part of a comparative graph, leaves Piketty vulnerable to charges of data manipulation or contrivance. Most researchers, when faced with two or more historical series of different lengths, would simply start the plot from the shorter series later on the graph at the point the data became available. Piketty instead decided to fill in his chart with numbers he pulled out of the air. Equally significant is that the missing data actually do exist, though he would have needed to do more than superficial

Figure 15.2

MISSING U.S. DATA POINTS IN PIKETTY'S FIGURE 13.1

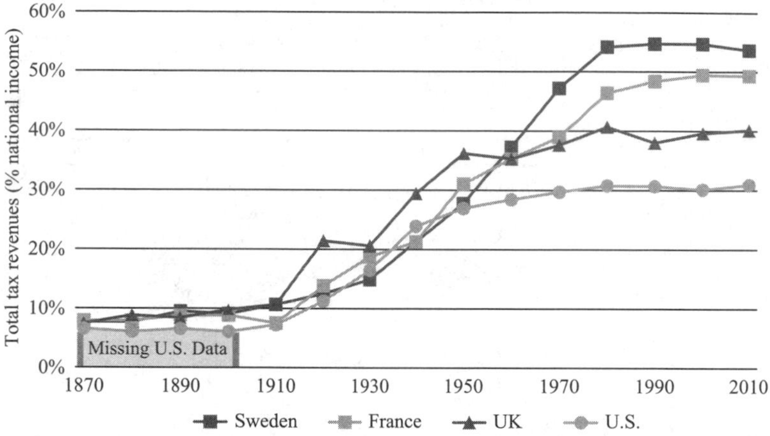

Total tax revenues were less than 10% of national income in rich countries until 1900–1910; they represent between 30% and 55% of national income in 2000–2010. Sources and series: see piketty.pse.ens.fr/capital21c.

SOURCE: Piketty (2014b), Figure 13.1, with 1870–1901 U.S. data gap denoted.

probing to incorporate them into his charts.[8] Thus, when other similarly questionable decisions pepper his data presentation in increasingly complex ways, with claims that carry greater interpretive significance to his theory of capital accumulation, there is legitimate cause for concern.

Another problem appears in Piketty's figure 11.12 (2014b, 423) and accompanying charts, which purport to illustrate wealth inheritance flows in the United Kingdom since the beginning of the 20th century. In this instance, Piketty uses a bizarrely creative averaging technique to obtain decennial averages for 1900 and 1910, deviating from the standard formula he uses for calculating the averages for the remainder of the 20th century. In Piketty's presentation, the two data points show a relatively flat and stable trend for about a decade prior to the sudden drop in inheritance flows allegedly precipitated by World War I, a seminal trigger event in the 20th century's dissipation of concentrated capital, according

Figure 15.3

UK Inheritance Flows, Piketty Chart vs. Corrected Decennial Average

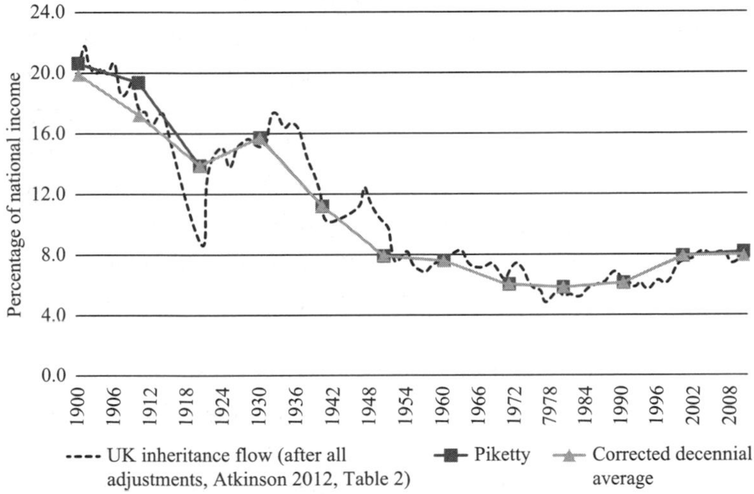

Source: Original data and corrections made using Piketty (2014b), Data Appendix, Table S11.3.

to Piketty's main argument. Figure 15.3 compares Piketty's constructed trend line (square data points in dark gray) against the raw annual source data he uses, as well as our own "corrected decennial average" using the same source data.

Notice that our corrected decennial average, included for comparison against Piketty's alterations, both tracks the raw source numbers more carefully and shows a much sharper downward trend between 1900 and 1910. That outcome is not accidental. Whereas Piketty's other decennial averages encompass the represented decade, as do our corrections (e.g., his 1920s figure averages the years 1920–1929), he appears to have intentionally back loaded his calculations for the 1900 and 1910 data points with numbers that are actually taken from their respective preceding decades. Deviating from the consistent decennial calculations of later decades, Piketty's resulting chart actually presents 1896–1902 figures in its average for the "1900s" and 1904–1910 figures for the "1910s," without any annotation or indication that he performed this backward shift. His intent is difficult to discern, but these discretionary modifications do produce a picture that is more amenable to a grand narrative about a static, capital-hording aristocracy in the Belle Époque. Alternatively, a modest but already-declining inheritance flow pattern in the decade and a half before the war—as suggested in the raw data—might present a wrinkle that requires a more nuanced investigation than Piketty's sweeping theory of capital accumulation permits.

From Theoretical Arguments to Data Illustrations

At this point, it is fair to ask whether the issues discussed so far, even if acknowledged as problematic to Piketty's historical narrative, pose a larger challenge to his theoretical argument. Briefly summarized, Piketty posits that capitalism is afflicted by an internal "contradiction" wherein an inherent propensity exists for the rate of return on capital—and thus the wealth of its owners—to outpace overall economic growth, and with it the employment income of workers (2014b, 571). The implication of this theory is a long-term divergence between a "rentier" class of capital-sustained wealthy elite and those who rely on their labor to earn income, perhaps best epitomized by the wealth disparities of the late "Gilded Age." Piketty appends this argument with a historical explanation for decreasing wealth inequality in the 20th century, which he attributes to the ravages of two world wars and an intervening depression on the previous century's capital-hording aristocracies, as well as the "progressive" era rise of confiscatory taxation. His predictive and prescriptive arguments, in turn, contend that this dissipation is at an end because of policy changes and trends in the global economy. Rounding out this argument, he claims that the experience of the late 20th century through the present day begins to resemble an oft-referenced "U-shaped" trend wherein capital-accumulation-fueled wealth disparities are presently on course to return to their Victorian levels, or something similar.

Piketty formalizes his narrative into a set of quasi-scientific "laws" of capitalism, each representing specific characteristics of capital accumulation and its return. Those theoretical underpinnings have proven fertile ground for criticism, and while further inquiry of that vein is certainly warranted, it falls beyond the scope of our present examination.[9] We accordingly view the theoretical line of scrutiny as a distinct issue with Piketty's work, although one that is complementary in its conclusions to our assessment of his empirics.

Returning to Piketty's data, their function is fundamentally evidentiary: that is, his data-driven historical analysis supplies the numbers that validate his theorizing about the nature of capital. He goes about the task through multiple examples drawn mostly from France, Britain, and the United States. When his data are examined as a century-long time series, his argument thus rests on demonstrating the U-shaped trend amid metrics that attest to capital accumulation and wealth distributions in a country or region. A U-shaped resurgence in wealth disparity between the highest levels and the rest of society might accordingly indicate the long-term effects of returns on capital, r, outpacing the rate of growth, g. A U-shaped curve, showing a divergent ratio between privately owned capital and national income, might similarly validate Piketty's claimed causal source for concurrent inequality trends—that is, a reconstitution of the capital stock that he places at the center of his late–20th century narrative and forecasts for the 21st century.

Dissecting Piketty's data in their entirety would exceed the scope of a single article, so our discussion will focus on two iterations of the U shape that cut to the core of his evidentiary claims. The first is Piketty's widely cited figure 10.5 (2014b, 347), in which he purports to represent 200 years of wealth inequality in the United States. The figure's title is itself a misnomer, as the entire first century of Piketty's graph is based on only two data points, 1810 and 1870, connected by linear interpolation. He attempts to weave a story of 19th-century America as something of a paradise lost, where an initially tempered disparity of wealth grew to resemble the high-water mark of European aristocracy by the close of the century. But the quantitative evidence he offers is far too sporadic to sustain the case in any detail. The subsequent course is more subdued than its counterparts in Britain and France, but is one with both causal claims and predictive implications for the United States.

Turning to his post-1910 data, the familiar U shape begins to emerge: a pre–World War I peak in wealth disparity dissipates across the 20th century. Spurred by a "pioneering" progressive tax policy, that trend continues until reaching a stable bottom in the 1970s. It is then depicted as following a gradual yet sustained and certain uptick into the present day. Piketty explains the graph (figure 10.5) with a very specific historical claim: "In the United States . . . a (white) patrimonial middle class already existed in the nineteenth century. It suffered a setback during the Gilded Age, regained its health in the middle of the twentieth century, and then suffered another setback after 1980. This 'yo yo' pattern is reflected in the history of U.S. taxation" (2014b, 350).

After lauding the United States for revolutionizing the practice of "confiscatory taxation of excessive incomes" (2014b, 505)—a narrative he constructs from his faulty recounting of Depression-era tax history—Piketty attempts to pin the observed uptick in inequality since the 1980s squarely on Reagan-era tax cuts. He even claims it implies an "explosion of executive salaries" (2014b, 508, 335), thus validating his theories of capital accumulation.

But is Piketty's figure 10.5, which is at the root of his American wealth disparity narrative, even accurate? Wealth inequality is a notoriously difficult concept to quantify, though two common estimation techniques do allow approximations. The first uses historical estate-tax records to estimate wealth shares annually. The second samples wealth distributions using the Federal Reserve's Survey of Consumer Finances (SCF), though only at the less-frequent intervals permitted by the survey's collection. Piketty's central graph is really a composite of other studies, based on variations of these two techniques.

When Piketty's book went to press, the most complete study of U.S. wealth inequality at that time was a 2004 article by Wojciech Kopczuk and Emmanuel Saez, who used estate-tax records to estimate wealth distributions from 1916 to 2000. Their time series, reprinted below as Figure 15.4, shows a late–20th century trend that is at odds with Piketty's narrative.

Whereas Piketty's figure 10.5 depicts a sharp uptick in inequality beginning in the 1980s—which fits his narrative that

Figure 15.4

KOPCZUK AND SAEZ ESTATE-TAX ESTIMATE OF U.S. WEALTH INEQUALITY
THE TOP 1% WEALTH SHARE IN THE UNITED STATES, 1916–2000

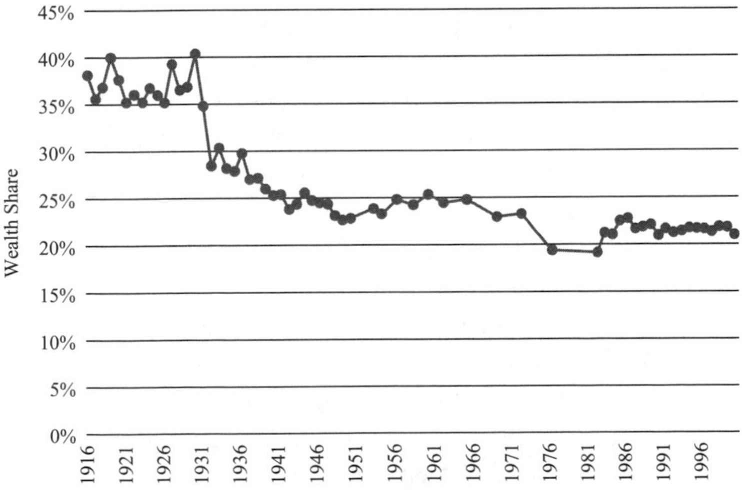

SOURCE: Kopczuk and Saez (2004), figure 2.

tax cuts for the wealthy drive the trend in inequality—the Kopczuk and Saez estate-tax study displays a trend that is at best ambiguous and appears to be flat through the end of the 20th century.

A closer examination of the source data in Piketty's figure 10.5 reveals that most of its root data are actually taken from the Kopczuk and Saez study. However, they are "augmented" and extended through 2010 with other studies based on the SCF as well as a number of opaque adjustments that are simply hard-coded into Piketty's source files. Unfortunately, neither Piketty's annotation nor the supplemental document that he released in response to data criticisms contains an adequate or transparent explanation of how he performed those "augmentations" (Piketty 2014a, 6–7). By reconstructing his graph from the provided data tables, however, it quickly becomes apparent that he is not so much an aggregator of the existing literature as a cherry picker.

Beginning with the raw Kopczuk and Saez data set for the top 1 percent of the wealth distribution, Piketty first reconciles it upward through "corrective" adjustments to match other studies using the SCF methodology. Converting his output into decennial averages to account for gaps in the data, he retains Kopczuk and Saez from 1910 through 1950. He then merges their data with a single 1962 data point from an SCF-based study by Edward Wolff (1994), bringing the Kopczuk and Saez average for the 1960s into line with the SCF. Without citing that change in sources, and in fact suggesting otherwise in his limited annotation, Piketty then migrates back to a figure derived from Kopczuk and Saez for the 1970s, obtained by weighting the SCF-reconciled 1960s data point with a marked drop-off shown in their estate tax series.[10] That switch introduces a problematic dimension to his decennial averaging technique, as the 1970s contain the largest modern data gap in Kopczuk and Saez, who cite only two years for the entire decade. Though the Kopczuk and Saez series improves for the 1980s and 1990s with 8 and 10 full years of data, respectively, those decades are also the point at which their inequality trend line flattens out, which is at odds with Piketty's U-shaped expectations. Piketty therefore quietly abandons Kopczuk and Saez from 1980 onward, migrating back to Wolff (1994, 2010), and then to separate SCF-based studies by Kennickell (2009) and Kennickell et al. (2011). See Figure 15.5.

The two sets of SCF-based studies do suggest a very modest increase in wealth inequality over the last two decades, but Piketty's unconventional combination and rotation of them with the Kopczuk and Saez estate-tax estimate removes a substantial amount of ambiguity to suggest a pronounced upward trend into the present day. The pivot to the Kopczuk and Saez 1970s data

Figure 15.5

SOURCE DATA RECONSTRUCTION OF PIKETTY'S FIGURE 10.5 ON INEQUALITY IN THE UNITED STATES, 1910–2010

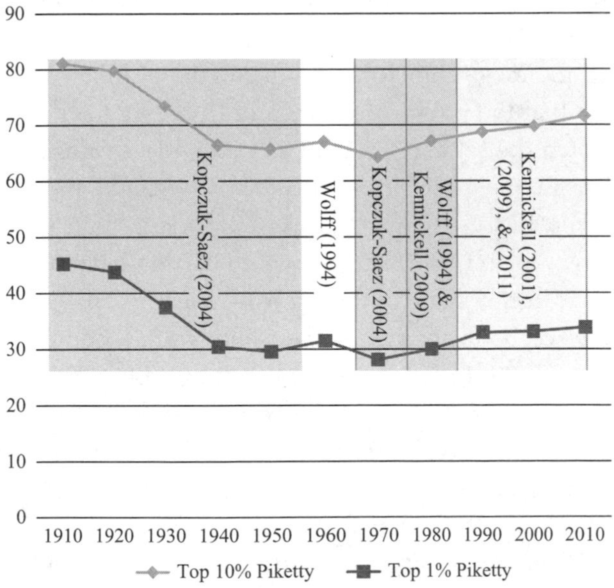

SOURCES: Piketty (2014b), Figure 10.5 and Data Appendix, Table TS10.1DetailsUS.

point adds an accentuating effect to Piketty's chart, as it produces a clear bottom point of the U shape. When merged with the later survey sources, that point gives the illusion of a steeper rebound than the post-1990 SCF studies show when taken alone. Piketty's assembly process for his figure 10.5 continues from there as he extrapolates a second wealth distribution for the top 10 percent. He begins by simply appending a fixed 36 percentage points to his top 1 percent series from 1910 to 1950, and again in 1970, without alerting the reader that this (large) portion of his trend line is based not on underlying data but on the mere addition of a fixed number to the lower trend line.[11] He then reconciles the new line with SCF data for the remaining decades. The end product is a Frankenstein graph, assembled from bits and pieces of the existing literature that seem to be added or dropped for the convenience of the trend line he wishes to see at the moment his preferred historical narrative expects it to appear.[12]

A Useful Digression: Estimating Wealth Distribution Using Estate vs. Income Tax Data

One of the most unfortunate outgrowths of Piketty's popular acclaim is that the public and much of the economics profession has accepted the settled "fact" of significantly increasing wealth inequality in the past three decades. In reality, the evidence for that conclusion is much more ambiguous than its loudest champions—including Piketty—would have us believe. In this section, we outline some of the controversies.

As Piketty's book zoomed to bestseller status soon after its release in April 2014, the academics and pundits who disagreed with its policy conclusions were caught somewhat flat-footed. After all, the book was a dense economics tome running almost 700 pages. Critics raised objections but were drowned out by the constant drumbeat that Piketty's empirical work was of the highest caliber. People argued about the truth and significance of $r > g$, but few doubted the accuracy of the historical charts that

Piketty had assembled. The charts showed a rising concentration of wealth (in both the top 10 percent and the top 1 percent), which Piketty warned would continue if drastic policy countermeasures were not taken.

Then on May 23, 2014, Chris Giles of the *Financial Times* (FT) launched a major broadside against Piketty's empirical work, arguing (among other things) that Piketty's chart for U.S. wealth inequality conveniently sampled from various disparate data sets to give the appearance of an increase in wealth concentration that the original data sets lacked. As we showed in the preceding section, that selective sampling is largely responsible for the U shape of Piketty's figure 10.5. We reproduce Giles's U.S. chart in Figure 15.6 to illustrate the ambiguity of the chart's disparate components and other similar studies when taken apart.

Figure 15.6

COMPARATIVE U.S. WEALTH INEQUALITY METRICS FROM THE *FINANCIAL TIMES* ANALYSIS

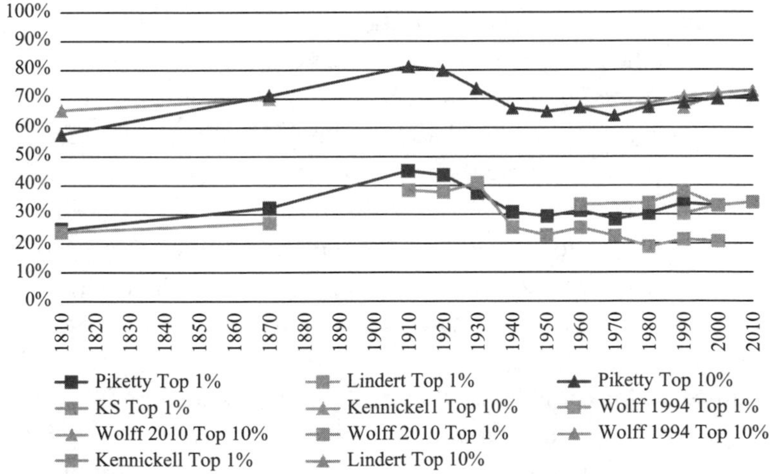

SOURCE: Giles (2014).

In Giles's chart, the two continuous lines represent Piketty's estimates as presented in his book. They are based on a blending of the various light gray data sets. The disconnected lines represent various source estimates. Note the lower source lines in particular, showing the concentration of wealth among the top 1 percent of wealth holders. Starting in 1910, Piketty's line tracks one of the source lines fairly closely (though overstating it). Yet, from the 1970s data point to the present, Piketty's line and that original source diverge sharply. At that point, Piketty performs his pivot to the other data sets, which do not go back as far. Had Piketty's line continued to track the original source line, Piketty would have shown that, as of 2000 at least, the wealth concentration in the upper 1 percent in the United States was just about the lowest and most stable it had been in recorded history, save for a slight dip in the 1980s.

After Giles challenged Piketty, Piketty directed his critics to a PowerPoint presentation based on a paper (not yet released at the time) from economists Emmanuel Saez—the coauthor of Kopczuk's 2004 study—and Gabriel Zucman. We reproduce a key slide from the Saez and Zucman PowerPoint presentation in Figure 15.7.

Far from accounting for his own questionable judgment calls on how to blend the various data sets in his figure 10.5, Piketty answered the FT critiques by claiming vindication in the Saez and Zucman PowerPoint results and retorting, "If anything, my book underestimates the rise in [U.S.] wealth inequality" (2014a, 2).

It is important to note the methodologies of the two series: the Kopczuk and Saez (2004) study uses estate tax data to estimate wealth concentration; the Saez and Zucman (2014b) PowerPoint series, which was released in full as part of a National Bureau of Economic Research working paper in October 2014, uses data on capital *income* and rates of return (by asset class) to generate a new estimate of the capital base that generated such income flows.

The amazing thing about the slide shown in Figure 15.7 is that the two methods—directly assessing wealth from estate tax data vs. computing the wealth by dividing capital income by the

Figure 15.7

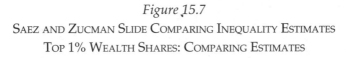

SAEZ AND ZUCMAN SLIDE COMPARING INEQUALITY ESTIMATES
TOP 1% WEALTH SHARES: COMPARING ESTIMATES

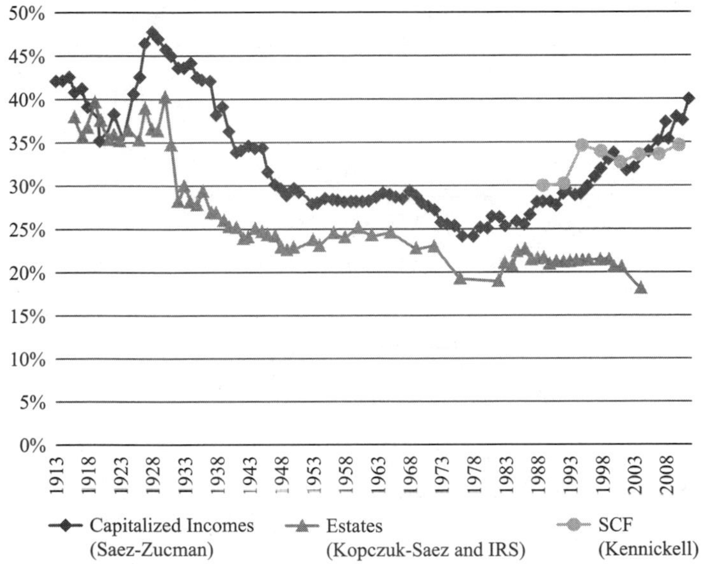

SOURCE: Saez and Zucman PowerPoint presentation, "Estate Tax Returns Fail to Capture Rising Top Wealth Shares," March 2014, http://gabriel-zucman.eu/files/SaezZucman2014Slides.pdf. Saez and Zucman 2014b; Kopczuk and Saez 2004; Kennickell et al. 2011.

relevant rate of return—tracked each other decently from the 1920s through the 1970s. The consistency of this tracking is even more pronounced when considering only the top 0.1 percent of wealth ownership. That comparison is shown in Figure 15.8, constructed from Kopczuk and Saez (2004), Saez and Zucman (2014b), and the SCF-based study by Kennickell et al. (2011).

In 1985, the two studies diverge sharply, with the estate tax–based Kopczuk and Saez estimates remaining flat and even falling through the early 2000s, while the new Saez and Zucman (2014b) estimate zooms upward about 10 percentage points in the same time period.[13] A similar divergence follows in the SCF

Figure 15.8

Saez and Zucman Divergence from Alternative Estimates
Comparison of Estimates: Wealth Inequality in the United States, Top 0.1%

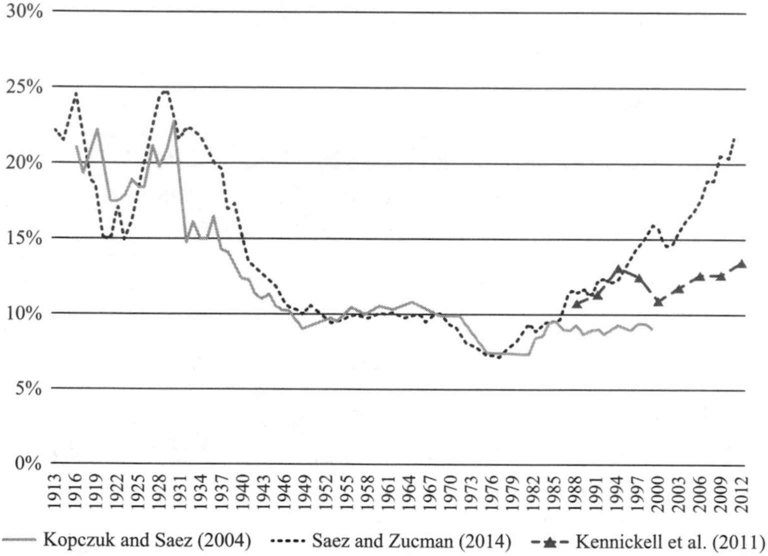

Source: Compiled from Saez and Zucman (2014b), Data Appendix.

study in 1991. This major discrepancy between the new Saez and Zucman PowerPoint results and both of the older techniques for estimating wealth inequality received almost no acknowledgement from Piketty or his defenders in the rush to claim vindication for Piketty's prior findings in his figure 10.5.

Although it is not essential for our present purpose, we can note several plausible explanations for the huge discrepancy between the capitalization method and the estate-tax data. On the one hand, the income inequality estimates—such as the (reputedly) definitive series produced by Piketty and Saez (2003)—may themselves be distorted because of the significant changes to the U.S. federal income tax code introduced in the 1980s. The sharp reduction in the top marginal personal income-tax rate (from 70 percent in 1980 to 28 percent by 1988) gave an incentive to high-income earners to reorganize their businesses as S corporations and other pass-through entities, allowing what was previously considered business income (then taxed at the corporate rate) to be taxed under the new personal income rates. Thus, the surge in income inequality during the 1980s may have been partly an artifact of a mere rearrangement of income that was there all along.

On the other hand, much of the middle class's capital income (such as capital gains, dividends, and interest earnings) disappeared from the tax data in the 1980s because of the rise of tax-deferred investment vehicles. Such capital income had been reported in the 1970s, meaning that the middle class's capital income was artificially understated by comparison in the 1980s. After discussing all of these factors (and more), Alan Reynolds concluded, "It is extremely deceptive to compare tax-based estimates of income distribution from 1970 to 1979 with any year after 1986" (2006, 80) To be clear, Reynolds was writing in the mid-2000s and was not addressing our present controversy. However, if his hypothesis about *income* inequality measures is right, then it also may be a major explanation for the divergence in *wealth* inequality measures. Specifically, Reynolds thinks the standard income inequality series became skewed in the mid-1980s and beyond—precisely when the estate-tax method diverged sharply from the capitalization method for wealth inequality, after tracking each other tolerably well for the previous 60 years.

Saez and Zucman, of course, consider their new results to be correct. A glance back at their PowerPoint slide shows that it is titled, "Estate tax returns fail to capture rising top wealth shares." In other words, they are sure that their results (at least the general trend) are correct: if the estate-tax method disagrees, then the estate-tax method must be wrong—it is missing the "rising top wealth shares" that Saez and Zucman are confident must really be there.

How do Saez and Zucman explain that the estate-tax method mimicked their preferred approach for decades but then went wildly adrift starting in the 1980s? In their October 2014 paper, Saez and Zucman suggest that the older Kopczuk and Saez (2004) data set went awry by failing to account for a substantial mortality gradient between the super wealthy and the merely wealthy (Saez and Zucman 2014b). If, in fact, the wealthiest 1 percent live significantly longer than the wealthiest 10 percent, then assuming a constant mortality rate would—using the estate-tax method—understate the true concentration of wealth among the living.

In December 2014, Kopczuk himself published a working paper addressing all of these issues, presenting the strengths and weaknesses of the main approaches to estimating wealth inequality (in addition to the capitalization, estate tax, and SCF methods, he also assesses a fourth method of ranking the wealthiest individuals, as published in the Forbes 400 list). Kopczuk is balanced in his treatment, though he notes that both the SCF and estate-tax methods show at best a modest increase in inequality since the mid-1980s, whereas the capitalization method shows a dramatic increase. He brings up Saez and Zucman's (2014b) theory that different mortality rates explain the discrepancy in the results, then comments:

> This explanation is conceptually plausible, but the estimated gap in mortality rates for the very wealthy is so large and unexplored elsewhere in the literature, that the subject clearly requires further research. For example, an alternative possible explanation for their finding of such a large mortality advantage at the very top of the wealth distribution rests on the observation that, by construction, they report mortality rates for individuals with high capital income (which they interpret as high wealth). If high capital income represents active rather than passive returns, because it is a form of compensation for actively running or managing a business, for example,

> then individuals with high capital income are partially selected on health—it is being healthy that allows them to be active beyond retirement. On the flip side, individuals who are sickly may instead have an incentive to engage in tax planning and not realize capital income; in particular, there is a strong tax incentive not to realize capital gains until death in order to benefit from the step up of the basis of capital gains at death. As I will argue in what follows, it is likely that individuals at the top of the wealth distribution have become increasingly self-made, so that one might plausibly expect that this type of selection has become stronger over time (Kopczuk 2014, 18).

Our purpose in walking through the debate in the inequality literature is not to single out one method or data series as the best. Rather, we are documenting that there is still lively debate among the top scholars in the field over Piketty's stated "fact" of rapidly increasing wealth inequality since the 1980s. The debate stands in marked contrast to the portrayal of Piketty by his progressive champions. Paul Krugman, for example, recently credited Piketty's "historical depth" for "demonstrating that we really are living in a new Gilded Age" and noted his detractors' purported inability to mount a "substantive" challenge to that claim (2014a). Krugman further characterizes Piketty's critics as peddlers of "inequality denial" on the conspiratorial payroll of "powerful groups with a strong interest in rejecting the facts, or at least creating a fog of doubt" (2014b); yet, he evinces little awareness of the widespread ambiguity that presently characterizes the academic literature outside of Piketty on this very subject. As a final word on this topic, let us repeat that Piketty and his defenders retorted by endorsing a PowerPoint presentation from an unreleased and little-vetted study when challenged by critics. That presentation has subsequently been appended by no more than a working paper, and one that creates more unanswered research questions about its own methods than it resolves for Piketty's claimed trend line. When it comes to the allegation of a rapid increase in wealth inequality in recent decades, the mismatch between the actual strength of the empirical evidence and the rhetorical flourishes with which it is communicated to the public is breathtaking.

Capital–Income Ratios, Soviet Distortions, and Intentional Mischief

Much of the debate around Piketty's inequality figures is methodological in nature, as may be seen in the following passage he wrote in response to Giles and the *Financial Times*:

> What is troubling about the FT methodological choices is that they use the estimates based upon estate-tax statistics for the older decades (until the 1980s), and then they shift to the survey-based estimates for the more recent period. This is problematic because we know that in every country wealth surveys tend to underestimate top wealth shares as compared to estimates based upon administrative fiscal data (2014a, 8).

The excerpt refers to the FT's own attempts to compare differing inequality measurement methods for the United Kingdom. Yet, also notice this: Is Piketty not guilty of the very same methodological charge in his United States series? He first enlisted the estate-tax figures of Kopczuk and Saez (2004) before shifting to the SCF-based survey estimate for the more recent period when selective use of the latter seemed to validate his narrative. Methodological concerns should weigh upon any evaluation of admittedly imprecise measurement tools, but such uneven and inconsistent applications suggest a severe confirmation bias at play throughout Piketty's book. He selectively pivots between methods that affirm his story while criticizing others for lesser indulgences in the same.

Indeed, most of the examples we have considered thus far display elements of confirmation bias, whether found in sloppy misstatements of simple tax rates and dates to augment Piketty's historical narrative or cherry-picked data points to construct a trend line that mirrors his predictions. Such errors, though sufficiently serious to call into question the claimed empirical soundness of his work, are quite distinct from acts of intentional mischief in the presentation of data. One final example warrants closer examination for reasons that may extend beyond simple biases, because it is qualitatively more dubious than the previous examples of questionable choices we have documented. We thus turn to the second U-shaped trend that Piketty enlists to support his central argument of $r > g$ and its implications.

As a multipronged attack on inequality and its theorized roots in the private capital stock, Piketty attempts to demonstrate his thesis by applying his argument globally and, with it, test his "second law" of capitalism, wherein he predicts an intrinsic tendency of the ratio of capital to national income to increase over time. Piketty depicts this "world" ratio for the years 1870 to 2100 in his figure 5.8; the same figure reappears as figure 12.4 to illustrate a projected "international convergence" in the proportions of capital accumulation around the globe over the coming century (hence the title of Piketty's book). As the last 90 years of this graph are Piketty's predictions, we will focus only on the historical data. Piketty's historical interpretation of figure 5.8/12.4 takes on the familiar narrative of the U-shaped trend he claims for the 20th century, as Figure 15.9 shows.

Piketty posits a global divergence of capital to national income at the peak of the Gilded Age, followed by a flattening of the capital stock from World War I and ensuing events (including the imposition of heavy progressive taxation), and then a rebound from the 1970s to the present. The growth in capital to income ratios for the developing world is said to reflect this reconstitution of the capital stock as well as drive future divergence in the cumulative ratio as the global capital stock stabilizes around

Figure 15.9

GLOBAL CAPITAL–INCOME RATIO, AS ESTIMATED BY PIKETTY

THE WORLD CAPITAL–INCOME RATIO, 1870–2100

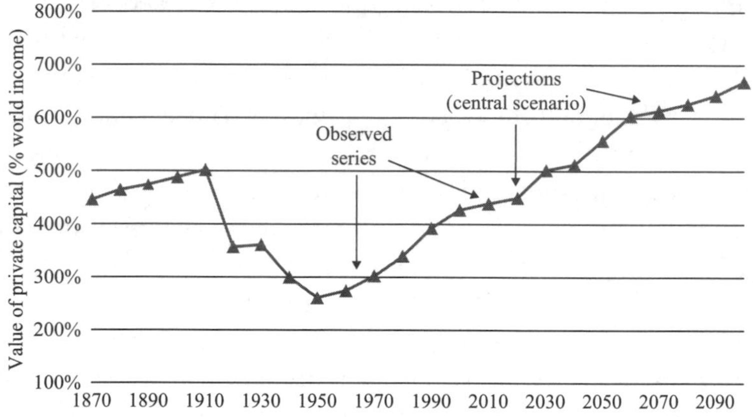

According to the simulations (central scenario), the world capital–income ratio might be near to 700% by the end of the 21st century. Sources and series: see piketty.pse.ens.fr/capital21c.

SOURCE: Piketty (2014b), Figure 12.4.

developed-world levels. If that upswing were to continue on the course his forecast lays out, the "entire planet could look like Europe at the turn of the twentieth century, at least in terms of capital intensity" (Piketty 2014b, 196).

Piketty's derivation of figure 5.8/12.4 poses a challenge, as it is poorly sourced and annotated in ways that are even less transparent than his U.S. wealth inequality example. His technical appendix annotates figure 5.8, the first iteration of the graph, as follows: "The series used to construct figure 5.8, replicated in the book on p. 196, are available in table S12.4 (see appendix to chapter 12). All the details about the assumptions on which the series are built, especially for the period 2010–2100, are specified in the book, as well as in the corresponding excel file" (Piketty 2014c, 34). When one turns to figure 12.4 and the corresponding Excel table S12.4, the accompanying note sends the reader on a circular return to the original note for figure 5.8: "These estimates are based on assumptions already presented in chapter 5 and in the appendix to chapter 5" (Piketty 2014c, 71).

The product is nonetheless presented as clear evidence of the predicted U-shaped trend and, thus, validation of his theory of capital stock accumulation and, by extension, its theorized inequality link. In reconstructing this figure, it helps to examine Piketty's derivation in steps, as questionable data decisions mar each one. To begin, because Piketty is working with capital data at the national level (where such data exist), he needs to bring those figures together for a global metric. To do so, he aggregates national income data by region to determine its respective percentage of the "world output distribution" in a given year. He uses those percentages, in turn, to weight each region's capital–income ratio, the cumulative result being the curve in the figure.

A closer examination of Piketty's regional weights (found in table S12.4b of his data set) reveals the first of many problems. Piketty has few data points to perform this basic calibration and resorts to extreme dependence on linear interpolation to fill the gaps. Of 15 decennial data points between 1870 and 2010, 9 of them are actually interpolated. The source from the remaining six "decades" is referenced to another table, S1.1, which reveals them to be distributions for 6 individual years out of the 150 covered in the resulting graph, each presented as representative of its nearest decade mark. The following images of Piketty's data tables (Figure 15.10) illustrate the source years, along with his corresponding regional output weights. Interpolated years are shaded, whereas weights are taken from individual years in the first table and transferred directly into the six noninterpolated rows.

While remaining fully cognizant that data limitations do indeed impinge on our ability to assemble a comprehensive multicentury time series of this sort, to use only 6 individual years for a 150-year examination is almost as astounding as it is incomprehensible. Indeed, one of the largest gaps in Piketty's output distribution places

Figure 15.10

PIKETTY'S WORLD OUTPUT DISTRIBUTION SOURCE CHARTS

	A	B	C	D	E	F
6						
7		**World output**	Europe	America	Africa	Asia
8	0	**100%**	18%	2%	8%	73%
9	1000	**100%**	14%	4%	11%	71%
10	1500	**100%**	25%	3%	8%	64%
11	1700	**100%**	30%	2%	7%	61%
12	1820	**100%**	33%	4%	5%	59%
13	1870	**100%**	46%	12%	4%	39%
14	1913	**100%**	47%	24%	3%	26%
15	1950	**100%**	39%	36%	4%	21%
16	1970	**100%**	40%	32%	4%	24%
17	1990	**100%**	34%	33%	4%	29%
18	2012	**100%**	25%	29%	4%	42%
19						

Table S12.4a. Private capital/national income ratio for the world, 1870-2100 (estimate) (series used for figure 12.4)

private capital / national income	World	Europe	America	Africa	Asia
1880	100%	46%	18%	4%	32%
1890	100%	46%	18%	4%	32%
1900	100%	46%	18%	4%	32%
1910	100%	47%	24%	3%	26%
1920	100%	43%	30%	3%	23%
1930	100%	43%	30%	3%	23%
1940	100%	43%	30%	3%	23%
1950	100%	39%	36%	4%	21%
1960	100%	39%	34%	4%	23%
1970	100%	40%	32%	4%	24%
1980	100%	37%	33%	4%	27%
1990	100%	34%	33%	4%	29%
2000	100%	29%	31%	4%	36%

SOURCE: Piketty (2014b), Data Appendix, Tables S1.1 and S12.4.

him without *any* data points with which to estimate his output distributions between 1913 and 1950 (note the distance between years in the first column of the first table shown in our Figure 15.10). That deficiency leaves Piketty making the absurdly untenable assumption that the regional distribution of world output remained static and fixed throughout both world wars and the Great Depression.

Piketty turns next to the individual ratios of capital to national income by country and again encounters a problem of nonexistent data. He at least partially acknowledges the issue in his text: for most of the world there are "no truly reliable estimates" (2014b, 195) of private capital until the late 20th century. Still, he is left with little more than figures for parts of Western Europe and North America across the 1870–2010 span, plus the addition of Japan, Australia, and New Zealand from 1970 onward. As with the regional output distributions he uses to weight the figures, the devil is in the missing details. Piketty simply "guesstimates" for the remaining countries by approximating where he expects them to be and assigning a value, as seen in the shaded cells in our Figure 15.11. Naturally, they all follow an assumed U shape, thereby reinforcing his expected trend when merged with the Western European and North American data.

More troubling, though, is a case of what appears to be some mischief in Piketty's approximations as he accounts for the communist regimes of the mid-20th century. Starting with the Soviet Union in 1920 and adding in Eastern Europe and China after 1950, Piketty arbitrarily reduces his estimates of their capital–income ratios to parity between the two indicators, thus implying a full reduction in the capital stock in these countries. This ratio reduction, shaded in dark in our Figure 15.12, is represented as 100 percent, or 1:1 for parity, for the duration of each region's rigid communist period.

Although a scenario in which the onset of communism is highly disruptive to the capital stock is plausible, Piketty offers no explanation for the assumption in his annotation of the chart and no accounting for the unique ratio parity he assigns to the

Figure 15.11

EXISTENT VS. ESTIMATED DATA FOR PIKETTY'S CAPITAL–INCOME RATIOS

private capital/ national income	Western Europe	Eastern Europe	Russia (+Ukraine/ Belarus/ Moldavia	North America	Latin America	Northern Africa	Sub-Saharan Africa	China	India	Japan	Australia/ NZ	Middle East (y.c. Turkey)	Central Asia	Other Asian countries
1870	680%	300%	300%	446%	300%	300%	200%	300%	300%	600%	300%	300%	300%	300%
1880	671%	325%	325%	437%	325%	325%	250%	325%	325%	600%	325%	325%	325%	325%
1890	643%	350%	350%	478%	350%	350%	300%	350%	350%	600%	350%	350%	350%	350%
1900	662%	375%	375%	448%	375%	375%	350%	375%	375%	600%	375%	375%	375%	375%
1910	659%	400%	400%	440%	400%	400%	400%	400%	400%	600%	400%	400%	400%	400%
1920	343%	200%	100%	407%	400%	400%	400%	400%	400%	600%	400%	400%	400%	400%
1930	386%	200%	100%	485%	300%	300%	300%	300%	300%	600%	400%	300%	300%	300%
1940	328%	200%	100%	328%	300%	300%	300%	300%	300%	500%	300%	300%	300%	300%
1950	232%	100%	100%	356%	300%	300%	300%	100%	300%	200%	300%	300%	300%	300%
1960	267%	100%	100%	361%	300%	300%	300%	100%	300%	300%	300%	300%	300%	300%
1970	285%	100%	100%	332%	400%	400%	400%	100%	400%	372%	343%	400%	400%	400%
1980	331%	100%	100%	357%	400%	400%	400%	100%	400%	531%	351%	400%	400%	400%
1990	403%	200%	200%	392%	400%	400%	400%	200%	400%	616%	407%	400%	400%	400%
2000	490%	300%	300%	447%	400%	400%	400%	300%	400%	586%	500%	400%	400%	400%
2010	545%	400%	400%	410%	400%	400%	400%	400%	400%	601%	518%	400%	400%	400%

NOTE: External source data are depicted in white. Rough "guesstimation" figures as determined by Piketty are indicated by the shade.

SOURCE: Piketty (2014b), Data Appendix, Table TS12.4.

Figure 15.12

ASSUMPTION OF COMMUNIST CAPITAL–INCOME PARITY IN PIKETTY'S SOURCE CHARTS

private capital/ national income	Western Europe	Eastern Europe	Russia (+Ukraine/ Belarus/ Moldavia	North America	Latin America	Northern Africa	Sub-Saharan Africa	China	India	Japan	Australia/ NZ	Middle East (y.c. Turkey)	Central Asia	Other Asian countries
1870	680%	300%	300%	446%	300%	300%	200%	300%	300%	600%	300%	300%	300%	300%
1880	671%	325%	325%	437%	325%	325%	250%	325%	325%	600%	325%	325%	325%	325%
1890	643%	350%	350%	478%	350%	350%	300%	350%	350%	600%	350%	350%	350%	350%
1900	662%	375%	375%	448%	375%	375%	350%	375%	375%	600%	375%	375%	375%	375%
1910	659%	400%	400%	440%	400%	400%	400%	400%	400%	600%	400%	400%	400%	400%
1920	343%	200%	100%	407%	400%	400%	400%	400%	400%	600%	400%	400%	400%	400%
1930	386%	200%	100%	485%	300%	300%	300%	300%	300%	600%	400%	300%	300%	300%
1940	328%	200%	100%	328%	300%	300%	300%	300%	300%	500%	300%	300%	300%	300%
1950	232%	100%	100%	356%	300%	300%	300%	100%	300%	200%	300%	300%	300%	300%
1960	267%	100%	100%	361%	300%	300%	300%	100%	300%	300%	300%	300%	300%	300%
1970	285%	100%	100%	332%	400%	400%	400%	100%	400%	372%	343%	400%	400%	400%
1980	331%	100%	100%	357%	400%	400%	400%	100%	400%	531%	351%	400%	400%	400%
1990	403%	200%	200%	392%	400%	400%	400%	200%	400%	616%	407%	400%	400%	400%
2000	490%	300%	300%	447%	400%	400%	400%	300%	400%	586%	500%	400%	400%	400%
2010	545%	400%	400%	410%	400%	400%	400%	400%	400%	601%	518%	400%	400%	400%

NOTE: External source data are depicted in white. Rough "guesstimation" figures as determined by Piketty are indicated in the lighter shade. Piketty's communist world data assumption of 1:1 capital–income parity is indicated in the darker shade for the applicable decades.

SOURCE: Piketty (2014b), Data Appendix, Table TS12.4.

communist regions outside of a possible vague allusion appearing much later in the book.[14] Nor does he attempt to justify the inclusion of an assumed data point from multiple communist economies with the premise of his U-shaped-curve argument, which purports to illustrate the characteristics of global capitalism. In doing so, he evinces what may be a naïve apriorism toward the claimed effects of the collectivization of capital under communist ideological systems. The effect nonetheless registers prominently in Piketty's figure 5.8/12.4. When evaluated for their effects on the global index he purports to construct, his decisions with regard to the Soviet Union and other communist regimes exert a strong downward pull upon the U-shaped curve to coincide with its claimed mid-century trough.

The following graph, Figure 15.13, displays the three communist regions overlaid with Piketty's depiction of the global

Figure 15.13

EFFECTS OF COMMUNIST DISTORTION ON PIKETTY'S GLOBAL CAPITAL–INCOME RATIO

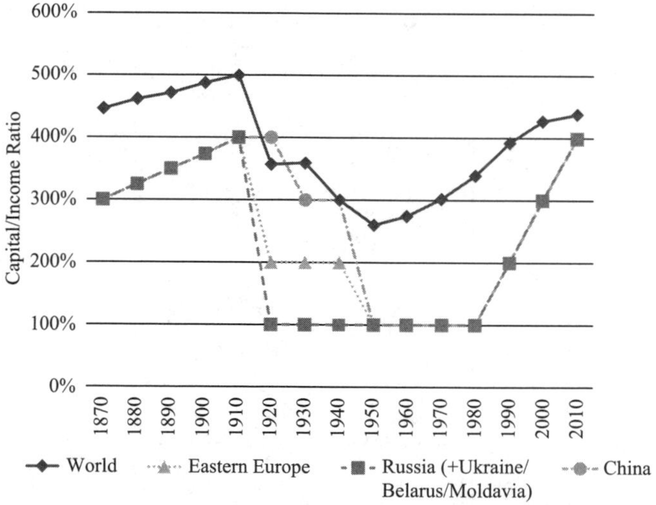

SOURCE: Figure created from Piketty (2014b), Data Appendix, Table TS12.4.

capital–income ratio. As the "world" index is, in effect, a time series constructed from weighted decennial averages, the inclusion of the communist bloc and the assumptions made about capital–income ratios therein end up being downwardly distortive to the constructed trend line.

The distortion is significant. At the 1950 trough, the weighting Piketty assigns to communist regimes is a sizable 17 percent of global output (compared with 27 percent for Western Europe and 29 percent for North America, making it the third largest bloc). With a 1:1 ratio falling far below either the North American ratio (3.6:1) or the Western European ratio (2.3:1) in the same year, the communist world's inclusion in Piketty's weighted average is biasing, severe, and unaccounted for in his book's text or annotation. Rather, it is quietly hard-coded some three spreadsheets deep into his data file, well beyond the awareness of even the most diligent reader.

Similarly, the apparent rebound of the (formerly) communist countries after 1990 obviously pushes up the world capital–income ratio. Yet, most readers would be surprised to see that the huge and identical shift among those countries (with a ratio of 1:1 rising to 4:1 over just three decades) does not derive from calculations performed on underlying data sources, but rather occurs because Piketty typed them directly into his Excel sheet.

A point of contrast may also be seen in the disaggregated ratios for Western Europe and North America, which form the substance of his actual data sources in the cumulative world graph. Although a U shape is indeed present for Western Europe when the two series are separated, a number of pertinent observations become clear. First, the bulk of the Western European U shape is attributable to a single decade's movement coinciding with World War I. Second and perhaps more important, the North American data actually defy the century-long U-shaped prediction. As Figure 15.14 shows, the North American ratio hovers around a comparatively stable and flat 4:1 for the entire 20th century, with only mild fluctuations as happened in the Depression era. When considering these regional trends alone, Piketty applies a misleading descriptor to the North American case, portraying it as a U shape that is simply "smaller in amplitude in the United States than in Europe" (Piketty 2014b, 154). In actuality, the century-long ratios for the two regions display two completely divergent trends, as Figure 15.14 shows.

A true weighted average drawn only from the two regions would show the effect of North America stabilizing and somewhat flattening the overall U shape found in the Western European data, particularly in conjunction with the former's dramatically ascendant share of total global economic output (and thus an increase in its weighting) at mid-century. Piketty's aggregate presentation shows the opposite effect, though, and precisely because it includes the distortive Soviet, Chinese, and Eastern European data points. The observed global U shape in Piketty's figure 5.8/12.4 is

Figure 15.14

COMPARATIVE CAPITAL–INCOME RATIOS IN PIKETTY'S SOURCE DATA

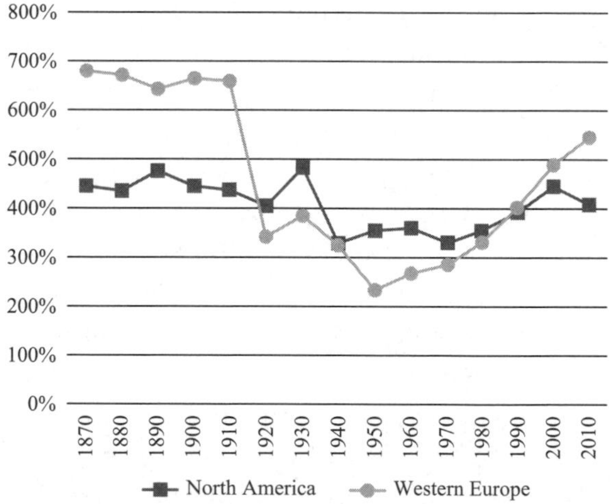

SOURCE: Figure created from Piketty (2014b), Data Appendix, Table TS12.4.

not a result of careful data analysis or even reasoned and articulated methodologies to account for its many data gaps; rather, it is the product of opaque and highly questionable assumptions. Piketty has simply written in his estimates for the rest of the world, with his unexplained communist region modifications exerting their strongest downward distortions precisely in sync with the 1950 bottom point of the claimed U.

Conclusions

In light of the foregoing analysis, it is evident that, under closer scrutiny, a sizable fissure exists between the bold data claims Piketty makes at the outset of *Capital in the 21st Century* and his actual empirics. We have highlighted a number of specific factual errors in the book as well as two of Piketty's larger evidentiary representations in the form of supposedly U-shaped patterns across the 20th century, one for wealth inequality in the United States and another pertaining to estimated capital–income ratios worldwide. Though these issues represent only a slice of Piketty's work, they exemplify the problems with the historical narrative that he uses to explain the 20th century and to make predictive claims about the coming century. They severely undermine his justification for a heavy-handed global "correction" of prescriptive tax policy, and they invalidate several core pieces of empirical evidence behind his larger theoretical argument about the nature of the capital stock in a market economy.

Our study is by no means exhaustive, and the public prominence of Piketty's work has at a minimum called attention to an important and ongoing line of research into economic history. We have focused on his claims about the United States, in particular, and those most central to his larger historical narrative and to United States tax policy, the latter being both a premise of the former and the primary implication of his policy prescriptions. Although we have not exhaustively scrutinized Piketty's data claims in the other regions and countries he examines, we have noted that other investigations have found similar patterns of historical mistakes of fact and questionable methods in his data presentation (see, for example, Sahlén and Furth [2014]).

Whereas other data critiques, including that of the *Financial Times*, have raised important normative and methodological questions about Piketty's data presentations, the issues highlighted here suggest an even more fundamental problem. His reliance on factually mistaken data claims, unsupported assertions of validity, and certain dubious chart constructions only make sense in service to a preconceived narrative. The discrepancies we identify are pervasive in the book, beginning with misstatements of basic historical fact and extending to an abundance of political distortion and confirmation bias in his data selection and methodological choices. In his use of communist data assumptions to accentuate the shape of a desired trend line, ostensibly explaining a hypothesized characteristic of capitalism, for example, it is difficult to maintain a noble opinion of the scholarship involved. These problems afflict *Capital in the 21st Century*'s historical narrative in ways that are both large and small. And the frequency with which they occur is sufficient to warrant deep skepticism of the book as a whole and especially the many instances where Piketty substitutes an appeal to the reader's trust for annotation that is—at best—murky. Curiously, the early reaction to *Capital* credited its data analysis despite other reservations with its contents and prescriptions. Now, to the contrary, an abundance of questionable and problematic data claims may well mean that empirics are the book's weakest point.

References

Auerbach, Alan, and Kevin Hassett. 2015. "Capital Taxation in the 21st Century." National Bureau of Economic Research Working Paper no. w20871.

Fleenor, Patrick. 1994. *A History and Overview of Estate Taxes in the United States*. Washington, D.C.: The Tax Foundation.

Furchtgott-Roth, Diana. 2014. "Piketty's Historic Minimum Wage Errors." *e21* (blog), Manhattan Institute, April 22.

Giles, Chris. 2014. "Piketty Findings Undercut by Errors." *Financial Times*, May 23.

Hayek, F. A. 1954. *Capitalism and the Historians.* Chicago: University of Chicago Press.

Henderson, David R., Robert McNab, and Tamás Rózsás. 2005. "The Hidden Inequality in Socialism." *Independent Review* 9 (3): 389–412.

Hoover, Herbert. 1952. *The Memoirs of Herbert Hoover: The Great Depression, 1929–1941*. New York: Macmillan.

Kennickell, Arthur B. 2001. "Modeling Wealth with Multiple Observations of Income: Redesign of the Sample for the 2001 Survey of Consumer Finance," working paper, Board of Governors of the Federal Reserve System. http://www.federalreserve.gov/pubs/oss/oss2/papers/scf2001.list.sample.redesign.9.pdf.

______. 2009. "Ponds and Streams: Wealth and Income in the U.S., 1989 to 2007." Working paper, Finance and Economics Discussion Series, Federal Reserve Board, Washington, D.C.

Kennickell, Arthur, Jesse Bricker, Brian K. Bucks, Traci L. Mach, and Kevin Moore. 2011. "Drowning or Weathering the Storm? Changes in Family Finances from 2007 to 2009." National Bureau of Economic Research Working Paper no. 16985.

Kopczuk, Wojciech. 2014. "What Do We Know about Evolution of Top Wealth Shares in the United States?" National Bureau of Economic Research Working Paper no. 20734, December.

Kopczuk, Wojciech, and Emmanuel Saez. 2004. "Top Wealth Shares in the United States, 1916–2000: Evidence from Estate Tax Returns." *National Tax Journal* 57 (2): 445–88.

Krugman, Paul. 2014a. "The Piketty Panic." *New York Times*, April 25.

______. 2014b. "On Inequality Denial." *New York Times*, June 1.

McCloskey, Deirdre. 2014. "Measured, Unmeasured, Mismeasured, and Unjustified Pessimism: A Review Essay of Thomas Piketty's *Capital in the 21st Century*." *Erasmus Journal of Philosophy and Economics* 7 (2): 73–115.

Piketty, Thomas. 2014a. "Addendum: Response to FT." May 28, http://piketty.pse.ens.fr/files/capital21c/en/Piketty2014TechnicalAppendixResponsetoFT.pdf.

______. 2014b. *Capital in the 21st Century*. Cambridge, MA: Belknap Press.

______. 2014c. "Technical Appendix of the Book *Capital in the 21st Century*." March. http://piketty.pse.ens.fr/files/capital21c/en/Piketty2014TechnicalAppendix.pdf.

Piketty, Thomas, and Emmanuel Saez. 2003. "Income Inequality in the United States, 1913–1998." *Quarterly Journal of Economics* 118 (1): 1–39.

Reynolds, Alan. 2006. *Income and Wealth*. London: Greenwood Press.

Saez, Emmanuel, and Gabriel Zucman. 2014a. "Exploding Wealth Inequality in the United States." Washington, D.C.: Washington Center for Equitable Growth, October 20.

———. 2014b. "Wealth Inequality in the United States since 1913: Evidence from Capitalized Income Tax Data." National Bureau of Economic Research Working Paper no. 20625, October.

Sahlén, Malin, and Salim Furth. 2014, "Piketty Is Misleading about the Swedish Case." *Timbro*, November 7. It is also reprinted with permission in this volume, Chapter 14.

U.S. Department of Labor. 2016. "History of Federal Minimum Wage Rates under the Fair Labor Standards Act, 1938–2009." Wage and Hour Division, http://www.dol.gov/whd/minwage/chart.htm.

Wolff, Edward N. 1994. "Trends in Household Wealth in the United States, 1962–83 and 1983–89." *Review of Income and Wealth* 40 (2): 143–74.

———. 2010. "Recent Trends in Household Wealth in the United States: Rising Debt and the Middle-Class Squeeze—An Update to 2007." Levy Economics Institute Working Papers Series no. 159.

Part 3. Theory and Policy

While its empirical analysis at first glance seemed to constitute the strength of Piketty's book, Part 2 showed that we could cast serious doubts in this regard. What about its theoretical aspect? The famous $r > g$ formula which seems, alone, to summarize the conceptual contribution of Piketty's *Capital* while explaining the empirical trends that the author claims to exhibit, acquired a scientific aura that is almost as famous as Einstein's formula on relativity.

But what are the theoretical concepts behind it? Are they realistic? Of course a theory is by definition a model of reality that isolates certain elements and abstracts others. The issue of "realism" in economics therefore should rather focus on the ability of a theory to correctly describe the *essential* processes of reality. From this point of view, what is the value of Thomas Piketty's theory? The French economist's processes of conceptualization and abstraction are strongly imbued with Marxist method. To what extent does historical determinism acquire a "superhuman" autonomy, making the theorist oblivious to endogenous social processes, in particular based on institutions?

This theoretical obliviousness seems to be also at play in the case of the consequences of the economic policies developed by our French socialist intellectual. Can a lack of understanding of the institutional and economic processes that really govern the evolution of capitalism lead to the formation of informed public policy? To what extent would these policies have a negative impact? What are the alternatives?

Section 6. The Dangers of the Historicist Method

Like Karl Marx before him, Thomas Piketty claims to discover the great laws of capitalism that explain the dynamics of inequality and allow the French economist to make catastrophic predictions for the 21st century. However, the intellectual tendency to produce grand laws of history has not proved especially enlightened if we consider the success of past predictions. Could that also be the case for Piketty?

Piketty has not conducted statistical tests to check the validity of his theory in the past. Other authors have performed those tests and discovered that his theory is not verified. Making predictions for the 21st century on the basis of a theory that is not even verified with past data seems risky.

In fact, Piketty's very deterministic "macro" theoretical framework overlooks complex microeconomic realities that require an understanding of the impact of institutional frameworks on human behavior. An analysis of economic evolution is incomplete without an institutionalist perspective. "Micro" reasoning brings us back down to earth from the aggregative heights of concepts such as capital or wealth. An institutional analysis also means government itself needs to be questioned as a potential source of inequality. This section addresses such questions and flushes out many flaws in Piketty's analysis.

16. The Rise and Decline of the General Laws of Capitalism

Daron Acemoglu and James A. Robinson

Economists have long been drawn to the ambitious quest of discovering the general laws of capitalism.[1] David Ricardo, for example, predicted that capital accumulation would terminate in economic stagnation and inequality as a greater and greater share of national income accrued to landowners (1817). Karl Marx followed him by forecasting the inevitable immiseration of the proletariat. In his tome, *Capital in the 21st Century*, Thomas Piketty emulates Marx in his title, his style of exposition, and his critique of the capitalist system (2014). Piketty is after general laws that demystify our modern economy and elucidate the inherent problems of the system—and point to solutions.

But the quest for general laws of capitalism is misguided because it ignores the key forces shaping how an economy functions: the endogenous evolution of technology and of the institutions and the political equilibrium that influence not only technology but also how markets function and how the gains from various economic arrangements are distributed. Despite his erudition, ambition, and creativity, Marx was led astray because of his disregard of these forces. The same is true of Piketty's sweeping account of inequality in capitalist economies.

Therefore, we will first review Marx's conceptualization of capitalism and some of his general laws, then turn to Piketty's approach to capitalism and his general laws. We will point to various problems in Piketty's interpretation of the economic relationships underpinning inequality. But the most important shortcoming is that, though he discusses the role of certain institutions and policies, he allows for neither a systematic role for institutions and political factors in the formation of inequality nor the endogenous evolution of those institutional factors. That disregard implies that his general laws have little explanatory power. We illustrate the point by using regression evidence to show that Piketty's central economic force, the relationship between the interest rate and the rate of economic growth, is not correlated with inequality (in particular, with a key variable he focuses on, the share of national income accruing to the richest 1 percent, henceforth, the top 1 percent share). We then use the examples of the South African and Swedish paths of inequality over the 20th century to demonstrate two things: (1) using the top 1 percent share may miss the big picture about inequality; and (2) it is impossible to understand the dynamics of inequality in those societies without systematically bringing in institutions and politics and their endogenous evolution. We conclude by outlining an alternative approach to inequality that eschews general laws in favor of a conceptualization in which both technology and factor prices are shaped by the evolution of institutions and political equilibria—and institutions themselves are endogenous and partly influenced by, among other things, the extent of inequality. We then apply that framework to the evolution of inequality and institutions in South Africa and Sweden.

We should note at this point that we do not believe the term *capitalism* is useful for the purposes of comparative economic or political analysis. By focusing on the ownership and accumulation of capital, the term distracts from the characteristics of societies that are more important in determining their economic development and the extent of inequality. For example, both Uzbekistan and modern Switzerland have private ownership of capital, but the two societies have little in common in terms of prosperity and inequality because the nature of their economic and political institutions differs so sharply. In fact, Uzbekistan's capitalist economy has more in common with avowedly noncapitalist North Korea than Switzerland, as we argued in Acemoglu and Robinson (2012). That said, given the emphasis in both Marx and Piketty on capitalism, we have opted to bear with this terminology.

Capital Failures

Though many important ideas in social science can be traced to Karl Marx's oeuvre, his defining approach was to seek certain hard-wired features of capitalism—what Marx called general laws of capitalist accumulation. That approach was heavily shaped by the historical context of the middle 19th century in which Marx lived and wrote. Marx experienced first-hand both the bewildering transformation of society with the rise of industrial production and the associated huge social dislocations.

Marx developed a rich and nuanced theory of history. But the centerpiece of his theory, historical materialism, rested on how material aspects of economic life, together with what Marx called forces of production—particularly technology— shaped all other aspects of social, economic, and political life, including the relations of production. For example, Marx famously argued in his 1847 book, *The Poverty of Philosophy*, that "the hand-mill gives you society with the feudal lord; the steam-mill society with the industrial capitalist" (as reprinted in McLellan 2000, 219–20). Here the hand-mill represents the forces of production while feudalism represents the relations of production, as well as a specific set of social and political arrangements. Changes in the forces of production (technology) destabilized the relations of production and led to contradictions and to social and institutional changes that were often revolutionary in nature. As Marx put it in 1859 in *A Contribution to the Critique of Political Economy*:

> The sum total of these relations of production constitutes the economic structure of society—the real foundation, on which rise legal and political superstructures and to which correspond definite forms of social consciousness. The mode of production of material life conditions the

> general character of the social, political and spiritual processes of life. At a certain state of their development the material forces of production in society come into conflict with the existing relations of production or—what is but a legal expression of the same thing—with the property relations within which they had been at work before. From forms of development of the forces of production these relations turn into fetters. Then comes the epoch of social revolution. With the change of the economic foundation the entire immense superstructure is more or less rapidly transformed (Marx [1859], 2000, 425).

Marx hypothesized that the forces of production, sometimes in conjunction with the ownership of the means of production, determined all other aspects of economic and political institutions: the de jure and de facto laws, regulations, and arrangements shaping social life. Armed with that theory of history, Marx made bold predictions about the dynamics of capitalism based just on economic fundamentals—without any reference to institutions or politics, which he generally viewed as derivative of the powerful impulses unleashed by the forces of production.[2]

Most relevant to this discussion are three of Marx's predictions concerning inequality. In *Capital* ([1867] 1990), Marx developed the idea that the reserve army of the unemployed would keep wages at subsistence level, making capitalism inconsistent with steady improvements in the living standards of workers. His exact prediction is open to different interpretations. Though Marx viewed capitalism as the harbinger of "misery, agony of toil, slavery, ignorance, brutality, and mental degradation" for working men, it is less clear whether that was meant to rule out real wage growth ([1867] 1990, 799). Blaug (1996) points out that Marx never claimed that real wages would be stagnant, but rather that the share of labor in national income would fall: as Marx says, "real wages... never rise proportionately to the productive power of labor" ([1867] 1990, 753). Foley (2008), however, argues that Marx did start by asserting that real wages would not rise under capitalism, but then weakened this claim to a falling labor share when he realized that wages were indeed increasing in Great Britain. Thus, we are motivated to state this law in both a strong and a weak form. Under either its strong or its weak form, the law implies that any economic growth under capitalism would almost automatically translate into greater inequality—as capitalists benefit and workers fail to do so. We combine that law with a second general law of capitalism from Volume III of *Capital* and a third law, less often stressed but highly relevant, presented in Volume I of *Capital*. Thus, three key predictions from Marx are as follows:

1. *General Law of Capitalist Accumulation*. Strong Form: Real wages are stagnant under capitalism. Weak Form: The share of national income accruing to labor falls under capitalism.
2. *General Law of Declining Profit*: As capital accumulates, the rate of profit falls.
3. *General Law of Decreasing Competition*: Capital accumulation leads to increased industrial concentration.

Marx's general laws did not fare well. As Marx was writing, real wages, which had remained constant or had fallen during the first decades of the 19th century, had already been rising, probably for about two decades (Allen 2001, 2007, 2009a; Clark 2005; Feinstein 1998). The share of labor in national income, which had fallen to less than half by 1870, also started to increase thereafter, reaching two-thirds in the 20th century. Robert Allen's (2009a) calculation of the real rate of profit suggests that the profit rate was comparatively low at the end of the 18th century and rose until around 1870, reaching a maximum of 25 percent, but then fell back to around 20 percent, where it stabilized until World War I. Robert Matthews, Charles Feinstein, and John Odling-Smee (1982, 187–88) suggest that these rates did not fall in the 20th century, though there is a lot of heterogeneity across sectors. (The third law's performance was no better as we discuss below.)

Why did Marx's general laws fail? They failed mostly because they ignored both the endogenous evolution of technology (despite his great emphasis on the forces of production) and also the role of institutions and politics in shaping markets, prices, and the path of technology. The increase in real wages in Great Britain, for example, was in part a consequence of the change in the pace and nature of technological change, rapidly increasing the demand for labor (Crafts 1985; Allen 2009b; Mokyr 2012). The rationalization of property rights, dismantling of monopolies, investment in infrastructure, and creation of a legal framework for industrial development (including the patent system) were among the institutional changes contributing to rapid technological change and its widespread adoption in the British economy (Acemoglu and Robinson 2012; Mokyr 2012).

The distribution of the gains from new technologies was also shaped by an evolving institutional equilibrium. The Industrial Revolution went hand in hand with major political changes, including the development of the state and the Reform Acts of 1832, 1867, and 1884, which transformed British political institutions and the distribution of political power. For example, in 1833 a professional factory inspectorate was set up, enabling the enforcement of legislation on factory employment. The political fallout of the 1832 democratization also led in 1846 to the repeal of the Corn Laws (tariffs limiting imports of lower-priced foreign corn), lowering the price of bread, raising real wages, and simultaneously undermining land rents (Schonhardt-Bailey 2006). The Factory Act of 1847 took the radical step of limiting working hours in the textile mills to 10 hours per day for women and teenagers. The Reform Act of 1867, which massively expanded voting rights, led to the abolition of the Masters and Servants Act in 1875—which had imposed on workers legally enforceable duties of loyalty and obedience, and limited mobility—illustrating the role of pro-worker labor market legislation that increased real wages (Naidu and Yuchtman 2013).

Another telling example is the failure of Marx's third general law—the prediction of increased industrial concentration—in the United States. After the end of the U.S. Civil War came the age of the robber barons and the huge concentration of economic ownership and control. By the end of the 1890s, companies such as Du Pont, Eastman Kodak, Standard Oil, and International Harvester dominated the economy, in several cases capturing more than 70 percent of their respective markets (Lamoreaux 1985, 3–4). It looked like a Marxian prediction come true—except that the situation was transitory and was duly reversed as popular mobilization, triggered in part by the increase in inequality, changed the political equilibrium and the regulation of industry (Sanders 1999). The Interstate Commerce Act of 1887 and then the Sherman Anti-Trust Act of 1890 began to curtail the power of larger corporations; both were used in the early 20th-century trust-busting efforts against Du Pont, the American Tobacco Company, the Standard Oil Company, and the Northern Securities Company, then controlled by J. P. Morgan. The reforms continued with the completion of the breakup of Standard Oil in 1911; the ratification of the Sixteenth Amendment in 1913, which introduced the income tax; and the Clayton Anti-Trust Act in 1914, which created the Federal Trade Commission. Those changes not only stopped further industrial concentration but reversed it (Collins and Preston 1961; Edwards 1975). White (1981) shows that U.S. industrial concentration in the post–World War II period changed little (see White [2002] for an update).

Crucially, the political process that led to the institutional changes transforming the British economy and inequality in the 19th century was not a forgone conclusion. Nor was the rise in inequality in 19th century America after the Civil War an inevitable consequence of capitalism. The reversal in inequality starting in the early 1900s was equally dependent on an evolving institutional equilibrium. In fact, while the power of monopoly and inequality were being curtailed in the United States, inequality continued to increase rapidly in neighboring Mexico under the authoritarian rule of Porfirio Diaz, culminating in revolution and civil war in 1910 and demonstrating the central role of endogenous and path-dependent institutional dynamics.

Marx's general laws failed for the same reason that previous general laws by other economists also performed poorly. The laws were formulated in an effort to compress the facts and events of their times into a grand theory aiming to be applicable at all times and places, with little reference to institutions and the (partly institutionally determined) changing nature of technology. For example, when David Ricardo published *On the Principles of Political Economy and Taxation* in 1817 and predicted that a rising share of national income would accrue to land, he had been living through a period of rapidly rising land rents in Britain. But soon thereafter, the share of national income accruing to land started a monotonic decline; by the 1870s, real rents started a rapid fall, which would last for the next 60 years (Turner et al. 1999; Clark 2002, 2010).

In short, Marx's general laws, like those of his predecessors, failed because they relied on a conception of the economy that did not recognize the endogenous evolution of technology and the role of changing economic and political institutions, shaping both technology and factor prices. In fact, even Marx's emphasis on the defining role of the forces of production, so emblematic of his approach, was often inadequate not only as the engine of history, but also as a description of history, including his paradigmatic example of "hand-mills" and "steam-mills" ([1847] 2000). For example, Marc Bloch (1967) argued persuasively that the hand-mill did not determine the nature of feudal society, nor did the steam-mill determine the character of the postfeudal world.

Seeking 21st Century Laws of Capitalism

Thomas Piketty is also an economist of his milieu. His thinking is heavily colored by increasing inequality in the Anglo-Saxon world and more recently in continental Europe—and in particular compared with the more equal distribution of labor and total incomes seen in France in the 1980s and 1990s. A large literature in labor economics had done much to document and dissect the increase in inequality that started sometime in the 1970s in the United States (see the surveys and the extensive references to earlier work in Katz and Autor [1999] and Acemoglu and Autor [2011]). The literature demonstrates that the increase in inequality has taken place throughout the income distribution and that it can be explained reasonably well by changes in the supply and demand for skills and in labor market institutions. Piketty and Emmanuel Saez (2003) brought a new and fruitful perspective to the literature by using data from tax returns, confirming and extending the patterns the previous literature had uncovered, and placing heavy emphasis on rising inequality at the very top of the income distribution.

In *Capital in the 21st Century*, Piketty goes beyond that empirical and historical approach to offer a theory of the long-run tendencies of capitalism. Though Piketty's data confirm the finding of the previous literature that widening inequality in recent decades, at least in advanced economies, had been driven by rising inequality of labor incomes, his book paints a future dominated by capital income, inherited wealth, and rentier billionaires. The theoretical framework used to reach that conclusion is a mix of Marxian economics with Solow's growth model. Piketty defines capitalism in the same way that Marx does and has a similarly materialist approach that links the dynamics of capitalism to the ownership of the means of production (in particular capital) and the ironclad nature of technology and exogenous growth dynamics. It is true that Piketty sometimes mentions policies and institutions (for example, the wealth tax and the military and political developments that destroyed capital and reduced the ratio of wealth-to-income during the first half of the 20th century). But their role is ad hoc. Our argument is that, to explain inequality, those features and their endogenous evolution have to be systematically introduced into the analysis.

Piketty's approach shapes his analysis and predictions about the nature of capitalism. *Capital in the 21st Century* starts by introducing two "fundamental laws," but the more major predictions flow from what Piketty calls a "fundamental force of divergence" (2014, 351) or sometimes the "fundamental inequality" (2014, 25), comparing the (real) interest rate of the economy with the growth rate. The first fundamental law is just a definition: capital share of national income = $r \times (K/Y)$, where r is the net real rate of return on capital (which can be viewed as a real interest rate), K is the capital stock, and Y is gross domestic product (GDP) (or, equivalently, national income as the economy is taken to be closed). The second fundamental law is slightly more substantial. It states that $K/Y = s/g$, where s is the saving rate and g is the growth rate of GDP. As we explain in the Online Appendix that accompanies this chapter (available at http://dx.doi.org/10.1257/jep.29.1.3), a version of this law does indeed follow readily from the steady state of a Solow-type model of economic growth (but see Krusell and Smith 2015; Ray 2014). At an intuitive level, the growth rate of the capital stock K is given by net investment, which in a closed economy is equal to saving, sY. Thus, the ratio K/Y reflects the ratio "change in K to change in Y" over time that is due to economic growth, which is s/g.

Let us follow Piketty here and combine the two fundamental laws to obtain capital share of national income = $r \times (s/g)$. Piketty posits that, even as g changes, r and s can be taken to be approximate constants (or at least that they will not change as much as g). That point leads to what can be thought of as his first general law: when growth is lower, the capital share of national income will be higher.

The first law is not as compelling as one might at first think, however. After all, one must consider whether a change in the growth rate g might also alter the saving rate s or the rate of return r, because they are all endogenous variables that are linked in standard models of economic growth. Piketty argues that r should not change much in response to a decline in g because the elasticity of substitution between capital and labor is high, resulting in an increase in the capital share of national income.[3]

However, the vast majority of existing estimates indicate a short-run elasticity of substitution significantly less than one (for example, Hamermesh 1993; Mairesse et al. 1999; Chirinko, Fazzari, and Meyer 1999; Krusell, Ohanian, Rios-Rull, and Violante 2000; Chirinko 1993; Antràs 2004; Klump et al. 2007; Oberfield and Raval 2014). The case is also plausible on intuitive grounds: given technology, the ability to substitute capital for labor would be limited (for example, if one reduces labor to zero, for a given production process, one would expect output to fall to zero as well). Though this elasticity could be higher in longer horizons, Robert Chirinko (2008) as well as Chirinko and Debdulal Mallick (2014) find it to be significantly less than one in the long run. One reason why the long-run elasticity of substitution might be greater than one is the endogeneity of technology (for example, Acemoglu 2002, 2003). In that context, it is worth noting that in the only recent paper estimating an elasticity of substitution greater than one, Loukas Karabarbounis and Brent Neiman (2014) use long-run cross-country variation related to changes in investment prices, making their estimates much more likely to correspond to endogenous-technology elasticities. Nevertheless, as Matthew Rognlie (2014) points out, even an elasticity of substitution significantly greater than one would not be sufficient to yield the conclusions that Piketty reaches.

Moreover, although the capital share of national income has indeed risen, that does not seem to be related to the forces emphasized in *Capital in the 21st Century*. In particular, Odran Bonnet and others (2014) demonstrate that the rise in the capital share is due to housing and the increased price of real estate, shedding doubt on the mechanism Piketty emphasizes.

The second general law of *Capital in the 21st Century* is formulated as $r > g$, stating that the (real) interest rate exceeds the growth rate of the economy. Theoretically, in an economy with an exogenous saving rate, or with overlapping generations (for example, Samuelson 1958; Diamond 1965), or with incomplete markets (for example, Bewley 1986; Aiyagari 1994), the interest rate need not exceed the growth rate. It will do so in an economy that is *dynamically efficient*, meaning in an economy in which it is impossible to increase the consumption at all dates (thus achieving a Pareto improvement). Whether an economy is dynamically efficient is an empirical matter—for example, François Geerolf (2013) suggests that several economies in the Organisation for Economic Co-operation and Development (OECD) might be dynamically inefficient—and dynamic inefficiency becomes more likely when the capital–output ratio is very high as *Capital in the 21st Century* predicts it to be in the future.

Finally, Piketty's third and most important general law is that whenever $r > g$, inequality will tend to rise. Capital income will tend to increase at the rate of interest, r, while national income (and the income of noncapitalists) increases at the rate g. Because capital income is unequally distributed, that will translate into a capital-driven increase in inequality, taking us back to the age of Jane Austen and Honoré Balzac. In the words of Piketty (2014, 25–26): "This fundamental inequality [$r > g$] will play a crucial role in this book. In a sense, it sums up the overall logic of my conclusions. When the rate of return on capital significantly exceeds the growth rate of the economy, then it logically follows that inherited wealth grows faster than output and income." He elaborates on the point later, writing: "The primary reason for the hyper-concentration of wealth in traditional agrarian societies and to a large extent in all societies prior to World War I is that these were low-growth societies in which the rate of return on capital was markedly and durably higher than the rate of growth" (2014, 351). On that basis, he proposes an explanation for the rise in inequality over the next several decades: "The reason why wealth today is not as unequally distributed as in the past is simply that not enough time has passed since 1945" (Piketty 2014, 372).[4]

As with the first two general laws, there are things to quibble with in the pure economics of the third general law. First, as already mentioned, the emphasis on $r - g$ sits somewhat uneasily with the central role that labor income has played in the rise in inequality. Second, as we show in the Online Appendix, $r > g$ is fully consistent with constant or even declining inequality. Third, $r - g$ cannot be taken as a primitive on which to make future forecasts, as both the interest rate and the growth rate will adjust to changes in policy, technology, and the capital stock. Finally, in the presence of a modest amount of social mobility, even very large values of $r - g$ do not lead to divergence at the top of the distribution (again, as we show in the Online Appendix).

But our major argument is about what the emphasis on $r > g$ leaves out: institutions and politics. Piketty largely dismisses the importance of institutions against the crushing force of the fundamental inequality, writing that "the fundamental inequality $r > g$ can explain the very high level of capital inequality observed in the 19th century, and thus in a sense the failure of the French Revolution. The formal nature of the regime was of little moment compared with the inequality $r > g$" (2014, 365). In passing, we should note that the available empirical evidence suggests that the French Revolution not only led to a decrease in inequality (Morrisson and Snyder 2000), but also profoundly changed the path of institutional equilibria and economic growth in Europe (Acemoglu et al. 2011).

If the history of grand pronouncements of the general laws of capitalism repeats itself—perhaps first as tragedy and then farce, as Marx colorfully put it—then we may expect the same sort of frustration with Piketty's sweeping predictions as they fail to come true, in the same way that those of Ricardo and Marx failed in the past. We next provide evidence suggesting that this outcome is quite likely as the existing evidence goes against Piketty's predictions.

Cross-Country Data on $r > g$ and Top-Level Inequality

Piketty's major contribution, often together with Emmanuel Saez, has been to bring to the table a huge amount of new data on inequality (Piketty and Saez 2003). The reader may come away from the data, presented at length in Piketty's book, with the impression that the evidence supporting his proposed laws of capitalism is overwhelming. However, Piketty does not present even basic correlations between $r - g$ and changes in inequality, much less any explicit evidence of a causal effect. Therefore, as a first step we show that the data provide little support for the general laws of capitalism he advances.

We begin by using as a dependent variable the top 1 percent share (see Alvaredo et al. 2011). We combine that variable with GDP data from Angus Maddison's data set. (See the Maddison project web page at http://www.ggdc.net/maddison/maddison-project/home.htm.) For the first part of our analysis, we do not use explicit data on interest rates, which gives us an unbalanced panel spanning 1870–2012. For the rest of our analysis, our panel covers the post–World War II period and uses GDP data from the Penn World Tables (available at http://cid.econ.ucdavis.edu/pwt.html).[5]

Table 16.1 reports regressions using three different measures of $r - g$. First, we assume that all capital markets are open and all of the countries in the sample have the same (possibly time-varying) interest rate. Under that assumption, cross-country variation in $r - g$ will arise only because of variation in the growth rate, g. The first three columns in panel A of the table simply exploit variation in g using annual data (that is, we set $r - g = -g$ by normalizing $r = 0$). Throughout, the standard errors are corrected for arbitrary heteroskedasticity and serial correlation at the country level; and because the number of countries is small (varying between 18 and 28), they are computed using the pairs-cluster bootstrap procedure proposed by Colin Cameron and others (2008), which has better finite-sample properties than the commonly used clustered standard errors. (The same results, with "traditional" standard errors that assume no heteroskedasticity and residual serial correlation, are reported in the Online Appendix Table A1 and show very similar patterns.) In column 1, we look at the relationship between annual top 1 percent share and annual growth in a specification that includes a full set of year dummies and country dummies—so that the pure time-series variation at the world level is purged by year dummies and none of the results rely on cross-country comparisons. Piketty's theory predicts a positive and significant coefficient on this measure of $r - g$: that is, in countries with higher g, the incomes of the bottom 99 percent will grow more, limiting the top 1 percent share.[6] Instead, we find a negative estimate that is statistically insignificant.

In column 2, we include five annual lags of top 1 percent share on the right-hand side to model the significant amount of persistence in measures of inequality. Specifications that include the lagged dependent variable on the right-hand side are potentially subject to the bias described by Stephen Nickell (1981). However, given the length of the panel, that issue is unlikely to arise (since the bias disappears as the time dimension becomes large). The test at the bottom of the table shows that lagged top 1 percent share is indeed highly significant. In this case, the impact of $r - g$ is negative and significant at 10 percent—the opposite of the prediction of *Capital in the 21st Century*. Column 3 includes five annual lags of GDP as well as five lags of top 1 percent share simultaneously. There is once more no evidence of a positive impact of $r - g$ on top inequality. On the contrary, the relationship is again negative, as shown by the first lag and also by the long-run cumulative effect reported at the bottom.

What matters for inequality may not be annual or five-year variations exploited in panel A, but longer-term swings in $r - g$.

Table 16.1

REGRESSION COEFFICIENTS OF DIFFERENT PROXIES OF $r - g$

(DEPENDENT VARIABLE IS THE TOP 1 PERCENT SHARE OF NATIONAL INCOME)

	No cross-country variation in r			OECD data on interest rates			r = MPK − δ		
	(1)	(2)	(3)	(4)	(5)	(6)	(7)	(8)	(9)
Panel A: Estimates using annual panel									
Estimate of $r - g$ at t	−0.006	−0.018*	−0.018*	−0.066**	−0.038**	−0.040*	0.029	−0.004	−0.011
	(0.012)	(0.010)	(0.011)	(0.027)	(0.017)	(0.021)	(0.033)	(0.009)	(0.008)
Estimate of $r - g$ at $t - 1$			0.001			−0.003			0.005
			(0.009)			(0.015)			(0.014)
Estimate of $r - g$ at $t - 2$			0.005			0.010			−0.012
			(0.008)			(0.019)			(0.008)
Estimate of $r - g$ at $t - 3$			−0.002			−0.012			0.014*
			(0.008)			(0.024)			(0.008)
Estimate of $r - g$ at $t - 4$			−0.005			−0.005			0.006
			(0.007)			(0.013)			(0.010)
Joint significance of lags			4.55			7.47			12.40
[*p*-value]			[0.47]			[0.19]			[0.03]
Long-run effect		−0.16	−0.18		−0.39	−0.47		−0.04	0.03
[*p*-value estimate > 0]		[0.13]	[0.15]		[0.29]	[0.34]		[0.68]	[0.89]
Persistence of top		0.89	0.89		0.90	0.89		0.90	0.92
1 percent share		[0.00]	[0.00]		[0.31]	[0.30]		[0.11]	[0.18]
[*p*-value estimate < 1]									

Observations	1,646	1,233	1,226	627	520	470	1,162	905	860
Countries	27	27	27	19	18	18	28	26	26
Panel B: Estimates using 10-year (columns 1, 2, 4, 5, 7, 8) and 20-year (columns 3, 6, 9) panels									
Average $r - g$	0.055	−0.036	−0.252	−0.114	−0.121	−0.110	0.069	0.148	0.238
	(0.110)	(0.118)	(0.269)	(0.138)	(0.132)	(0.320)	(0.118)	(0.100)	(0.164)
Long-run effect		−0.05			−0.25			0.29	
[p-value estimate > 0]		[0.76]			[0.44]			[0.22]	
Persistence of top 1 percent share		0.32			0.52			0.48	
[p-value estimate < 1]		[0.00]			[0.02]			[0.00]	
Observations	213	181	106	82	80	43	135	124	61
Countries	27	25	24	18	18	17	27	25	22

NOTE: MPK = marginal product of capital; OECD = Organisation for Economic Co-operation and Development. The table presents estimates of different proxies of $r - g$ on the top 1 percent share of national income. The dependent variable is available from 1871 onward for the countries covered in the *World Top Incomes Database*. We use different proxies of $r - g$: Columns 1–3 use growth rates from Maddison and assume no variation in real interest rates across countries. Those data are available from 1870 onward. Columns 4–6 use real interest rates computed by subtracting realized inflation from nominal yields on long-term government bonds and growth rates from the Penn World Tables. Those data are only available since 1955 for OECD countries. Columns 7–9 use r = MPK − δ, constructed as explained in the text using data and growth rates from the Penn World Tables. Those data are available for 1950 onward. Panel A uses an unbalanced yearly panel. Columns 2, 5, and 8 add five lags of the dependent variable and report the estimated persistence of the top 1 percent share of national income and the estimated long run effect of $r - g$ on the dependent variable. Columns 3, 6, and 9 add four lags of $r - g$ on the right-hand side, and also report the long-run effect of a permanent increase of 1 percent in $r - g$ and a test for the joint significance of those lags (with the corresponding χ^2 statistic and p-value). Panel B uses an unbalanced panel with observations every 10 years (columns 1, 2, 4, 5, 7 8) or 20 years (columns 3, 6, 9). Columns 1, 2, 4, 5, 7, and 8 present estimates from a regression of the top 1 percent share of national income at the end of each decade in the sample (that is, 1880, 1890, ..., 2010, depending on data availability) on the average $r - g$ during the decade. Columns 2, 5, and 8 add one lag of the dependent variable on the right-hand side. Finally, columns 3, 6, and 9 present estimates from a regression of the top 1 percent share of national income at the end of each 20-year period in the sample (that is, 1890, 1910, ..., 2010, depending on data availability) on the average $r - g$ during the period. All specifications include a full set of country and year fixed effects. Standard errors allowing for arbitrary heteroskedasticity and serial correlation of residuals at the country level are computed using the pairs-cluster bootstrap procedure proposed by Cameron and others (2008) and are reported in parentheses. Asterisks—* and **—indicate 10 and 5 percent levels of significance, respectively.
SOURCE: Maddison data from The Maddison Project, http://www.ggdc.net/maddison/maddison-project/home.htm, 2013 version.

Panel B investigates that possibility by looking at 10-year (columns 1, 2, 4, 5, 7, 8) and 20-year data (columns 3, 6, 9).[7] But those specifications do not provide any evidence of a positive relationship between this measure of $r - g$ and top 1 percent share either.

In columns 4–6 in panel A, we work with a different measure of $r - g$ based on the realized interest rate constructed from data on nominal yields of long-term government bonds and inflation rates from the OECD. The relationship is again negative and now statistically significant at 5 percent in columns 4 and 5, and at 10 percent in column 6. In panel B, when we use 10-year and 20-year panels, the relationship continues to be negative but is now statistically insignificant.

One concern with the results in columns 4–6 is that the relevant interest rate for the very rich may not be the one for long-term government bonds. Motivated by this possibility, columns 7–9 use the procedure proposed by Francesco Caselli and James Feyrer (2007) to estimate the economy-wide marginal product of capital minus the depreciation rate, using data on aggregate factors of production, and construct $r - g$ using those estimates. Now the relationship is more unstable. In some specifications it becomes positive but is never statistically significant.

The Online Appendix Tables A2 and A3 show that those results are robust to including, additionally, GDP per capita (as another control for the business cycle and its impact on the top 1 percent share), population growth, and country-specific trends, and to the use of the top 5 percent measure of inequality as the dependent variable. The Online Appendix Table A4 verifies that the results are similar if we limit the analysis to a common sample consisting of OECD countries since 1950, and the Online Appendix Table A5 shows that focusing on the capital share of national income, rather than the top 1 percent share, leads to a similar set of results, providing no consistent evidence of an impact from $r - g$ to inequality.[8]

This evidence is tentative, and, obviously, we are not pretending to estimate any sort of causal relationship between $r - g$ and the top 1 percent share. However, it is quite striking that such basic conditional correlations provide no support for the central emphasis of *Capital in the 21st Century*. That is not to say that a higher r is not a force toward greater inequality in society—it probably is. But many other forces promote inequality, and our regressions suggest that, at least in a correlational sense, those other forces are quantitatively more important than $r - g$.

A Tale of Two Inequalities: Sweden and South Africa

We now use the histories of inequality during the 20th century in Sweden and South Africa to illustrate how the dynamics of inequality appear linked to the institutional paths of those societies—rather than to the forces of $r > g$. In addition, the two cases illustrate that the share of national income going to the top 0.1 percent or top 1 percent can give a distorted view of what is actually happening to inequality more broadly. Indeed, the focus on inequality at the top inevitably leads to a lesser and insufficient focus on what is taking place in the middle or the bottom of the income distribution. (See Figure 16.1.)

Figure 16.1 shows the evolution of the share of the top 1 percent in national income in Sweden and South Africa since the early 20th century. There are, of course, some differences. Sweden started out with a higher top 1 percent share than South Africa, but its top 1 percent share fell faster, especially following World War I. The recent increase in the top 1 percent also starts earlier in Sweden and is less pronounced than what we see in South Africa in the 1990s and 2000s. But in broad terms, the top 1 percent share behaves similarly in the two countries, starting high, then falling almost monotonically until the 1980s, and then turning up. Such common dynamics for the top 1 percent share in two such different countries—one, the birthplace of European social democracy, and the other, a former colony with a history of coerced labor and

Figure 16.1
TOP 1 PERCENT SHARES OF NATIONAL INCOME IN SWEDEN AND SOUTH AFRICA

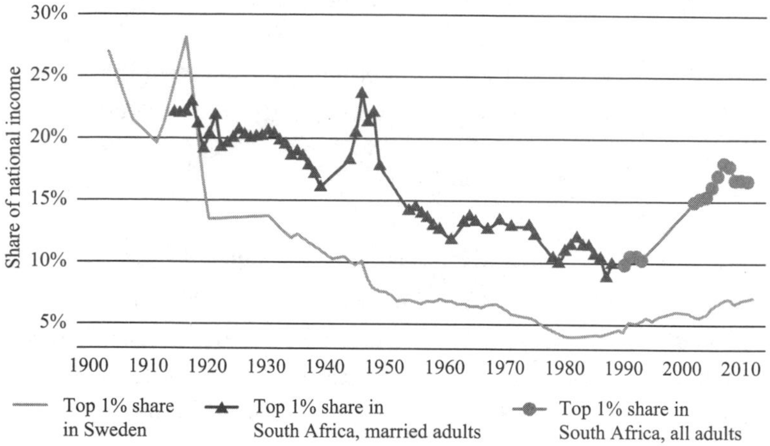

SOURCES: The data series for South Africa is from Alvaredo and Atkinson (2010). The data series for Sweden is from Roine and Waldenström (2009).

land expropriation, ruled for much of the 20th century by a racist white minority—would seem to bolster Piketty's case that the general laws of capitalism explain the big swings of inequality, with little reference to institutions and politics. Perhaps one could even claim, as in Piketty's example of the French Revolution, that the effects of apartheid and social democracy are trifling details against the fundamental force of $r > g$.

However, the reality is rather different. In South Africa, for example, the institutionalization of white dominance after 1910 quickly led to the Native Land Act in 1913, which allocated 93 percent of the land to the "white economy" and left blacks (around 59 percent of the population) with 7 percent. In the white economy, it became illegal for blacks to own property or a business, and many types of contractual relations for blacks were explicitly banned. By the

1920s, the "color bar" blocked blacks from practically all skilled and professional occupations (Van der Horst 1942; Feinstein 2005). After 1948, the apartheid state became even stronger, implementing a wide array of measures to enforce social and educational segregation between whites and blacks. Finally, in 1994, the apartheid institutions collapsed as Nelson Mandela became South Africa's first black president. However, a naïve look at Figure 16.1 would seem to suggest that South Africa's apartheid regime, which was explicitly structured to keep black wages low and to benefit whites, was responsible for a great decrease in inequality, while the end of apartheid caused an explosion in inequality!

How can that be? The answer is that measuring inequality by the top 1 percent share can give a misleading picture of inequality dynamics in some settings. Figure 16.2 shows the top 1 percent

Figure 16.2

TOP INCOME SHARES AND BETWEEN-GROUP INEQUALITY IN SOUTH AFRICA

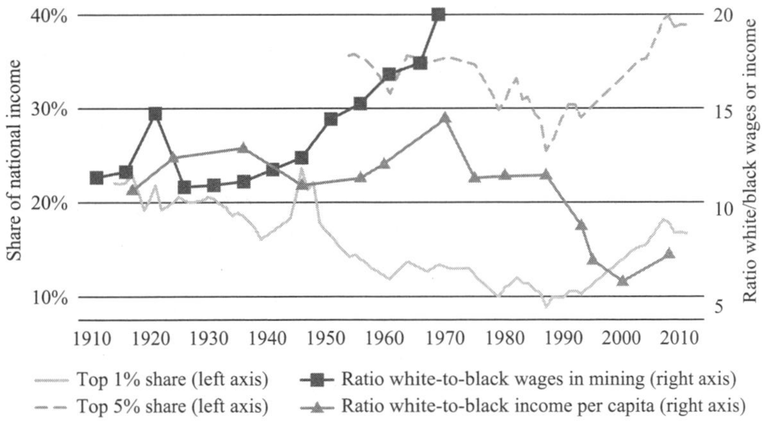

SOURCES: The left axis shows the top 1 and 5 percent shares of national income for South Africa on the left axis (obtained from Alvaredo and Atkinson 2010). The right axis shows the ratio between whites' and blacks' wages in mining (obtained from Wilson 1972), and the ratio between whites' and blacks' income per capita (obtained from Leibbrandt et al. 2010).

share together with other measures of inequality in South Africa, which behave quite differently. Inequality between whites and blacks widened massively during the 20th century as measured by the ratio of white-to-black wages in gold mining, a key engine of the South African economy at the time (from the wage series of Wilson 1972); that result represents a continuation of 19th-century trends (discussed in de Zwart 2011). The pattern is confirmed by the white-to-black per capita income ratio from census data, which has some ups and downs but exhibits a fairly large increase—from about 11-fold to 14-fold, from 1911 until 1970. Thereafter, it shows a rapid decline. Even the top 5 percent share behaves somewhat differently than the top 1 percent share (though available data for that variable start only in the 1950s).

Thus, changes in labor market institutions and political equilibria appear much more relevant than *r* and *g* to understanding economic inequality in South Africa. Indeed, the alternative measures of inequality in Figure 16.2 show that during the time the share of the top 1 percent was falling, South Africa became one of the most unequal countries in the world. As we will discuss, the turning points in inequality in South Africa actually have institutional and political roots.

Figure 16.3 shows that in Sweden, the decline in the top 1 percent share from 1965 to 1980 was accompanied by a much more pervasive fall in inequality as measured by the Gini coefficient for household disposable income. And over the entire period, the two series for the Gini index have trends similar to the top 1 percent and top 5 percent shares. However, in the Swedish case as well, the story of inequality seems related not to supposed general laws of capitalism and changes in *r* and *g*, but rather to institutional changes (Bengtsson 2014). The initial fall in the top 1 percent share coincided with large changes in government policy—for example, a rapid increase in redistribution in the 1920s from practically nothing in the 1910s (Lindert 1994), and an increase in top marginal tax rates from around 10 percent in

Figure 16.3

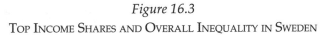

TOP INCOME SHARES AND OVERALL INEQUALITY IN SWEDEN

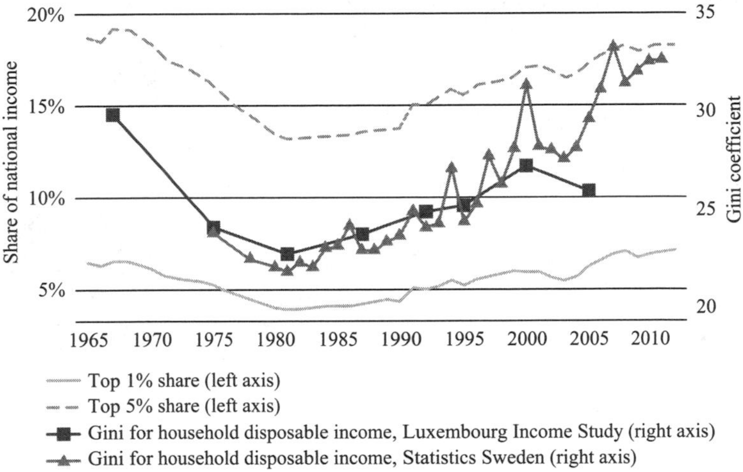

SOURCES AND NOTE: The figure plots the top 1 and 5 percent shares of national income for Sweden on the left vertical axis, obtained from Roine and Waldenström (2009). The right axis plots the Gini coefficient for household disposable income, from the Luxembourg Income Study (Milanovic 2013), and from Statistics Sweden (SCB, http://www.scb.se/en_/).

1910 to 40 percent by 1930 and 60 percent by 1940 (Roine et al. 2009, 982). The expanding role of the government and of redistributive taxation plausibly had a negative impact on the top 1 percent share. The data in Figures 16.1 and 16.3 are for pretax inequality, but they are likely to be affected by taxes, which influence effort and investment (see the evidence in Roine et al. 2009), and also directly by the wage compression created by Sweden's labor market institutions. Indeed, union density rose rapidly from around 10 percent of the labor force during World War I to 35 percent by 1930 and to over 50 percent by 1940 (Donado and Wälde 2012).

Piketty emphasizes the role of the destruction of the capital stock and falling asset prices in the aftermath of the two world wars as key factors explaining the decline of top inequality during much of the 20th century. But such factors can hardly account for the trends in Sweden or South Africa. Sweden was neutral in both wars, and though South Africa provided troops and resources for the Allied powers in both, neither economy experienced any direct destruction of its capital stock.

Toward an Institutional Framework

A satisfactory framework for the analysis of inequality should take into account both the effect of different types of institutions on the distribution of resources and the endogenous evolution of those institutions. We now flesh out such a framework and then apply it to the evolution of inequality—and institutions—in Sweden and South Africa. The framework we present is based on the one we proposed in Acemoglu et al. (2005). Adapting figure 1 from that paper, our framework can be represented schematically as follows:

$$\left.\begin{array}{l}\text{political institutions}_t \Rightarrow \text{de jure political power}_t\ \&\\ \text{inequality}_t \Rightarrow \text{de facto political power}_t\end{array}\right\} \Rightarrow \begin{cases}\text{economic institutions}_t \Rightarrow \left.\begin{array}{c}\text{technology}_t,\\ \text{skills}_t, \ \&\\ \text{prices}_t\end{array}\right\} \Rightarrow \left\{\begin{array}{c}\text{economic performance}_t\\ \&\\ \text{inequality}_{t+1}\end{array}\right.\\ \text{political institutions}_{t+1}\end{cases}$$

In this approach, the prevailing political institutions at a certain time determine the distribution of de jure political power (Acemoglu and Robinson 2000, 2008; Acemoglu 2008; Acemoglu et al. 2012, 2015): for example, which groups are disenfranchised, how political power is contested, how constrained the economic and political elites are, and so on. Political institutions also affect, together with inequality in society, the distribution of de facto political power. For instance, de facto power—which designates political power and constraints generated by access to the means of violence, collective action, informal institutions, and social norms—depends on the extent to which different social and economic groups are organized, how they resolve their collective action problems, and how resources influence their ability to do so. De facto and de jure power together determine economic institutions and also the stability and change of political institutions.

In turn, economic institutions affect the supply of skills—a crucial determinant of inequality throughout history and even more so today. Economic institutions also influence goods and factor prices through regulation of both prices and market structure (by taxation or by affecting the bargaining power of different factors of production and individuals). Finally, economic institutions affect technology, including whether and how efficiently existing technologies are utilized, as well as the evolution of technology through endogenous innovations and learning by doing. For example, Joseph Zeira (1998) and Acemoglu (2010) show how low wages, resulting from either supply or institutional factors, can sometimes reduce technology adoption or even technological progress; Richard Hornbeck and Suresh Naidu (2014) provide evidence consistent with that pattern. Through their joint impact on technology, the supply of skills, and relative prices, economic institutions affect not only r and g, but more important, inequality. In this approach, inequality should not be thought of as always summarized by a single statistic, such as the Gini index or the top 1 percent share. Rather, the economic and political factors stressed here determine the distribution of resources more generally.

We do not mean to suggest that this framework determines the evolution of institutions, technology, and inequality deterministically. The arrows designate influences, which are mediated by various stochastic events and political economy interactions; similar economic developments will result in very different institutional responses, depending on the prevailing political equilibrium, as evidenced by the contrasting histories of Mexico and the United States in the 20th century (noted earlier). Nor do we imply that the framework captures all economic implications of import—or all of those that are relevant for inequality. Most centrally, technology will evolve over time not only because of institutional factors, but also because of scientific developments and because it responds to other economic changes, including factor prices, the abundance and scarcity of different types of skills, and market structure (for example, Acemoglu 2002, 2003, 2010). Technological developments may, in turn, affect institutional dynamics (for example, Acemoglu et al. 2001; Hassler et al. 2003). Nevertheless, this simple framework is useful for highlighting the potentially important role of institutional equilibria, and their changes, in shaping inequality.

Let us now apply the framework to South Africa. Before 1910, nonwhites could vote in the Cape and Natal as long as they fulfilled certain wealth, income, or property restrictions (Natal was more heavily restricted). After 1910, a specifically white franchise was established in the Transvaal and Orange Free State and gradually extended to the rest of the country; in 1936, blacks were definitively disenfranchised in the Cape. The de jure institutions of the apartheid state cemented the political power of the white minority, and segregationist laws and other aspects of the regime created economic institutions, such as the skewed distribution of land and the "color bar," aimed at furthering the interests of the white minority. Why, then, did the flourishing of social apartheid after 1948 lead to a fall in the top 1 percent share?

The primary reason is that political dynamics in South Africa at the time cannot be fully captured as a conflict between monolithic groups of whites and blacks. Rather, apartheid should be viewed as a coalition between white workers, farmers, and mineowners—at the expense of blacks but also white industrialists who had to pay very high wages for white workers (Lundahl 1982; Lipton 1985). Thus, one reason for a reduction in the top 1 percent share was that profits were squeezed by wages for white labor. Moreover, by depriving industrialists of a larger pool of skilled workers and tilting the price of white labor higher (because the supply of labor was artificially restricted), the rules further stunted South African economic development.

In addition, there were forces within apartheid for redistribution from the very rich toward poorer whites. Indeed, South Africa's political discussions in the 1920s that led to the further spread of the "color bar" and subsequently to the victory of the National Party in 1948 were related to what was called the "poor white problem," highlighting the importance of the specific coalition underpinning apartheid. Alvaredo and Atkinson (2010) discuss other factors, such as the gold price.

The compression of the huge wage gaps between South Africa's whites and blacks starting in the 1970s (see Figure 16.2) should be viewed within the context of the political weakening of the apartheid regime and its increasing economic problems (Wilson 1980; Mariotti 2012). The domestic turning point was the ability of black workers to organize protests and riots and to exercise their de facto power, particularly after the Soweto uprising of 1976, which led to the recognition of black trade unions. That process was aided by mounting international pressure, which induced British and U.S. firms based in South Africa to push back against workplace discrimination. Ultimately, the de facto power forced the collapse of the apartheid regime, leading to a new set of political institutions and the enfranchisement of black South Africans. The new set of economic institutions, and their consequences for inequality, flowed from those political changes. Consistent with our framework, the institutions of apartheid may have also fed back into the evolution of technology, for example, in impeding the mechanization of gold mining (Spandau 1980). As the power of apartheid started to erode in the 1970s, white businessmen responded rapidly by substituting capital for labor and moving technology in a labor-saving direction (Seekings and Nattrass 2005, 403).

As can be seen from Figure 16.1, the top 1 percent share in South Africa shows a steep rise after 1994, coinciding with the final overthrow of the formidable extractive institutions of apartheid. No clear consensus has yet emerged on the causes of the postapartheid increase in inequality; however, one reason relates to the fact that after the end of apartheid, the artificially compressed income distribution of blacks started widening as some portion of the population started to benefit from new business opportunities, education, and aggressive affirmative action programs (Leibbrandt et al. 2010). Whatever the details of those explanations, it is hard to see the post-1994 rise in the top 1 percent share as representing the demise of a previously egalitarian South Africa.

The role of de facto and de jure political power in shaping political and economic institutions is no less central in Sweden, where the important turning point was created by the process of democratization. Adult male suffrage came in 1909, but true parliamentary democracy developed only after the Reform Act of 1918, with significant curbs on the power of the monarchy and more competitive elections. Both the 1909 reform and the emergence of parliamentary democracy in 1918 were responses to unrest, strikes, and the de facto power of disenfranchised workers, especially in the atmosphere of uncertainty and social unrest following World War I (Tilton 1974). Ruth Collier (1999, 83) explains: "It was only after the economic crisis of 1918 and ensuing worker protests for democracy led by Social Democrats that the Reform Act was passed. Indeed, in November 1918, labor protests reached such a point as to be perceived as a revolutionary threat by Sweden's Conservative Party and upper classes."

Swedish democracy then laid the foundations for modern labor market institutions and the welfare state and created powerful downward pressure on inequality, including the top 1 percent share. However, democratic conflict in Sweden was not a simple contest between monolithic groups of workers and businesses. As Karl Moene and Michael Wallerstein (1995, 2006) characterize it, social democracy was a coalition of the ends of the income distribution—businessmen and unskilled workers—against the middle class and skilled workers (for theories about the emergence of such political coalitions, see also Gourevitch 1986; Luebbert 1991; Saint-Paul 2000). In consequence, Swedish economic institutions strongly compressed skilled wages relative to unskilled wages, underpinning the rapid decline in broad-based measures of inequality. Some businesses benefited from those arrangements, particularly in sectors exposed to international competition, which used centralized wage bargaining as a tool to stop wage push from non-traded sectors, such as construction (Swenson 1991, 2002). Swedish labor market institutions also likely affected the path of technology. For instance, Moene and Wallerstein (1997) emphasize that wage compression acted as a tax on inefficient plants and stimulated new entry and rapid technological upgrading. In the face of high unskilled wages and the institutions of the welfare state, it is not surprising that the top 1 percent share declined in Sweden as well, even if businessmen also did well with some aspects of Swedish labor market institutions.

Why does the top 1 percent share appear to increase not just in South Africa and Sweden, but in almost all OECD economies over the past 20 years or so? Factors left out of our framework—globalization, skill-biased technological changes, and the increase in the size of large corporations—are likely to be important. But those forces are themselves not autonomous and have likely responded to other changes in the world economy. For example, Acemoglu (2002) argues that skill-biased technological change cannot be understood without the increase in the supply of skilled workers in the United States and the world economy, making those types of technologies more profitable; and globalization and the increasing size of global corporations are themselves consequences of regulatory and technological changes of the last several decades. These points simply underscore that the framework presented here cannot capture the dynamics of all dimensions of inequality—or the rich dynamics of political and economic institutions for that matter. Nevertheless, the basic forces that the framework stresses appear to be important not just in the context of Sweden and South Africa, but much more generally (as we argue in Acemoglu and Robinson 2006, 2012).

The framework also helps clarify why we might care about inequality at the very top of the income and wealth distributions. Most relevant is that the factors undergirding a high share of income for the top 1 percent might also represent a lack of equality of opportunity or a lack of a level playing field. Extending the framework, we argued in Acemoglu and Robinson (2012) that lack of a level playing field, including limited social mobility, is likely to hold back countries in their investments, innovation, and efficiency of resource allocation. However, the top 1 percent share may not be the most relevant dimension of the distribution of income for evaluating equality of opportunity and barriers to the efficient allocation of talent and resources in society. For example, if a small number at the top became wealthier—say, Bill Gates and Warren Buffett became twice as wealthy—at the expense of other rich individuals, would that make U.S. society notably less meritocratic? That seems unlikely. Indeed, Raj Chetty and others ("Where Is the Land of Opportunity," 2014) as well as Chetty and others ("Is the United States Still a Land of Opportunity," 2014) show that social mobility at the commuting-zone level in the United States is unrelated to income inequality, especially inequality at the top. Their evidence that U.S. social mobility has stayed the same even as the top 1 percent share has increased rapidly over the past several decades further corroborates that intuition. Other types of inequalities, such as the gap between whites and blacks in South Africa or between the bottom and the middle class in the United States, may be more relevant for thinking about whether there have been changes in social mobility and the angle of the playing field.

One dimension of political economy where the top 1 percent share may be central is the health of political institutions. It may be difficult to maintain political institutions that create a dispersed distribution of political power and political access for a wide cross section of people in a society in which a small number of families and individuals have become disproportionately rich.

A cautionary tale about the dangers created by that type of inequality is discussed in Puga and Trefler (2014) and Acemoglu and Robinson (2012): the story of late medieval Venice. There, the economic power of the most prosperous and well-established families ultimately made it possible for them to block the access of others to political power; once they monopolized political power, they could change economic institutions for their benefit by blocking the entry of other families into lucrative businesses and banning contracts that had previously made it possible for individuals with limited capital to enter into partnerships for long-distance trade. The change in political institutions, feeding into a deterioration of economic institutions, heralded the economic decline of Venice.

Yet, if the primary threat from the top 1 percent share is political, then the main response should be related to monitoring and containing the political implications of the increase in top-level inequality—not necessarily catch-all policies such as the wealth taxes advocated by Piketty. Such policies should be explicitly related to the institutional fault lines of the specific society and should be conceived in the context of strengthening institutional checks against any potential power grab.

Conclusion

Thomas Piketty's (2014) ambitious work proffers a bold, sweeping theory of inequality applicable to all capitalist economies. Though we believe that the focus on inequality and the ensuing debates on policy are healthy and constructive, we have argued that Piketty goes wrong for exactly the same reasons that Marx, and before him Ricardo, went astray. The quest for general laws ignores both institutions and politics, and the flexible and multifaceted nature of technology, which make the responses to the same stimuli conditional on historical, political, institutional, and contingent aspects of the society and the epoch, vitiating the foundations of theories seeking fundamental, general laws. We have argued, in contradiction to that perspective, that any plausible theory of the nature and evolution of inequality has to include political and economic institutions at center stage, recognize the endogenous evolution of technology in response to both institutional and other economic and demographic factors, and attempt to model how the response of an economy to shocks and opportunities will depend on its existing political and institutional equilibrium.

References

Acemoglu, Daron. 2002. "Directed Technical Change." *Review of Economic Studies* 69 (4): 781–809.

———. 2003. "Labor- and Capital-Augmenting Technical Change." *Journal of the European Economic Association* 1 (1): 1–37.

———. 2008. "Oligarchic versus Democratic Societies." *Journal of the European Economic Association* 6 (1): 1–44.

———. 2010. "When Does Labor Scarcity Encourage Innovation?" *Journal of Political Economy* 118 (6): 1037–78.

Acemoglu, Daron, Philippe Aghion, and Giovanni L. Violante. 2001. "Deunionization, Technical Change and Inequality." *Carnegie-Rochester Conference Series on Public Policy* 55 (1): 229–64.

Acemoglu, Daron, and David Autor. 2011. "Skills, Tasks and Technologies: Implications for Employment and Earnings." In *Handbook of Labor Economics Volume 4B*, ed. Orley Ashenfelter and David Card, pp. 1043–171. Amsterdam: Elsevier, North-Holland.

Acemoglu, Daron, Davide Cantoni, Simon Johnson, and James A. Robinson. 2011. "The Consequences of Radical Reform: The French Revolution." *American Economic Review* 101 (7): 3286–307.

Acemoglu, Daron, Georgy Egorov, and Konstantin Sonin. 2012. "Dynamics and Stability of Constitutions, Coalitions, and Clubs." *American Economic Review* 102 (4): 1446–76.

———. 2015. "Political Economy in a Changing World." *Journal of Political Economy* 123 (5): 1038–86.

Acemoglu, Daron, Simon Johnson, and James A. Robinson. 2005. "Institutions as a Fundamental Cause of Long-Run Growth." In *Handbook of Economic Growth Volume 1A*, ed. Philippe Aghion and Steven N. Durlauf, pp. 385–472. Amsterdam: Elsevier, North-Holland.

Acemoglu, Daron, and James A. Robinson. 2000. "Why Did the West Extend the Franchise? Democracy, Inequality, and Growth in Historical Perspective." *Quarterly Journal of Economics* 115 (4): 1167–99.

———. 2006. *Economic Origins of Dictatorship and Democracy*. New York: Cambridge University Press.

———. 2008. "Persistence of Power, Elites, and Institutions." *American Economic Review* 98 (1): 267–93.

———. 2012. *Why Nations Fail: The Origins of Power, Prosperity, and Poverty*. New York: Crown.

Aiyagari, S. Rao. 1994. "Uninsured Idiosyncratic Risk and Aggregate Saving." *Quarterly Journal of Economics* 109 (3): 659–84.

Allen, Robert C. 2001. "The Great Divergence in European Wages and Prices from the Middle Ages to the First World War." *Explorations in Economic History* 38 (4): 411–47.

———. 2007. "Pessimism Preserved: Real Wages in the British Industrial Revolution." Oxford University Department of Economics Working Paper no. 314. http://www.nuffield.ox.ac.uk/users/Allen/unpublished/pessimism-6.pdf.

———. 2009a. "Engels' Pause: Technological Change, Capital Accumulation, and Inequality in the British Industrial Revolution." *Explorations in Economic History* 46 (4): 418–35.

———. 2009b. *The British Industrial Revolution in Global Perspective*. New York: Cambridge University Press.

Alvaredo, Facundo, and Anthony B. Atkinson. 2010. "Colonial Rule, Apartheid and Natural Resources: Top Incomes in South Africa, 1903–2007." Centre for Economic Policy Research Discussion Paper no. 8155. http://www.parisschoolofeconomics.eu/IMG/pdf/DP8155_SouthAfrica.pdf.

Alvaredo, Facundo, Tony Atkinson, Thomas Piketty, and Emmanuel Saez, compilers. 2011. *World Top Incomes Database*. http://www.parisschoolofeconomics.eu/en/news/the-top-incomes-database-new-website/.

Antràs, Pol. 2004. "Is the U.S. Aggregate Production Function Cobb–Douglas? New Estimates of the Elasticity of Substitution." *Contributions to Macroeconomics* 4 (1).

Bengtsson, Erik. 2014. "Labour's Share in Twentieth Century Sweden: A Reinterpretation." *Scandinavian Economic History Review* 62 (3): 290–314.

Bewley, Truman F. 1986. "Stationary Monetary Equilibrium with a Continuum of Independently Fluctuating Consumers." In *Contributions to Mathematical Economics in Honor of Gérard Debreu*, edited by Werner Hildenbrand and Andreu Mas-Colell, pp. 79–102. Amsterdam: Elsevier North-Holland.

Blaug, Mark. 1996. *Economic Theory in Retrospect*, 5th ed. New York: Cambridge University Press.

Bloch, Marc. 1967. *Land and Work in Medieval Europe: Selected Papers*. Translated by J. E. Anderson. New York: Harper Torchbooks.

Bonnet, Odran, Pierre-Henri Bono, Guillaume Chapelle, and Étienne Wasmer. 2014. "Does Housing Capital Contribute to Inequality? A Comment on Thomas Piketty's *Capital in the 21st Century*." Sciences Po Department of Economics Discussion Paper no. 2014-07. http://www.insee.fr/en/insee-statistique-publique/connaitre/colloques/acn/pdf15/ACN2014-Session5-4-texte-3.pdf.

Cameron, A. Colin, Jonah B. Gelbach, and Douglas L. Miller. 2008. "Bootstrap-Based Improvements for Inference with Clustered Errors." *Review of Economics and Statistics* 90 (3): 414–27.

Caselli, Francesco, and James Feyrer. 2007. "The Marginal Product of Capital." *Quarterly Journal of Economics* 122 (2): 535–68.

Chetty, Raj, Nathaniel Hendren, Patrick Kline, and Emmanuel Saez. 2014. "Where Is the Land of Opportunity? The Geography of Intergenerational Mobility in the United States." *Quarterly Journal of Economics* 129 (4): 1553–623.

Chetty, Raj, Nathaniel Hendren, Patrick Kline, Emmanuel Saez, and Nicholas Turner. 2014. "Is the United States Still a Land of Opportunity? Recent Trends in Intergenerational Mobility." *American Economic Review* 104 (5): 141–47.

Chirinko, Robert S. 1993. "Business Fixed Investment Spending: Modeling Strategies, Empirical Results, and Policy Implications." *Journal of Economic Literature* 31 (4): 1875–1911.

———. 2008. "σ: The Long and Short of It." *Journal of Macroeconomics* 30 (2): 671–86.

Chirinko, Robert S., Steven M. Fazzari, and Andrew P. Meyer. 1999. "How Responsive Is Business Capital Formation to Its User Cost? An Exploration with Micro Data." *Journal of Public Economics* 74 (1): 53–80.

Chirinko, Robert S., and Debdulal Mallick. 2014. "The Substitution Elasticity, Factor Shares, Long-Run Growth, and the Low-Frequency Panel Model." CES-IFO Working Paper no. 4895. https://ideas.repec.org/p/ces/ceswps/_4895.html.

Clark, Gregory. 2002. "Land Rental Values and Agrarian History: England and Wales, 1500–1912." *European Review of Economic History* 6 (3): 281–308.

———. 2005. "The Condition of the Working Class in England, 1209–2004." *Journal of Political Economy* 113 (6): 1307–40.

———. 2010. "The Macroeconomic Aggregates for England, 1209–2008." In *Research in Economic History* Volume 27, edited by Alexander J. Field, pp. 51–140. Bingley, UK: Emerald Group Publishing.

Collier, Ruth B. 1999. *Paths toward Democracy: Working Class and Elites in Western Europe and South America*. New York: Cambridge University Press.

Collins, Norman R., and Lee E. Preston. 1961. "The Size Structure of the Largest Industrial Firms, 1909–1958." *American Economic Review* 51 (5): 986–1011.

Crafts, Nicholas F. R. 1985. *British Economic Growth during the Industrial Revolution*. Oxford: Clarendon Press.

Diamond, Peter A. 1965. "National Debt in a Neoclassical Growth Model." *American Economic Review* 55 (5): 1126–50.

Donado, Alejandro, and Klaus Wälde. 2012. "How Trade Unions Increase Welfare." *Economic Journal* 122 (563): 990–1009.

Edwards, Richard C. 1975. "Stages in Corporate Stability and the Risks of Corporate Failure." *Journal of Economic History* 35 (2): 428–57.

Feinstein, Charles H. 1998. "Pessimism Perpetuated: Real Wages and the Standard of Living in Britain during and after the Industrial Revolution." *Journal of Economic History* 58 (3): 625–58.

———. 2005. *An Economic History of South Africa: Conquest, Discrimination and Development*. New York: Cambridge University Press.

Foley, Duncan K. 2008. *Adam's Fallacy: A Guide to Economic Theology*. Cambridge, MA: Belknap Press.

Geerolf, François. 2013. "Reassessing Dynamic Efficiency," Sciences Po. https://dl.dropboxusercontent.com/u/7363883/Efficiency_Emp.pdf.

Gourevitch, Peter. 1986. *Politics in Hard Times: Comparative Responses to International Economic Crises*. New York: Cornell University Press.

Hamermesh, David S. 1993. *Labor Demand*. Princeton, NJ: Princeton University Press.

Hassler, Jon, José V. Rodríguez Mora, Kjetil Storesletten, and Fabrizio Zilibotti. 2003. "The Survival of the Welfare State." *American Economic Review* 93 (1): 87–112.

Hornbeck, Richard, and Suresh Naidu. 2014. "When the Levee Breaks: Black Migration and Economic Development in the American South." *American Economic Review* 104 (3): 963–90.

Karabarbounis, Loukas, and Brent Nieman. 2014. "The Global Decline of the Labor Share." *Quarterly Journal of Economics* 129 (1): 61–103.

Katz, Lawrence F., and David H. Autor. 1999. "Changes in the Wage Structure and Earnings Inequality." In *Handbook of Labor Economics*

Volume 3A, edited by Orley C. Ashenfelter and David Card, pp. 1463–555. Amsterdam: Elsevier, North-Holland.

Klump, Rainer, Peter McAdam, and Alpo Willman. 2007. "Factor Substitution and Factor– Augmenting Technical Progress in the United States: A Normalized Supply-Side System Approach." *Review of Economics and Statistics* 89 (1): 183–92.

Krusell, Per, Lee E. Ohanian, José-Víctor Ríos-Rull, and Giovanni L. Violante. 2000. "Capital-Skill Complementary and Inequality: A Macroeconomic Analysis." *Econometrica* 68 (5): 1029–53.

Krusell, Per, and Anthony A. Smith, Jr. 2015. "Is Piketty's 'Second Law of Capitalism' Fundamental?" *Journal of Political Economy* 123 (4): 725–748. http://aida.wss.yale.edu/smith/piketty1.pdf.

Lamoreaux, Naomi R. 1985. *The Great Merger Movement in American Business, 1895–1904*. New York: Cambridge University Press.

Leibbrandt, Murray, Ingrid Woolard, Arden Finn, and Jonathan Argent. 2010. "Trends in South African Income Distribution and Poverty since the Fall of Apartheid." OECD Social, Employment and Migration Working Paper no. 101.

Lindert, Peter H. 1994. "The Rise of Social Spending, 1880–1930." *Explorations in Economic History* 31 (1): 1–37.

Lipton, Merle. 1985. *Capitalism and Apartheid: South Africa, 1910–84*. London: Gower/Maurice Temple Smith.

Luebbert, Gregory M. 1991. *Liberalism, Fascism, or Social Democracy: Social Classes and the Political Origins of Regimes in Interwar Europe*. New York: Oxford University Press.

Lundahl, Mats. 1982. "The Rationale of Apartheid." *American Economic Review* 72 (5): 1169–79.

Mairesse, Jacques, Bronwyn H. Hall, and Benoit Mulkay. 1999. "Firm-Level Investment in France and the United States: An Exploration of What We Have Learned in Twenty Years." *Annales d'Economie et de Statistique* 55–56 (December): 27–67.

Mariotti, Martine. 2012. "Labour Markets during Apartheid in South Africa." *Economic History Review* 65 (3): 1100–1122.

Marx, Karl. [1847] 2000. *The Poverty of Philosophy*. Reprinted in *Karl Mark: Selected Writings*, edited by David McLellan. New York: Oxford University Press.

———. [1859] 2000. *A Contribution to the Critique of Political Economy*. Reprinted in *Karl Marx: Selected Writings*, edited by David McLellan. New York: Oxford University Press.

———. [1867] 1990. *Capital: Critique of Political Economy*. Vols. I, II, and III. New York: Penguin.

———. [1883] 2016. *The Eighteenth Brumaire of Louis Napoleon*. New York, Wallachia.

Marx, Karl, and Friedrich Engels. [1848] 2007. *Communist Manifesto*. Radford VA, Wilder Publications.

Matthews, Robert C. O., Charles H. Feinstein, and John C. Odling-Smee. 1982. *British Economic Growth, 1856–1973: The Post-War Period in Historical Perspective*. Palo Alto, CA: Stanford University Press.

Milanovic, Branko. 2013. *All the Ginis Dataset*. The World Bank. http://econ.worldbank.org/WBSITE/EXTERNAL/EXTDEC/EXTRESEARCH/0,,contentMDK:22301380%7EpagePK:64214825%7EpiPK:64214943%7EtheSitePK:469382,00.html.

Moene, Karl Ove, and Michael Wallerstein. 1995. "How Social Democracy Worked: Labor-Market Institutions." *Politics and Society* 23 (2): 185–211.

———. 1997. "Pay Inequality." *Journal of Labor Economics* 15 (3): 403–30.

———. 2006. "Social Democracy as a Development Strategy." In *Globalization and Egalitarian Redistribution*, edited by Pranab Bardhan, Samuel Bowles, and Michael Wallerstein. Princeton, NJ: Princeton University Press/Russell Sage Foundation.

Mokyr, Joel. 2012. *The Enlightened Economy: An Economic History of Britain 1700–1850*. New Haven, CT: Yale University Press.

Morrisson, Christian, and Wayne Snyder. 2000. "The Income Inequality of France in Historical Perspective." *European Review of Economic History* 4 (1): 59–83.

Naidu, Suresh, and Noam Yuchtman. 2013. "Coercive Contract Enforcement: Law and the Labor Market in Nineteenth Century Industrial Britain." *American Economic Review* 103 (1): 107–44.

Nickell, Stephen. 1981. "Biases in Dynamic Models with Fixed Effects." *Econometrica* 49 (6): 1417–2

Oberfield, Ezra, and Devesh Raval. 2014. "Micro Data and Macro Technology." Unpublished paper, Princeton University. http://economics.mit.edu/files/9861.

Piketty, Thomas. 2014. *Capital in the 21st Century*. Cambridge, MA: Belknap Press.

Piketty, Thomas, and Emmanuel Saez. 2003. "Income inequality in the United States, 1913–1998." *Quarterly Journal of Economics* 118 (1): 1–39.

Puga, Diego, and Daniel Trefler. 2014. "International Trade and Institutional Change: Medieval Venice's Response to Globalization." *Quarterly Journal of Economics* 129 (2): 753–821.

Ray, Debraj. 2014. "Nit-Piketty: A Comment on Thomas Piketty's *Capital in the 21st Century*." http://www.econ.nyu.edu/user/debraj/.

Ricardo, David. 1817. *On the Principles of Political Economy and Taxation*, 1st ed. London: John Murray.

Rognlie, Matthew. 2014. "A Note on Piketty and Diminishing Returns to Capital." http://www.mit.edu/~mrognlie/piketty_diminishing_returns.pdf.

Roine, Jesper, Jonas Vlachos, and Daniel Waldenström. 2009. "The Long-Run Determinants of Inequality: What Can We Learn from Top Income Data?" *Journal of Public Economics* 93 (7–8): 974–88.

Roine, Jesper, and Daniel Waldenström. 2009. "Wealth Concentration over the Path of Development: Sweden, 1873–2006." *Scandinavian Journal of Economics* 111 (1): 151–87.

Saint-Paul, Gilles. 2000. *The Political Economy of Labour Market Institutions*. New York: Oxford University Press.

Samuelson, Paul A. 1958. "An Exact Consumption-Loan Model of Interest with or without the Social Contrivance of Money." *Journal of Political Economy* 66 (6): 467–82.

Sanders, Elizabeth. 1999. *Roots of Reform: Farmers, Workers, and the American State, 1877–1917*. Chicago, IL: University of Chicago Press.

Schonhardt-Bailey, Cheryl. 2006. *From the Corn Laws to Free Trade: Interests, Ideas, and Institutions in Historical Perspective*. Cambridge, MA: MIT Press.

Seekings, Jeremy, and Nicoli Nattrass. 2005. *Class, Race, and Inequality in South Africa*. New Haven, CT: Yale University Press.

Singer, Peter. 2000. *Marx: A Very Short Introduction*. New York: Oxford University Press.

Spandau, A. 1980. "Mechanization and Labour Policies on South African Mines." *South African Journal of Economics* 48 (2): 110–20.

Swenson, Peter. 1991. "Bringing Capital Back In, or Social Democracy Reconsidered: Employer Power, Cross-Class Alliances, and Centralization of Industrial Relations in Denmark and Sweden." *World Politics* 43 (4): 513–44.

———. 2002. *Capitalists against Markets: The Making of Labor Markets and Welfare States in the United States and Sweden*. New York: Oxford University Press.

Tilton, Timothy A. 1974. "The Social Origins of Liberal Democracy: The Swedish Case." *American Political Science Review* 68 (2): 561–71.

Turner, Michael E., John V. Beckett, and B. Afton. 1999. *Agricultural Rent in England, 1690–1914*. New York: Cambridge University Press.

Van der Horst, Sheila T. 1942. *Native Labour in South Africa*. London: Frank Cass and Co., Ltd.

White, Lawrence J. 1981. "What Has Been Happening to Aggregate Concentration in the United States?" *Journal of Industrial Economics* 29 (3): 223–30.

———. 2002. "Trends in Aggregate Concentration in the United States." *Journal of Economic Perspectives* 16 (4): 137–60.

Wilson, Francis. 1972. *Labour in the South African Gold Mines, 1911–1969*. New York: Cambridge University Press.

———. 1980. "Current Labor Issues in South Africa." In *The Apartheid Regime: Political Power and Racial Domination*, edited by Robert M. Price and Carl G. Rosberg. Berkeley, CA: University of California Press.

Zeira, Joseph. 1998. "Workers, Machines, and Economic Growth." *Quarterly Journal of Economics* 113 (4): 1091–117.

Zwart, Pim de. 2011. "South African Living Standards in Global Perspective, 1835–1910." *Economic History of Developing Regions* 26 (1): 49–74.

17. Get Real: A Review of Thomas Piketty's *Capital in the 21st Century*

Donald J. Boudreaux

Thomas Piketty's *Capital in the 21st Century* (2014) is a blockbuster. If today's thunderous applause from the left, booming criticism from the right, and nonstop attention from across the spectrum are any indication, Piketty's tome might soon stand with Karl Marx's *Capital* as one of the most influential economics book published in the past 150 years. But like those of Marx, Piketty's sweeping conclusions—economic "evolutions" and "social justice"—rest upon a fundamentally flawed economic logic that, if acted upon, will have deeply unfortunate results.

Gazing from his ivory-tower perch, Piketty sees only big statistics concerning such things as population growth and the share of national income "claimed" by the very rich. (For him, revealingly, income and wealth are always "claimed" or "distributed" and never earned or produced.) Piketty deserves credit, indeed, for bringing these statistical "structures," as he terms them, into sharper focus by dint of the painstaking compilation of two centuries worth of data. Nevertheless, the structures he uncovers reveal far too little about what is happening at ground level to form a basis for wise economic policies.

Instead of actually looking at the behavior behind his statistics, Piketty serves up ad hoc, and ultimately unpersuasive, theories about the behavior of his big statistics themselves—including such hulking, impersonal aggregates as the return on capital and the ratio of national wealth to national income.

He imagines that such aggregates interact through a logic of their own, unmoved by individual human initiative, creativity, and choice.

Consider Piketty's central theory that the rate of return on capital (*r*) tends to be greater than the rate of economic growth (*g*). For Piketty, the fact that $r > g$ (by several percentage points, according to his reckoning) alone seals capitalism's fate, because it implies (again, according to him) that owners of capital will get increasingly richer than nonowners. Because capital ownership is itself unevenly distributed across society, wealth and income disparities will in turn worsen, "impoverishing" (his word) the middle classes and the poor alike, while giving a relatively small number of rich elites both vast resources and disproportionate influence over government policymaking.

Despite the logical implications of $r > g$, Piketty doesn't think that the plutocraticization of society is inevitable. First of all, it can be arrested and even reversed by calamities such as world wars or Soviet-style communism, the destructive effects of which fall disproportionately on the rich. Alas, the welcome consequences (as Piketty sees them) of such correctives are only temporary. But another, more lasting and agreeable remedy is readily at hand: hard-hitting taxation. Piketty calls for greater and more progressive taxation not only of incomes but also of wealth, preferably to be enacted globally (lest differential tax burdens prompt plutocrats to flee from high-tax to low-tax jurisdictions). He isn't optimistic about the likelihood in the near term of the necessary government cooperation. But he's willing to settle for whatever steps more enlightened governments might take to soak the rich, especially such steps as might be accompanied by greater cross-border sharing of information about bank accounts and other investments owned by foreigners.

Flaws aplenty mar Piketty's account of capitalism's denouement—flaws that spring mainly from his disregard for basic economic principles. None looms larger than Piketty's mistaken notion of wealth.

What Is Wealth?

No principle of economics is more essential than the realization that, ultimately, wealth isn't money or financial assets; instead, wealth is ready access to real goods and services. (Every semester I ask my freshman students how wealthy they would be if they each were worth financially as much as Bill Gates but were stranded with all those stocks, bonds, property titles, and bundles of cash alone on a desert island. My students immediately see that what matters is not the amount of money they have but, rather, what the amount of money they have *can buy*.) Piketty seems barely aware of that reality. He's concerned overwhelmingly with differences in people's *monetary* portfolios. Piketty doesn't ask what people—rich, middle class, and poor—can *buy* with their money.

Yet, surely, the only economic inequalities that matter in the end are inequalities in access to real goods and services for consumption. Such "real" inequalities do exist—Bill Gates's house is larger and more elegantly furnished than is that of any American or Dane or Aussie of ordinary means. However, two relevant facts about ability to consume undermine Piketty's tale of capitalist woe. First, even the poorest people in market economies have seen their ability to consume skyrocket over time. Second, the poorer the person, the greater has been the absolute enhancement of his or her ability to consume.

Today, the middle classes in America (the country that is the bête noire of Piketty and other "progressives" obsessed with monetary inequality) take for granted their air-conditioned homes, cars, and workplaces—along with their smartphones, global positioning system (GPS) navigation, safe air travel, Lasik vision correction, and pills for ailments ranging from hypertension to erectile dysfunction. At the end of World War II, when income and wealth inequalities were lower than at any time in the past century, such goods and services were either unavailable to everyone or affordable only for the very rich. So, regardless of how many more dollars today's plutocrats have accumulated and stashed into their portfolios, the accumulation of riches by the elite has not prevented the living standards of ordinary people from rising spectacularly.

Furthermore, those improvements in real living standards have been undeniably *greater* for ordinary folks than for rich ones. In 1950, Howard Hughes and Humphrey Bogart could easily afford to pay for the likes of overnight package delivery, hour-long transcontinental telephone calls, and air-conditioned homes. For ordinary Americans, however, those things were out of reach. Yet, while today's tycoons and celebrities still have easy access to such amenities, so, too, do middle-class and even poor Americans.

If we follow the advice of Adam Smith and examine people's ability to consume, we discover that nearly everyone in market economies is growing richer. We discover also that the real economic differences separating the rich from the middle class and the poor are shrinking. Reckoned in standards of living—in ability to consume—capitalism is creating an ever-more-egalitarian society.

The shrinking gap between the real economic fortunes of the rich and the rest of us should calm concerns about the political dangers of the expanding inequality of monetary fortunes. If economic inequality is destined to dangerously destabilize our political institutions, it would have to be inequality that is readily noticeable. But the 1 percent's private art collections, solid gold Jacuzzis, and (least of all) bank accounts are not on display for the 99 percent to gaze upon enviously. Those things are invisible to the public. Unlike a hundred years ago when upper-income people (and only upper-income people) were regularly seen motoring in automobiles or strolling in their clean, pressed, and patch-free clothing into restaurants, even the super rich today are largely indistinguishable in public from middle-class Americans. If you happened past Jeff Bezos strolling down Fifth Avenue in

Manhattan, you'd have no clue that he's a billionaire. His dress, grooming, and physical health would look to the naked eye no different from that of countless middle-class Americans.

Piketty's book itself ironically supports this point: progressives hail *Capital in the 21st Century* as supplying the best evidence yet that the trend of economic inequality has become, as Piketty describes it, "potentially terrifying" (2014, 571). But if people have to read a book to learn just how great is economic inequality, then that inequality is not salient to their daily lives.

Is Return on Capital Automatic?

Flaws in the author's stratospheric viewpoint are also on display when we try to think in human terms about the inevitability of the return on capital, at 4 percent to 5 percent, exceeding the growth rate of the economy, at 1 percent to 1.5 percent. According to the author, that gap of a few percentage points, when compounded over many years, can greatly increase economic inequality. But two key factors make it quite difficult for that tendency to persist for very long in the lives of most individuals.

First, advance and retreat, rather than permanence, tend to characterize the pattern of most successful businesses. Sooner or later, the entry of competitors and of changing consumer tastes curbs their growth, sometimes reducing their size absolutely or even bankrupting them. In 2013 alone, more than 34,000 businesses in the United States filed for bankruptcy, a typical figure for a year of economic expansion (Oellermann and Douglas 2014). Second, and more important, successful capitalists rarely spawn children and grandchildren who match their elders' success; there is regression toward the mean. Note that the terrifyingly successful capitalist Bill Gates will likely not be succeeded by younger Gateses prepared to capitalize on his success.

Leave aside plans like those of Gates and Warren Buffett to give away much of their fortunes, or the redistributive role of philanthropy generally. The empirical data suggest that turnover—not the building of a permanent plutocracy—is the norm among wealthy capitalists. The IRS's list of "Top 400 Individual Tax Returns" (Perry 2011) provides evidence of instability at the top. Over the 18 years from 1992 through 2009, 73 percent of the individuals who appeared on the list did so for only one year. Only a handful of individuals made the list in 10 or more years. Wealth gets diluted over time when left to multiple heirs, and is further diluted by estate taxes, philanthropy, and changes in market conditions.

Piketty's pronouncements about the stability of capitalist wealth deny such realities. He writes, for example, "Capital is never quiet: it is always risk-oriented and entrepreneurial, at least at its inception, yet it always tends to transform itself into rents as it accumulates in large enough amounts—that is its vocation, its logical destination" (2014, 115–16). In other words, the risky, entrepreneurial element in business formation eventually recedes in importance until the business naturally evolves toward its logical destination—that of a perpetual cash machine that regularly spits out rents.

In a similar vein, Piketty observes, "What could be more natural to ask of a capital asset than that it produce a reliable and steady income: that is in fact the goal of a 'perfect' capital market as economists define it." (2014, 114) It may be natural to ask this of a capital asset. But only economists who talk of perfect capital markets are naïve enough to expect a "yes" answer.

If Piketty really believes in a perfect capital market that yields capitalists reliable and steady income, he might wonder why the bankrupt book-selling giant Borders is no longer around to sell his books, while Amazon.com has grown up to challenge all manner of brick-and-mortar retailers. In his world, capitalism is a system of profits; in the real world, it's a system of profit and loss.

The Pay of "Supermanagers"

Piketty's poor grasp of economics is also on display in his discussion of the rising pay of corporate executives in America.

Piketty blames that rising pay of what he calls "supermanagers" for driving most of the recent increase in U.S income inequality. According to Piketty, executive compensation, especially in America, has nothing to do with managers' productivity and everything to do with the cozy relationship between managers and corporate boards. Managers and board members are clubby friends scratching each other's well-massaged backs and setting each other's astronomically high salaries. He is content to blame rising executive compensation on American social norms that encourage toleration of such payments but strangely never asks why shareholders continue to invest in corporations that so wastefully spend shareholder funds.

Here's an even deeper mystery that escapes Piketty's notice: if current patterns of executive compensation serve no purpose except to further enrich unproductive corporate oligarchs, what explains the rising market value of the capital that Piketty believes to be the central driver of increasing wealth inequality? Piketty doesn't ask this question because, for him, wealth perpetuates itself. It grows automatically. So any amount of wealth that is "claimed" by Dick could otherwise have been "distributed" to Jane without reducing the total amount of wealth available to all.

Of course, wealth doesn't grow automatically. It must be created. And to grow—indeed, even to be sustained—wealth must be skillfully managed. If Piketty's theory of executive compensation were correct, corporate boards' inattention to the productivity of their management teams would cause the market value of corporations to plummet. Piketty's *r* would fall to zero. So, too, would *g*. Fortunately, neither the rich nor the rest of us are suffering any such lamentable impoverishment.

Had Piketty examined more carefully the empirical literature on executive compensation he would have discovered that compensation is indeed tied closely to managerial productivity. As University of Chicago professor Steven Kaplan reported not long ago in *Foreign Affairs*, having analyzed 1,700 firms, he "found that compensation was highly related to performance: the companies that paid their CEOs the most saw their stocks do the best, and those that paid the least saw their stocks do the worst" (Kaplan 2013).

Yet, an observer perched too high above reality can easily miss what really matters. And that's the ultimate problem with Piketty's narrative. Like Marx, Piketty writes passionately about big, all-encompassing social forces that allegedly spell doom for humanity unless wise and good government intervenes.[1] But also like Marx, Piketty's disregard for basic economic reasoning blinds him to the all-important market forces at work on the ground—market forces that, if left unencumbered by government, produce growing prosperity for all.

References

Kaplan, Steven N. 2013. "The Real Story Behind Executive Pay." *Foreign Affairs*, May/June. http://www.foreignaffairs.com/articles/139101/steven-n-kaplan/the-real-story-behind-executive-pay.

Oellermann, Charles M., and Mark G. Douglas. 2014. "The Year in Bankruptcy 2013." Jones Day, January. http://jonesday.com/-the-year-in-bankruptcy-2013-01-22-2014/.

Perry, Mark. 2011. "IRS Data from 1992–2008 on the Top 400 Show Significant Turnover: 73% Last for Only 1 Year." *Carpe Diem* blog post, November 8. http://mjperry.blogspot.com/2011/11/irs-data-from-1992-2008-on-top-400-show.html

Piketty, Thomas. 2014. *Capital in the 21st Century*. Cambridge, MA: Belknap Press.

18. The Role of Government in Creating Inequality

Jeffrey Miron

In *Capital in the 21st Century*, Thomas Piketty argues that capitalism inevitably enriches capitalists relative to workers, leading to ever-greater inequality of wealth (Piketty 2014). Piketty goes on to present data (for the United States, Great Britain, France, and other capitalist economies) that appear to confirm his predictions. Piketty concludes that government should enact large wealth taxes to moderate this inevitable tendency of capitalist economies toward ever-increasing inequality of material well-being.

As the papers in this volume and elsewhere document, Piketty's theoretical claim, his supporting evidence, and his policy conclusions are, at a minimum, debatable. I leave the reader to digest those critiques. Here I raise a different issue that has received comparatively little attention.

Even if every part of Piketty's analysis is right, his discussion of the interconnections between capitalism, inequality, and government policy is incomplete. Piketty's reasoning has three components. He argues that capitalism generates inequality; he takes as given that increased inequality, at least beyond some point, is undesirable; and he argues that government can and should reduce this inequality (in his view, via a global wealth tax).

What Piketty misses is that government plays a huge role in generating inequality, especially in producing differences in income that most people would regard as undesirable because they neither correspond to differences in productive ability nor arise as an unavoidable side effect from a policy that is overall beneficial.

Some policies are misguided on efficiency grounds and redistribute in arbitrary ways; those policies are difficult to defend. Other policies potentially accomplish a sensible goal but also generate unappealing differences in income as a side effect; for those policies, one may have to accept additional inequality as a necessary evil.

The unwanted differences in wealth that result from government, moreover, do not occur just within the middle and upper-middle income ranges or between people of similar incomes. A significant fraction of the truly rich owe much of their wealth to government interventions of one sort or another. Thus, had Piketty adopted a broader view about whether and which kinds of inequality are undesirable, and had he set out to discuss all the possible sources of unwanted differences in wealth or income, he would have written a different book: one that recognizes how much "bad" inequality results from government, not capitalism. A full account of the policies that generate inequality would take volumes; in my limited space, I highlight some key examples.

Trade restrictions such as tariffs and quotas protect the owners and employees of certain industries, generating higher profits and salaries than would occur under full competition. Thus, interference with free trade not only reduces economic efficiency, it also redistributes wealth toward the industries or sectors that win such protections. And though the era of tariffs and quotas in the United States is largely a relic of the past, certain imported products have recently been subjected to substantial tax rates, including tobacco, nuts, sneakers and leather shoes, and ship parts (*Business Insider* 2010). Standard arguments against free trade implicitly assume that the distribution occurring under a restricted-trade status quo is somehow natural or right. A more accurate view holds that industries that receive protection are stealing from the rest of the economy, and removing the restriction would return the pattern of wages and profits to its appropriate configuration—based on productivity rather than on trade policies.

Immigration restrictions similarly maintain high salaries for the jobs that would face greater competition in the presence of more open borders. This holds both for low-wage jobs, such as unskilled or semiskilled positions in agriculture, services, and manufacturing, and also for high-wage jobs in medicine, academia, technology, finance, and law. With unrestricted immigration for high-skill jobs, many high-income people would earn lower salaries. Thus, freer immigration not only enhances economic efficiency (by allowing domestic firms to hire labor more cheaply), it also implies a more just distribution of income, in which people get paid their marginal product and no more.

Occupational licensing, whether for hair-braiding, plumbing, medicine, law, or hundreds of other examples, generates higher incomes for those who obtain a license to practice these professions. Consumers pay higher prices for the goods and services offered in licensed professions. Even across different U.S. states, distinct medical or legal licensing standards effectively restrict the free flow of such workers and further raise the price of the services they offer. A 2014 study, for example, examined state-level insurance claims data and found that having more rigid occupational licensing requirements increased the average price of a generic child's medical exam by 3 to 16 percent (Kleiner et al. 2014). Thus, occupational licensing both redistributes away from those who want to work in a given profession but cannot obtain a license (e.g., because of costs) and redistributes from consumers to the licensed members of that profession. These effects may be a necessary evil if licensing keeps low-quality providers out of the market. The evidence that licensing promotes quality, however, is limited.

Prohibitions against drugs, prostitution, gambling, and other vices redistribute first by creating black markets in which those willing to break the law may get rich from the higher prices and profits under prohibition. If these goods were legal, the profit rate would be the same as in any other industry. Vice laws also create extra demand for police, lawyers, and prisons, enriching those groups at the expense of vice consumers and taxpayers. For instance, each year, marijuana prohibition laws in the United States result in an estimated $7.6 billion in additional state and local police expenditures, as well as $3.1 billion in added correctional spending and $853 million in extra judicial costs (St. Pierre 2005). These redistributions are almost impossible to defend; even if policy should aim to reduce the consumption of these goods, sin taxation accomplishes that goal while redistributing from vice consumers to general taxpayers, a superior outcome.

Modern tax codes also produce arbitrary and perverse redistributions. Many existing "tax preferences" (e.g., the home mortgage interest deduction, the preferential tax treatment of employer-paid health insurance, and the deductibility of charitable contributions) benefit high-income relative to low-income taxpayers. The incredible complexity of current tax codes also rewards those savvy enough to find loopholes and dishonest enough to bend or break the rules. Those individuals or businesses often escape penalty because of the difficulty of enforcing such messy and opaque rules. And many lawyers and accountants earn high incomes helping people navigate the tax code and take advantage of the loopholes. With a neutral tax code, those professionals would earn less, in line with their productivity.

Even the estate tax—often lauded as crucial for restraining inequality—may in fact have the reverse effect. An estate tax creates a demand for high-priced lawyers and accountants who can help those potentially subject to the tax escape its full impact. That demand comes from much more than the small fraction of estates that actually pay positive amounts of estate tax; many other taxpayers exert significant effort to legally avoid—or illegally evade—being subject to the tax. And again, the lawyers and accountants who benefit would face lower demand for their services without the estate tax, and many of those individuals earn moderate to high incomes.

Regulations produce unwanted redistributions by boosting the demand for lawyers, accountants, and lobbyists. Such redistribution may be a necessary evil if the regulation in question helps correct significant market failures, but in that case no criticism of the inequality is warranted. Regulation also redistributes across industries or across firms within an industry if regulated sectors can "capture" regulators and tilt regulation to their advantage. For example, much regulation imposes significant fixed costs that disadvantage small firms and new entrants relative to large firms and incumbents; regulation thereby creates or protects market power and generates excessive profits.

Intellectual property protection (IPP)—patents, copyrights, and trademarks—also generates differences in income that might be greater than necessary to maximize economic efficiency. IPP gives the patent or copyright owner a monopoly on production of the relevant good or service and thus allows that owner to charge a price in excess of marginal costs, which means inefficiently lower consumption of the good or service, conditional on its existence. IPP may be crucial to incentivizing the research and development or other investment that produces intellectual property in the first place; in that case, the IPP system can enhance productivity when viewed in the longer-term context. Thus, if the amount of intellectual property protection is about right, the high incomes earned by inventors or artists should be viewed as compensation for the investments and risks assumed. Real-world IPP systems, however, can easily be manipulated to provide excessive protection.

Agriculture subsidies have no efficiency justification; indeed, they distort the allocation of resources by encouraging domestic production of agricultural goods relative to the rest of the global economy. Subsidies mainly go to owners of large farms, not mom-and-pop operations. Domestic agricultural subsidies alone also cost U.S. taxpayers $20 billion each year, with most of the money subsidizing corn and soy, two crops that are already grown in bulk to support meat and processed foods (*The Economist* 2015). Worse, agricultural subsidies overwhelmingly benefit farmers in rich countries relative to farmers in poor countries. A 2015 study in the *International Journal of Food and Agricultural Economics* revealed that higher agricultural subsidies in Organisation for Economic Co-operation and Development (OECD) nations were associated with worsening poverty rates in some developing countries and negative impacts on those countries' food export industries (Tedesco et al. 2015).

Green energy subsidies provide a further example. By targeting particular kinds of energy, firms lucky enough to be in the subsidized sectors win while others lose, and the choice of which sectors to help often reflects politics more than economics. One example is the ethanol subsidy, which rewards corn farmers in the Midwest and big chemical companies that refine the corn into ethanol. An alternative approach to reducing use of fossil fuels—carbon taxation—would consistently raise the price of carbon but then let private factors determine which alternatives survive in the marketplace. Carbon taxation does reward suppliers of noncarbon-based energy relative to carbon-based, but that is inevitable given the goal. Carbon taxation avoids creating arbitrary winners and losers, such as Solyndra, a green energy company that received large sums of Department of Energy stimulus funds but ultimately went bankrupt as it attempted to compete with cheaper solar power technologies.

One could go on in this vein. Social Security redistributes toward those with longer life expectancy. Public schools favor families with many children. Federal support of low-income housing subsidizes shareholders of Fannie Mae and Freddie Mac (because the implicit guarantee from the Treasury allowed the agencies to borrow at low interest rates). Subsidies for museums, symphonies, zoos, skating rinks, parks, and so on help those who enjoy those goods at the expense of people who prefer nonsubsidized activities (e.g., mud-wrestling). In fact, virtually any government intervention affects the distribution of wealth—whether intentionally or not. So a full analysis of inequality must address government's role (which, typically, is restraining capitalism) rather than examining only capitalism's effect.

A skeptic might respond to the arguments above by suggesting that the inequalities discussed are modest and mainly between people in the middle of the income distribution. Thus, government policies do not explain the wealth of the truly rich, which is mainly a result of capitalism rather than interventionist government. On the contrary, it is difficult to identify any general category of the extremely rich that does not benefit substantially from government interventions. Many of these individuals or families would have high incomes regardless, but government helped make them even higher.

One category of the super-rich is star athletes. These individuals have enormous and scarce talents, so they would command high incomes even without government subsidies. State and city funding for stadiums, however, reduces the costs of producing professional sporting events, thereby expanding the market and generating even greater surplus for athletes and team owners. In the last two decades, more than $7 billion in public funding has been spent across the country on the construction and renovation of National Football League stadiums alone (Waldron 2015). State governments also fund professional sports through their subsidies for state colleges and universities, which effectively serve as the "farm systems" for professional teams. In the 2014–2015 school year, National Collegiate Athletic Association programs received more than $2.6 billion in institutional subsidies from publicly funded colleges and universities (*USA Today* 2015). Nearly 130 athletic departments rely on these subsidies for more than half their revenue (Wolverton et al. 2015).

Another category of the super-rich is executives of major commercial banks, investment banks, hedge funds, and other financial intermediaries. Some of those high incomes no doubt reflect skill at managing or trading. But Wall Street also gets a significant subsidy from the federal government's policy of too-big-to-fail, which provides implicit or explicit insurance against bankruptcies for large financial institutions. The recent 2008–2009 financial crisis is a textbook example. Although some chief executives and shareholders did lose much or all of their wealth, creditors generally received enormous protections from the Treasury bailouts and Federal Reserve asset purchases. Taxpayers footed an enormous bill to prevent the collapse of hundreds of large companies during the financial crisis, including AIG ($67 billion), General Motors ($50 billion), Citigroup ($45 billion), and Goldman Sachs ($10 billion) (ProPublica 2016).Even though most of the bailouts were repaid, they still prevented huge wealth transfers that would otherwise have occurred.

Whether too-big-to-fail is a desirable policy is a separate question. According to many economists, financial crises not only redistribute wealth from those who "bet right" to those who "bet wrong," crises also reduce the efficiency of the real economy by destroying the ability of the financial sector to identify and make productive loans and investments. In that case, the redistribution that results is one of the costs of too-big-to-fail but not a reason to oppose the policy completely. Thus, redistributions are something we have to accept for the greater good; they are not a reason to rail against evil Wall Street.

Still another category of the truly rich is authors, artists, and musicians who earn huge returns on their particular talents because of copyright protections. Had J. K. Rowling been unable to prevent bootlegging of her *Harry Potter* books, she would probably be worth far less than her reported $1 billion. One possibility, without copyright, is that she would have written the book anyway and just earned less. If most authors were in this category, then copyright protection would be generating wealth transfers (from customers to producers) without a substantial benefit in stimulating creative activity. A different possibility is that these high monopoly rents are necessary to generate artistic activity in the first place; in this scenario, redistribution is a necessary evil. Of course, artists knowingly enjoy—and profit from—these strong monopolies and often go out of their way to use them to their advantage. In recent years, some extremely wealthy musicians such as Taylor Swift, Adele, and Coldplay have pulled some or all of their albums from free streaming services like Spotify in an effort to boost their own sales revenue.

Similar considerations apply for patents. It is hard to imagine Bill Gates or Steve Jobs becoming nearly as rich as they did without the hundreds of patent protections they received for personal computers, laptop designs, media players, and operating systems such as iOS and Windows. The same is true for shareholders and executives of pharmaceutical companies behind blockbuster drugs such as Viagra, EpiPen, and Daraprim, all of which have been subject to tremendous price hikes. In what is perhaps the most infamous case, former pharmaceutical chief executive Martin Shkreli raised the price of his company's lifesaving drug from $13.50 to $750 per pill overnight. Shkreli recognized that regulatory barriers and the lack of competition made it possible for the company to profiteer from a 5,000 percent price hike, and lengthy Food and Drug Administration approval laws made it impossible for potential competitors to quickly enter the market (Surowiecki 2015). Thus, while patent laws generally exist to boost consumer safety, they can clearly be exploited and abused in ways that exacerbate fundamental inequalities.

Without quantitative analysis of the considerations raised here, it is impossible to discern whether capitalism or government is the greater source of inequality—and just as importantly, which kinds of inequality. Maybe Piketty's next book will address this issue.

References

Business Insider. 2010. "25 American Products that Rely on Huge Protective Tariffs to Survive." September 27. http://www.businessinsider.com/americas-biggest-tariffs-2010-9?op=1/#corative-glassware-38-tariff-16.

The Economist. 2015. "Milking Taxpayers: As Crop Prices Fall, Farmers Grow Subsidies Instead." http://www.economist.com/news/united-states/21643191-crop-prices-fall-farmers-grow-subsidies-instead-milking-taxpayers.

Kleiner, Morris M., Allison Marier, Kyoung Won Park, and Coady Wing. 2014. "Relaxing Occupational Licensing Requirements: Analyzing

Wages and Prices for a Medical Service." National Bureau of Economic Research Working Paper no. 19906. http://www.nber.org/papers/w19906.

Piketty, Thomas. 2014. *Capital in the 21st Century*. Cambridge, MA: Belknap Press.

ProPublica. 2016. "Bailout Tracker: Bailout Recipients." August 4. https://projects.propublica.org/bailout/list.

St. Pierre, Allen. 2005. "Executive Summary." In *Crimes of Indiscretion: Marijuana Arrests in the United States*, ed. Jon B. Gettman. Washington: National Organization for the Reform of Marijuana Laws. http://norml.org/library/item/executive-summary.

Surowiecki, James. 2015. "Taking on the Drug Profiteers." *New Yorker*, October 12. http://www.newyorker.com/magazine/2015/10/12/taking-on-the-drug-profiteers.

Tedesco, Ilaria, Alessandra Pelloni, and Giovanni Trovato. 2015. "OECD Agricultural Subsidies and Poverty Rates in Lower Income Countries." *International Journal of Food and Agricultural Economics* 3, no. 2, Special Issue (2015): 31–49. http://www.foodandagriculturejournal.com/vol3.no2.pp31.pdf.

USA Today. 2015. "2014–15 NCAA Finances." December 8. http://sports.usatoday.com/ncaa/finances/.

Waldron, Travis. 2015. "Taxpayers Have Spent a 'Staggering' Amount of Money on NFL Stadiums." *Huffington Post*, September 10. http://www.huffingtonpost.com/entry/taxpayers-nfl-stadiums_us_55f08313e4b002d5c077b8ac.

Wolverton, Brad, Ben Hallman, Shane Shifflett, and Sandhya Kambhampati. 2015. "Sports at Any Cost: College Students Are Bankrolling the Athletics Arms Race." *Huffington Post* and *Chronicle of Higher Education*, November 15. http://projects.huffingtonpost.com/ncaa/sports-at-any-cost.

Section 7. What Can We Conclude from r > g?

The "fundamental inequality" $r > g$ seems at first to form a solid foundation for Thomas Piketty's theory. It has contributed, in its simplicity and communicational aspect, to the success of the book. However, while the statement is not controversial in itself, the hyperbolic reasoning and the auxiliary hypotheses that Piketty places within it are very questionable. First, he implies that r, the rate of return on capital, is almost automatic; and he conceptually reverses the relationship between returns and capital. Second, even if $r > g$, would that necessarily lead to a spiraling inequality? This section will deal with these questions to better dissect the fundamental inequality and its pretensions within the framework set by Piketty.

19. Capital, Returns, and Risk: A Critique of Thomas Piketty's *Capital in the 21st Century*

Randall Holcombe

Thomas Piketty's *Capital in the 21st Century* is a surprising best seller (how many economics books make the *New York Times* best-seller list?) that has received considerable attention, both from economists and from the popular press. He has done a nice job of collecting a substantial amount of historical data for many countries and using it to demonstrate that there is, indeed, significant inequality in income and wealth, and that inequality has been growing over the past 30 years.

Piketty explains where he got the data, how various economic measures are constructed, and how they are related to each other in enough detail that I am persuaded he has done a good job of collecting and presenting the best data available on the subject. There has been some debate about the way he has adjusted the data, but I will leave that aside; he has presented his data on his website and explained what he has done, so he appears to have been completely transparent about the data he has used. The book is competently researched and written, but his conclusions do rest heavily on the data. So, questions about the data must be taken seriously. Nonetheless, I will set to one side such questions in my analysis of the book.

The book has obvious Marxist undertones. Piketty favorably cites Marx more than just in passing, and the class conflict pitting the owners of capital against those whose incomes come from labor has a clear Marxist slant. But Piketty also recognizes some problems with Marx's analysis. Ultimately, the places where I take issue with Piketty relate to his reliance on concepts more closely associated with neoclassical economics and his aggregation of economic measures without clearly thinking through the economic processes behind those measures.

The Nature of Capital

Capital does not just exist and produce a rate of return. It has to be employed productively, which Piketty acknowledges in his words but not in the empirical framework he uses to draw his conclusions. Therein lies the most fundamental problem with his analysis. His framework misrepresents the nature of capital, how it is valued, and how owners of capital earn their returns.

Piketty says the first fundamental law of capitalism is that the share of income going to capital, α, is equal to the return on capital, r, times the capital/income ratio, β, or in equation form, $\alpha = r \times \beta$. I can accept the formula as an accounting identity, although I have minor issues with it. I take greater issue with the way Piketty describes the interrelationships among the three variables.

One minor issue is that β measures capital as an aggregate monetary value, when, in fact, capital is a heterogeneous collection of producer goods that, combined with labor by entrepreneurs, produce output. So already, Piketty has oversimplified by aggregating a heterogeneous stock of capital and calling it equal to its money value.

Another issue, which is more relevant to Piketty's policy conclusions than his empirical analysis, is that capital's value comes from the anticipated value of the final goods it will produce. That is necessarily speculative. Nobody can know today how productive a capital asset will be years into the future, which is why capital markets provide an essential function in capitalism. The market value of capital assets is determined by a process in which people who anticipate that some specific capital goods will have a higher value buy assets from those who anticipate they will have a lower value. Both buyer and seller may be correct in their assessments. If the capital remained with the seller, it might have a lower value than if it is sold to the buyer because the buyer is able to use the capital more productively than the seller. That is why a capital market is essential to the operation of capitalism, and why interference with the capital market, such as the taxes Piketty recommends, lowers overall economic productivity.

The Relationship between Capital and Returns

A larger problem with Piketty's analysis is that he assumes capital earns some rate of return, r, so the share of income going to capital, α, is determined by the value of capital times the return it earns. That is exactly backwards.

Capital does not have some value, which then earns a return to provide income to the owners of capital. Rather, capital consists of productive assets that generate a return; the value of the stock of capital is determined by the return it generates, rather than, as Piketty depicts it, the return being determined by the value of capital.

The difference is important because Piketty misrepresents how capital owners earn their incomes. In fact, capital must be allocated to productive uses to generate a return, and the job of the capital owner is to allocate that capital as productively as possible. Successful owners of capital will earn higher returns, and unsuccessful owners may lose their investment altogether—and see the value of their capital drop to zero.

Those results are apparent even in the stock market. Stockholders do not just own capital and receive r as their rate of return. They look for promising investments, trying to buy into companies that will produce value for the economy, which will enable the company to earn income, leading to a higher stock price. The challenge is similar (perhaps greater) for managers of firms, who make investment decisions regarding building new plants and buying equipment, producing new product lines, and so forth. Capital does not just earn a return. The return is determined by how productively it is used.

The people who are making those decisions, whether they are management who make the decisions directly or stockholders who delegate the decisionmaking to the managers, are working in a competitive environment. If they make poor decisions, they can end up with a negative return and ultimately go bankrupt, in which case their capital becomes worthless.

Piketty's equation, $\alpha = r \times \beta$, aggregates all the individual decisions so that—while it is accurate in an accounting sense—it is misleading in an economic sense. Piketty makes it appear that because capitalists have β, they get α. That is not true. The point can be illustrated with an example from Piketty's book. He says the long-term return on capital, r, is around 4–5 percent per year and gives an example of a Paris apartment that is valued at 1 million Euros. The apartment "rents for slightly more than 2,500 Euros per month, or an annual rent of 30,000 Euros, which corresponds to a return on capital of only 3 percent per year.... This type of rent tends to rise until the return on capital is around 4 percent.... Hence this tenant's rent is likely to rise in the future" (Piketty 2014, 54)

As the example shows, Piketty assumes that the value of capital, β, determines the amount it earns, α. Surely, the reverse is actually the case.

Piketty uses the relationship $\alpha = r \times \beta$, but a more accurate way to depict the economic relationship is $\beta = \alpha / r$. The expressions are mathematically equivalent, but Piketty's way of showing it assumes that the value of capital determines its return, rather than the more economically accurate depiction in which the return produced by the capital determines its value.

The rent on an apartment will be determined by the supply and demand for apartments. In Piketty's example, α is €30,000 a year, which is determined by the market. If $r = 0.04$ as Piketty assumes, then because $\beta = \alpha / r$, $\beta = 30{,}000 / 0.04 =$ €750,000. The rental rate is determined by the supply and demand for apartments, so following Piketty's assumptions about the annual rent and the rate of return the landlord will earn, the apartment is worth €750,000 and will fall in value. The value of the apartment is determined by the rent it can command, and not the other way around.

This general idea—that capital does not just earn a rate of return, but has to be employed in productive activity by its owner—plays no role in the way Piketty analyzes his extensive data set on inequality. Piketty makes it appear that earning a return on capital is a passive activity in which, by virtue of owning capital that has some value β, capital owners receive a flow of income α. But capital has value only because it provides a flow of income to its owners, and it only provides that flow if the owners employ it productively.

Capital produces income only if it adds value to the economy. Wal-Mart has added value and provided a return to its owners. Circuit City failed to do so, and the value of its capital fell to zero. The value of capital is determined by the income it produces, so capital has value only because it adds value to the economy, which benefits everyone.

Inequality and Living Standards

Piketty laments the increase in inequality since 1980. But setting aside inequality for the moment, anyone who has lived in a capitalist economy since that time can see the increase in the standard of living that everybody—not just the economic elite—has enjoyed. That increase in the general standard of living has been due to the employment of capital in productive uses by its owners. And yet, this economic function of the owners of capital plays no role in Piketty's analysis.

Changes in the general standard of living are completely absent from Piketty's analysis. Piketty defines both the value of capital and the income from capital as a fraction of total income, so β is the value of capital divided by income and α is capital income as a fraction of total income. For this discussion, however, we can multiply both sides of the equation by income and refer to β as the value of the capital stock and α as the income it earns. That simplifies the discussion without misrepresenting the concepts Piketty discusses. Still, it is worth noting that, because Piketty always depicts the incomes of various groups as income shares, he never provides evidence or discussion of how general living standards have changed.

Casual observation shows that even people at the official poverty line today have mobile phones, microwave ovens, flat-screen color televisions, and a host of other goods that were available only to upper-income individuals half a century ago. Anyone focused on the standard of living of those in poverty or on the edge of poverty, would see a vast improvement in their quality of life over the time period Piketty examines; but he deliberately eliminates this point from consideration by looking only at income shares, not the absolute incomes, of various groups.

What about Risk?

Piketty recognizes that more risky investments will earn a higher return, but that idea plays no role in his empirical analysis that follows. In particular, the idea that capital owners make decisions to risk their capital and are not guaranteed any rate of return receives minimal consideration. As already noted, the income that capital owners earn from their capital depends on their investing it effectively in projects that create value for the economy.

Consider my rearranged fundamental law, $\beta = \alpha / r$. For a given return on capital, if α rises, then the value of capital, β, will also rise. The value of capital grows in proportion to the income it produces, whereas Piketty states that the income produced by the capital depends on the value of the capital.

What about the rate of return on capital? Piketty says it has been relatively constant over long periods of time, and I have no problem with that generalization as a stylized historical fact. One can see from looking at the equation that if the economic environment becomes more risky and owners of capital receive a higher return (r rises), then the value of capital will go down even if the income it earns remains constant. This is common sense: if there is more risk involved in owning capital, the capital will not be worth as much, confirming what the equation shows. For example, holding α constant, the higher return, r, going to riskier capital results in a lower value of β.

Likewise, if the economic environment becomes less risky, the owners of capital will receive a lower return, meaning that r falls, and the value of capital, β, will rise.

The Distorting Role of Monetary Policy

Risk is not the only factor that affects the return on capital. Government policy can also have a substantial effect. Piketty shows that β has increased substantially in the 21st century, which supports his argument of growing inequality. But consider that monetary policy in most of the 21st century has been geared toward keeping interest rates low, first during Alan Greenspan's tenure at the Federal Reserve in response to the recession in the early 2000s, and then after 2007 in response to the growing financial crisis.

A lower interest rate lowers the rate of return on capital. So, again looking at $\beta = \alpha / r$, the Fed's policy of lowering r has had the effect of increasing β, that is, of increasing Piketty's measure of inequality. The bulk of the growing inequality Piketty sees in the 21st century is not the result of anything inherent in capitalism, as he claims, but rather is the result of a deliberate policy on the part of the Federal Reserve and the European Central Bank.

The conventional wisdom in financial markets is that the low rate of return on fixed interest investments pushed money into the stock market, which was responsible, at least in part, for the stock market's rise following the crash after the recession. Piketty's law supports that view, because the Fed forced a lower rate of return on investment, lowering r and causing β to be higher for a given α.

That being the case, 21st-century data cannot be used to argue persuasively about rising inequality because β is rising, as Piketty argues. Interest rates can't be pushed lower, and when interest rates rise, that will increase r, and that will reduce β for any given α. The effect Piketty documents in the 21st century is temporary.

Capital for the Masses?

Piketty observes that growing inequality is the result of the return on capital being greater than the growth in wages (which is determined by aggregate economic growth). If people owned capital in proportion to the wages they earn, inequality would not increase; but because those at the top of the income distribution own significantly more capital, their incomes and wealth grow faster than those at the bottom.

One way to mitigate this inequality would be for those at the bottom of the income distribution to increase their ownership of capital. Indeed, Piketty notes that happened for the middle class in the 20th century. The middle class, which was almost as poor as the lower class at the beginning of the century, had accumulated substantial wealth by the end of the century. But the lower class remains with almost no wealth, which serves to increase inequality.

Inequality perpetuates itself and grows over time, Piketty argues, because of inherited wealth. The children of the rich start out with an advantage, because of their inheritances, while the children of the poor start with nothing because their parents had little to bequeath.

One reason the lower class (Piketty includes the bottom 50 percent here, so the term differs from what one might ordinarily consider poor) has little incentive to save is that the welfare state has taken much of that incentive away. A good reason to accumulate assets is for precautionary purposes. Examples include saving for retirement, for unexpected health care costs, and for the possibility of losing one's job. However, programs like Social

Security, Medicare, Medicaid, and unemployment compensation take away much of the incentive for precautionary saving.

The bottom half of the income distribution is wealthier than they appear from wealth statistics because they "own" a claim to future retirement and health care benefits—a claim that they have paid for in their current and past taxes. But the difference between the claims to future government payments and services compared with precautionary saving is that precautionary saving is an asset that (if there is any left at death) can be passed on to heirs. Government benefits end at death, and heirs get nothing.

Piketty supports government provision of health care benefits and pensions for everyone. That stance is not inconsistent with his dislike of inequality; but the more secure the welfare state makes people feel, the lower the incentive to set aside precautionary saving, which is the main reason people at the lower end of the income distribution have to save. The less they save, the greater the imbalance of capital ownership will skew toward those at the upper end.

Why set aside precautionary savings rather than take a vacation or buy a new car, when government programs exist to take care of those contingencies? The government policies Piketty advocates contribute toward the reason he cites for growing inequality.

Reducing Inequalities by Pulling Down Those at the Top?

Piketty recommends progressive taxes on income and capital as the remedy to the growing inequality he forecasts. He says, "the ideal policy for avoiding an endless inegalitarian spiral and regaining control over the dynamics of accumulation would be a global tax on capital" (2014, 471). The tax "ought to be a progressive annual tax on individual wealth" (2014, 516). Piketty makes clear that the purpose of the progressive taxes he recommends is not to provide funds to raise the incomes of those at the bottom, but rather to lower inequality by reducing the incomes of those at the top.

Recommending a progressive income tax with rates of 50–60 percent on incomes over $200,000 and a top marginal rate of

80 percent on incomes above $500,000–$1 million, Piketty says, "A rate of 80 percent applied to incomes above $500,000 or $1 million a year would not bring the government much in the way of revenue, because it would quickly fulfill its objective: to drastically reduce remuneration at this level" (2014, 513). Recommending a progressive tax on capital, Piketty says, "The primary purpose of the capital tax is not to finance the social state but to regulate capitalism" (2014, 518).

When one looks at the remarkable accomplishments of capitalism, an economic system that is roughly 250 years old, among its top accomplishments is how much it has done to improve the standard of living of average citizens and the working class. The rich have always been very comfortable, and capitalism has brought a level of comfort to working-class people today that would have been unimaginable to even the most well-off people a century and a half ago.

Why should average citizens be concerned about the wealth of the very well off if the system that makes them well off produces prosperity for everyone? Evidence suggests that most people are not that concerned. In big government countries ranging from Canada to Sweden, the government sector has shrunk with public support. In the United States, lower taxes and smaller government remain politically popular (even as the government increases its involvement in health care and energy).

Piketty promotes the politics of envy, in which greater equality is a goal in itself—as opposed to the goal of helping out those at the bottom of the income distribution. Piketty plainly states that the policies he recommends to reduce inequality would do so by pulling down those at the top rather than bringing up those at the bottom.

Reference

Piketty, Thomas. 2014. *Capital in the 21st Century*. Cambridge, MA: Belknap Press.

20. Piketty's World Formula

Hans-Werner Sinn

Thomas Piketty's book (2014) on inequality hit a sensitive spot with Americans.[1] It channeled the mounting dissatisfaction in a country that lacks a robust welfare system and a more progressive tax system.

His book has a whiff of Karl Marx, with his style of writing. And he resorts to a theory similar to Marx's when he decries the increasing inequality that results from an ever higher ratio of wealth to national income. Marx predicted the increase in this ratio with his law on the growing organic composition of capital.

Piketty attributes the growth in inequality to the $r > g$ formula, one of the few formulas that have made it to the international daily newspapers and which by now has attained a hallowed status among journalists akin to Einstein's $E = mc^2$. Piketty's formula states that interest in the form of the average return on capital, r, is persistently higher than the growth rate of the economy, g. The consequence, according to Piketty, is that the wealth of an economy accumulates faster than the growth in economic output. The formula is a hot topic of discussion everywhere.

In fact, the formula has been known for quite a long time now; it denotes a fundamental implication of the neoclassical theory of economic growth. Indeed, over the long run, the rate of return to capital usually lies above the growth rate of the economy, as Piketty asserts. If that were not the case, land prices would be infinite, there would be excessive consumption, and growth would eventually end. But the formula does not imply that wealth grows faster than economic output. Such a conclusion would only be warranted if the savings of an economy could be set equal to the economy's capital income, so that the rate of economic growth is the same as the interest rate. But that is not the case. Rather, savings are consistently smaller than the sum of all capital income. The wealthy consume substantial parts of their income, and the savings from labor income usually is small. Thus, the growth rate of wealth lies significantly below the interest rate; the fact that the interest rate exceeds the rate of economic growth in no way implies that wealth grows faster than the economy.

Indeed, a central finding of economic growth theory states that the interest rate of an economy, dependent on the savings rate, settles over the long term at a level in which the growth of capital equals the growth rate of output. The consequence is the long-term persistence of the ratio of wealth to economic output. The long-term constancy of the ratio is a basic ingredient of all growth theories.

Behind the long-term persistence of this ratio stands a simple mathematical law. If an economy saves a given portion of its income, the wealth resulting from the accumulation of those savings will increase in the long run at the same rate at which national income grows. Thus, the ratio of wealth to income cannot increase permanently.

The law is based on the fact that every increasing quantity can grow over the long run only at the rate at which its accretion grows. An example is the heaping of earth into a mound. Assume that in every period, a further spade of earth is added, and that the size of the spade itself grows at a given rate from one period to the next. The growth rate of the amount of earth in the mound converges toward the growth rate of the spade size. If we substitute the current savings of an economy for the amount of earth in the spade and wealth for the size of the mound, we obtain the long-run constancy of the ratio of wealth to income when a fixed share of income is saved.

It must be stressed that this law applies over the long run, over several decades. Wealth can well grow faster than the economy at given times. Piketty could then have a point.

But even when such is the case, there is hardly any reason for apprehension. When it comes to distributional issues, the important element is less the ratio of wealth to national income than the ratio of capital income to wage income, that is, the proportion of capital and wages in national income. The distributional shares of national income, as first observed by the left-leaning economist Joan Robinson in her 1942 book, *An Essay on Marxian Economics*, have remained fairly stable over time and follow no discernible trend.

Much more important than Piketty's theory of everything is the question of how many people share in the wage and capital income. If the number of wage earners increases faster than the number of wealth owners, a less desirable distributional pattern could emerge despite the constancy of the ratio of capital to wage income. That could be the case in the United States, with its large number of immigrants, and could be the reason for the current dissatisfaction among the populace. But there is no evidence to support this as a general law.

And if the risk should indeed exist that the number of people sharing the capital income grows too slowly compared with the number of people sharing the labor income, the best medicine is to improve the chances of upward mobility. The more people share the wealth and capital income, the smaller the distributional problem.

It helps for this reason if the rich have more children than the poor, since their wealth will eventually become spread among their heirs, solving the distributional problem at a stroke. A family income splitting system such as France's is one of the policy measures that a society might consider if it fears an undesirable concentration of wealth.

Regardless, a progressive taxation system is needed to check the growth in net income among the upper income echelons. Even in the absence of a fundamental trend toward greater inequality owing to the theory formulated by Piketty, inequality within the wealthy group can increase because some dynasties accumulate ever more wealth at the expense of other dynasties. Whether action is needed in this regard in Europe is open to debate, since progressive taxation is already present it will be hard to make the case for even more of it.

My conclusion is that Piketty, like Marx, caters to a longing, simmering among the people, but that he tries to underpin his policy proposals with a theory that does not substantiate what he asserts.

References

Piketty, Thomas. 2014. *Capital in the 21st Century*. Cambridge, MA: Belknap Press.

Robinson, Joan. 1942. *An Essay on Marxian Economics*. London: Macmillan Press Ltd.

21. A Controversial Assumption

Henri Lepage

The strength of Thomas Piketty's book, *Capital in the 21st Century*, is not just a matter of the rich documentary record to which it appeals.[1] The thesis that Piketty develops is embedded in a formal model, one expressed as a series of macroeconomic equations. It is very difficult for a professional economist to be taken seriously without an apparatus of that sort. The model is expressed by an inequality and two identities:

1. The inequality $r > g$, where r designates the rate of return on capital and g is the rate of growth of income and production. This inequality, Piketty asserts, expresses the "central contradiction" of capitalism itself (Piketty 2014, 571).
2. The identity (or the *first fundamental law* of capitalism): $\alpha = r \times \beta$, where α designates the income derived from capital as a fraction of annual income, r is again the rate of return on capital, and β is the value of an economy's accumulated capital stock as a fraction of annual national income (Piketty 2014, 52).
3. The identity (or the *second fundamental law* of capitalism): $\beta = s / g$, where β represents the ratio of capital to income, s is the savings rate, and g is the growth rate of a given economy (Piketty 2014, 166).

From those premises, Piketty derives the following conclusions:

1. If the rate of return on capital (r) displays a stable long-term tendency greatly to exceed the rate of growth (g) of income

and production, then it is likely that the distribution of wealth will be skewed in favor of the fraction of national income derived from capital.

2. That result leads inexorably to an increase in the fraction of income (α) derived from capital in an economy's annual income flow and, thus, to a cumulative process of enrichment and capital accumulation.
3. Given that the return on capital (r) is relatively stable over the long-term, any sustained slowdown in the growth rate (g) accelerates the rate of capital accumulation with respect to other economic factors. The return on capital (r) then gradually converges to a stable limiting value by virtue of the law of diminishing marginal utility and the relationship $\beta = s / g$.

In Piketty's view, that process determines the value of both the figures and the shape of the curves in his book, especially those from which he derives his alarming projections.

Piketty's model is simple, elegant, and consistent. No neoclassical model of growth had, before Piketty, integrated the production, accumulation, and distribution of wealth in such a pithy play of equations. Still, Piketty's model, it is important to observe, must meet certain very specific conditions if it is to justify his dynamic predictions. The model demands that the reduction or fall in the rate of return on capital induced by the expansion of capital accumulation be neither too strong nor too fast. If the descent is too rapid, for example, the tendency toward accumulation will result, in only a few years—not decades—in a reduction of the share of capital to annual income, even if the share of total assets continues to grow. Precisely the opposite is supposed to happen.

In turn, that implies the *coefficient of elasticity* between capital and labor must be greater than one. Only in that way can there be both an increase in the capital–income ratio (inventory effect) *and* an increase in capital income with respect to labor income (flow effect). If the coefficient of elasticity is less than one, then the increase in the capital–income ratio is offset by a reduction in the share of capital within the flow of income. The assumption of positive elasticity greater than one thus functions as a premise in Piketty's model, a claim about both the past and the future.

Piketty is well aware of the issue. He responds, "Over a very long period of time, the elasticity of substitution between capital and labor seems to have been greater than one.... On the basis of historical data, one can estimate an elasticity between 1.3 and 1.6" (2014, 220–21). That estimate has been severely contested among English-speaking economists (especially Rognlie 2014). The literature is extensive, and various claims are very often confused. Nonetheless, very little in that body of work supports Piketty's thesis that capital and labor elasticities are, or have been, greater than one. The rough consensus is that the ratio has a mean value between 0.40 and 0.60.

Most of the estimates, it is true, are derived from *gross* capital measures, which include depreciation. Piketty, though, uses *net* capital measures throughout, which exclude depreciation. That choice does little to strengthen his argument. *Net* elasticity is invariably less than *gross* elasticity. Piketty's appeal to historical data is, moreover, restricted to data that he himself has calculated. Empirical observations, he argues, confirm the dominant trend of high elasticity. But that is only true if a specific attribute of the model—stability of the real price of capital—is also to be found in the real world. Given the heterogeneous nature of capital, that is a very risky assumption.

The discussion (or debate) is ongoing. No one is yet entitled to draw firm conclusions. These issues will be debated for years among economists. If firm conclusions are not yet possible, a certain degree of caution with respect to Piketty's predictions is obviously desirable.

References

Piketty, Thomas. 2014. *Capital in the 21st Century*. Cambridge, MA: Belknap Press.

Rognlie, Matthew. 2014. "A Note on Piketty and Diminishing Returns to Capital." http://www.mit.edu/~mrognlie/piketty_diminishing_returns.pdf

22. An Infinite Growth of Large Fortunes? The Limits of Mathematics

Jean-Philippe Delsol

The postulate of Thomas Piketty in *Capital in the 21st Century* (2014) is that wealth disparity is growing inevitably because of a fundamental inequality expressed as $r > g$, where r is the return of capital yield (i.e., the average return in a year in the form of profits, dividends, interests, and rent as a percentage of its value) and g represents the rate of economic growth (i.e., the annual increase of income and production). Piketty starts by noting that growth in the past 2,000 years was always less than 1 percent, or even 0.2 to 0.5 percent before the 19th century—except in the 20th century when it was substantially higher. In contrast, during the past 2,000 years the return on capital was 4–5 percent before taxes (note that there was practically no wealth taxation before the 20th century).

> When the rate of return on capital significantly exceeds the growth rate of the economy (as it did through much of history until the nineteenth century and as is likely to be the case again in the twenty-first century), then it logically follows that inherited wealth grows faster than output and income. People with inherited wealth need save only a portion of their income from capital to see that capital grow more quickly than the economy as a whole. Under such conditions, it is almost inevitable that inherited wealth will...attain extremely high levels (Piketty 2014, 26).

He thus reckons that the hyperconcentration of wealth observed in traditional and agrarian societies, especially until World War I in Europe, is linked to the fact "that these were low-growth societies in which the rate of return on capital was markedly and durably higher than the rate of growth." He continues:

> Consider a world of low growth, on the order of, say, 0.5–1 percent a year, which was the case everywhere before the eighteenth and nineteenth centuries. The rate of return on capital, which is generally on the order of 4 or 5 percent a year, is therefore much higher than the growth rate. Concretely, this means that wealth accumulated in the past is recapitalized much more quickly than the economy grows, even when there is no income from labor. For example, if $g = 1\%$ and $r = 5\%$, saving one-fifth of the income from capital...is enough to ensure that capital inherited from the previous generation grows at the same rate as the economy" (Piketty 2014, 351).

Obviously, in that scenario, saving at more than 1 percent will tend to make wealth increase rapidly.

The Mathematical Boomerang

The mathematical formula employed by Piketty as a magic key to understand economic and social history becomes incoherent when applied over time. Piketty seriously argues that the rate of return on capital was 4 to 5 percentage points above economic growth for the past 2,000 years. If that were the case, how would capital have accumulated sustainably at a higher level than what the rate of economic growth allowed? Wealth cannot be seized by the richest, as Piketty believes, beyond the limits of existing wealth whose growth more or less reflects the general rate of growth. If during the past 2,000 years wealth increased by 4 percent a year on average while the rate of growth oscillated below 0.5 percent, it would quickly have become clear that the existing wealth was insufficient to satisfy the demand for increased wealth that savings would have "requested." Or the rate of return would at least have decreased much faster than Piketty imagines. To clarify, his formula, as the "alpha and omega" of his pseudodemonstration, cannot apply over the long term.

True, he admits:

> If the fortunes of wealthy individuals grow more rapidly than average income, the capital/income ratio will rise indefinitely, which in the long run should lead to a decrease in the rate of return on capital. Nevertheless, this mechanism can take decades to operate, especially in an open economy in which wealthy individuals can accumulate foreign assets, as was the case in Britain and France in the nineteenth century and up to the eve of World War I (Piketty 2014, 361).

Since he is intelligent, he raises the possible objection; but since he is also an ideologue, he does not take it into account when he develops his thinking and calculations.

Piketty estimates that the return on capital oscillates in the long term around 4–5 percent, or even 3–6 percent, with a small decrease from 4–5 percent, through the 18th and 19th centuries, to 3–4 percent in the 20th century. He also notes that the share of capital in the national income varies in the long term between 25 and 40 percent, whereas the difference (75–60 percent) represents the share of labor. The difference is obviously substantial and would tend to favor labor: "We find that capital's share of income was on the order of 35–40 percent in both Britain and France in the late eighteenth century and throughout the nineteenth, before falling to 20–25 percent in the middle of the twentieth century and then rising again to 25–30 percent in the late twentieth and early twenty-first centuries" (Piketty 2014, 200). Over the same period, the value of the stock of capital seems to fluctuate between 4 and 5 times the value of the annual national income, falling to less than 3 times national income in the 1950s as two world wars exhausted the capital stock and labor increased in importance as the postwar boom got under way. Piketty admits:

> The total value of the capital stock, measured in years of national income—the ratio that measures the overall importance of capital in the economy and society—appears not to have changed very much over a very long period of time. In Britain and France...national capital today represents about five or six years of national income, which is just slightly less than the level of wealth observed in the eighteenth and nineteenth centuries and right up to the eve of World War I (2014, 164).

Therefore, considering that, generally, the capital stock remains in the same proportion—more or less 5 times—the national income and considering that the wealth of a nation, or of the world, cannot exceed gross domestic product (GDP) growth in the long run, we have to admit that Piketty's formula does not work. If the rate of return was durably 4 to 5 percentage points higher than the rate of growth, that would mean that by saving just 1 percent per year of the 4 or 5 percent return, the wealthiest would soon run out of investments for their capital.

If a capital of $100 is invested at 1 percent, a hundred years later it will have increased from $100 to $270.48 and after 200 years from $100 to $731.60. Very likely, however, the wealthiest people—who according to Piketty hold most assets—do not consume all their income; to get richer they have to save. And if they saved a mere fifth of their capital income, they would multiply their assets by seven in 200 years; but that would not be possible if the wealthiest people already owned, as he claims, half of all assets.

The Limits of the Argument

The limits of the argument may be demonstrated in another way. Let us start with the situation in 2012 in France: the gross return is 2.81 percent, consumption of fixed assets is 0.5 percent, and GDP growth stands at 1.54 percent. What portion of my return should I reinvest to keep my share of income and assets in the GDP with a capital–output ratio that remains constant?

A constant capital–output ratio assumes that the rate of growth of capital is equal to GDP growth, g. My capital income K is $r.K$, where r is the rate of return. Now x is the share of my return, $r.K$, which I must reinvest and d is the rate of consumption of fixed capital. The equation is as follows:

$$g = \frac{\Delta K}{K} = \frac{x.r.K - dK}{K} = \frac{(x.r - d)K}{K} = xr - d.$$

Hence,

$$x = \frac{g + d}{r} = \frac{1.54\% + 0.5\%}{2.81\%} = 72.6\%.$$

Thus, I would need to reinvest more than 70 percent of my return to maintain my share of wealth in the national economy. Considering that the 2.81 percent average return is taxed at a minimum level of 15.5 percent corresponding to the French generalized social contribution, the income is reduced by at least 15.5 percent. Therefore, I have to reinvest close to 86 percent of my capital return. Assuming that my marginal tax rate is higher than 15 percent, I will not be able to maintain my share of capital, nor increase it—obviously.

Be that as it may, let us assume that my return figures are erroneous. Let us take those of Piketty (1 percent growth and a net return of 5 percent) and suppose that the wealthiest 1 percent, who own 17 percent of assets, decide to grab all available assets by reinvesting 100 percent of their wealth. With a constant capital–output ratio, the ambition of the richest 1 percent will stop in 2016, unless they are able to convince the other 99 percent to sell their assets.

Table 22.1
SIMULATION WITH 100 PERCENT OF CAPITAL INCOME REINVESTED BY WEALTHIEST 1 PERCENT

Year	Investment of the 99% (percent capital return)	Investment of the 1% (percent capital return)	Share of capital of the 99% (percent)	Share of capital of the 1% (percent)
2012	3.61	100	83.0	17.0
2013	2.83	100	82.3	17.7
2014	1.99	100	81.6	18.4
2015	1.11	100	80.9	19.1
2016	0.18	100	80.1	19.9
2017	−0.81	100	79.4	20.6

At that point, the desires of the 1 percent run into the absence of assets available and necessary to generate growth. (See Table 22.1.)

The situation presented in Table 22.1 may seem outrageous. Taking into account taxes and contributions, let us assume that the 1 percent may only invest 70 percent of their capital income. (See Table 22.2.)

This only means that the exhaustion of assets available for the rich to "grab" is postponed until 2034 and that from 2013 the 99 percent of households accept to reduce their investments each year. With a rate of return at 5 percent, it is hard to see why they would do so.

Only if the capital–output ratio were to increase could the share of the 1 percent increase without constraining the 99 percent, reducing their share. But in that case, the return would decrease and capital accumulation would slow down. In turn, opportunities would decrease—unless the share of profits increased, and that would be contrary to the trend documented since 1996. Piketty's theory crashes not only against the logic of math, but against reality.

Table 22.2

SIMULATION WITH 70 PERCENT OF CAPITAL INCOME REINVESTED BY WEALTHIEST 1 PERCENT

Year	Investment of the 99% (percent capital return)	Investment of the 1% (percent capital return)	Share of capital of the 99% (percent)	Share of capital of the 1% (percent)
2012	9.76	70	83.0	17.0
2013	9.45	70	82.6	17.4
2014	9.13	70	82.1	17.9
2015	8.81	70	81.7	18.3
2016	8.46	70	81.3	18.7
2017	8.11	70	80.8	19.2
2018	7.74	70	80.3	19.7
2019	7.36	70	79.8	20.2
2020	6.97	70	79.3	20.7
2021	6.56	70	78.8	21.2
2022	6.14	70	78.3	21.7
2023	5.69	70	77.8	22.2
2024	5.24	70	77.2	22.8
2025	4.76	70	76.6	23.4
2026	4.26	70	76.1	23.9
2027	3.75	70	75.5	24.5
2028	3.21	70	74.9	25.1
2029	2.65	70	74.2	25.8
2030	2.07	70	73.6	26.4
2031	1.46	70	72.9	27.1
2032	0.82	70	72.3	27.7
2033	0.16	70	71.6	28.4
2034	−0.53	70	70.9	29.1

Reference

Piketty, Thomas. 2014. *Capital in the 21st Century*. Cambridge, MA: Belknap Press.

Section 8. Taxation: Consequences of Piketty's Policies and Alternative Reforms

What are the logical consequences of a tax policy based on the recommendations of Thomas Piketty? He seems oblivious to the incentives for individuals and households that his proposed system would introduce, but the question is critical. Would Piketty's proposals not undermine the very foundations of policies that helped produce prosperity for the greatest number in the space of a few generations? And if tax reform is needed, what kind should it be—particularly in France, which is already a poster child of tax complexity?

23. Piketty's Plan for Equality Would Reduce Personal Freedom and Undermine Growth

James A. Dorn

Thomas Piketty, author of the bestseller *Capital in the 21st Century*, would like to see a radical leveling of incomes to ensure social justice. To reduce rising inequality of income and wealth, he would impose highly progressive income and wealth taxes on the rich and near-rich.

He proposes a top marginal tax rate of 80 percent on those making more than $500,000 a year, along with a 5 to 10 percent annual wealth tax on those with very high net worth (in excess of $1 billion). His plan would effectively confiscate the capital income of high net worth individuals who he assumes have no legitimate claim to such income. Piketty's mantra is that "capitalism and markets should be the slave of democracy and not the opposite." He wants to promote "progressive" policies so that "democracy can regain control over capitalism and ensure that the general interest takes precedence over private interests, while preserving economic openness" (Piketty 2014, 1).

Yet, his planned redistribution via government taxation of income and wealth would undermine the fabric of civil society, stem economic growth, and diminish economic and personal freedom. Government power would rise and human liberty decline.

The Effect on Human Capital and Growth

Capital is best understood as a bundle of ownership rights—in particular, the right to sell one's property and the right to receive the income from that property. When those rights are attenuated, capital is destroyed.

Gary Becker ([1964] 1993), the late Nobel laureate economist, showed the importance of human capital (i.e., the skills individuals acquire through education and training) for a person's future income and economic growth. High marginal income tax rates and wealth taxes dampen incentives to invest in human and nonhuman capital—and when investment slows so will economic growth. Imposing a 50 percent marginal tax rate on individuals with incomes starting at $200,000 and increasing that rate to 80 percent at $500,000, as Piketty proposes, would heavily penalize those who have invested in their human capital and discourage others from doing so.

Likewise, Piketty's proposed wealth tax would translate into a very high tax on the income from nonhuman capital. For example, with some simplifying assumptions, a 2 percent wealth tax is equivalent to a tax rate of 67 percent on capital income if the discount rate is 3 percent. Piketty proposes a 5 to 10 percent annual tax on the net worth of individuals with at least $1 billion in assets. A 10 percent wealth tax translates into a tax on capital income of 333 percent (assuming a discount rate of 3 percent). Such confiscatory tax rates would not raise much revenue because the rich would move to low tax regimes like Hong Kong that relish economic freedom. That is why Piketty wants a global wealth tax—but that's pie in the sky.

The high taxes on capital would ultimately harm workers in those countries that followed Piketty's policies, as incomes grew more slowly. Rich capitalists are not the enemy of poor workers. Capital freedom and private property allow for upward mobility.

Piketty does the economics profession a disservice by focusing on outcomes rather than institutions, incentives, and processes. He believes more in the power of government than in the power of markets to transform people's lives.

Rule of Law vs. Distributive Justice and the Pretense of Morality

As Adam Smith long ago explained, the wealth of a nation is best advanced by liberty and markets, not by government intervention and planning. The "invisible hand" of market competition under a just government protecting persons and property is more apt to lead to social and economic harmony than the "grabbing hand" of the state.

James Madison, the chief architect of the Constitution, made it clear that "persons and property are the two great subjects on which Governments are to act; and that the rights of persons, and the rights of property, are the objects, for the protection of which Government was instituted" (Madison 2006, 354). As government power grows and private property rights are attenuated by oppressive taxes and other takings, individual freedom diminishes. Equality under a just rule of law is replaced by some vague criterion of "social justice" and the politicization of economic life.

If Piketty's scheme were implemented, "legal plunder" (a term coined by the 19th century French liberal Frédéric Bastiat [1998]) would undermine the rule of law, which is meant to safeguard persons and property, and turn the concept of justice on its head. Instead of meaning the prevention of injustice (i.e., the protection of individual rights to liberty and property), justice has come to mean distributive justice—namely, the use of force to dictate some politically favored distribution of income and wealth.

Piketty also ignores the wisdom of the late development economist Peter Bauer who warned, "The unholy grail of economic equality would exchange the promised reduction or removal of differences in income and wealth for much greater actual inequality of power between rulers and subjects" (Bauer 1981, 8).

Piketty claims he is not a Marxist but rather a socialist with a belief in private property. Yet, the contradiction should be apparent: One cannot defend private property and at the same time call for a massive taking of property. The redistributive state is not only unjust (hence, the "pretense of morality," to use F. A. Hayek's term); it is detrimental to economic growth. Economic history has shown that the plight of the poor is more likely to improve by increasing economic freedom and growth, rather than by reducing the return to capital.

Lessons from China

A case in point is China's economic liberalization, which began in 1978. The opening of markets and growth of the nonstate sector, along with privatization of housing and other reforms, have led to rapid economic growth, the rise of a large middle class, and the possibility of becoming rich. Income inequality has increased, but the power of the state has decreased—and more than 500 million people have lifted themselves out of poverty as economic and personal freedom have advanced.

Martin King Whyte, a scholar at Harvard's Fairbank Center for Chinese Studies, has found that most of the Chinese people "feel optimistic about their own chances to get ahead. A majority also believe that talent, hard work, and schooling are the primary routes to mobility." At the same time, he found that the recent rise of mass citizen protests "are mainly a response to abuses of power and other procedural justice issues, rather than being fueled by feelings of distributive injustice and anger at the rich" (Whyte 2012, 234).

The injustices in China and elsewhere are those of the state against the people, not the rich against the poor. The market is not the enemy of the people; it is the engine of creativity and progress. Unfortunately, that message does not get the same spotlight in the media as Piketty's call for distributive justice.

Underlying Piketty's approach to equality is the false idea that the rich get richer at the expense of the poor. He ignores the reality that voluntary exchanges in the marketplace make parties to the trades better off and create new wealth. The principle of nonintervention or freedom contrasts sharply with Piketty's "social state" based on government power.

The real issue is where to draw the line between consent and coercion, and thus between the individual and the state. When government power is limited to the protection of rights to liberty and property, individuals are free to choose. Private free markets, bounded by a just rule of law, strengthen individual responsibility and improve people's lives. Piketty's redistributive state would do the opposite.

Instead of calling for higher taxes to reduce the return on capital, Piketty would be on firmer ground by arguing for an increase in economic freedom and more limited government to increase the range of choices open to people.

References

Bastiat, Frédéric. 1998. *The Law.* Irving-on-Hudson, NY: Foundation for Economic Education. First published 1850 as a pamphlet.

Bauer, Peter T. 1981. *Equality, the Third World, and Economic Delusion.* Cambridge, MA: Harvard University Press.

Becker, Gary S. [1964] 1993. *Human Capital: A Theoretical and Empirical Analysis, with Special Reference to Education*, 3rd ed. Chicago, IL: University of Chicago Press. First published by National Bureau of Economic Research and distributed by Columbia University Press.

Madison, James. 2006. "Speech, Virginia Convention, December 2, 1829." In *Selected Writings of James Madison*, edited by Ralph Ketcham. Indianapolis, IN: Hackett Publishing Company.

Piketty, Thomas. 2014. *Capital in the 21st Century.* Cambridge, MA: Belknap Press.

Whyte, Martin K. 2012. "China's Post-Socialist Inequality." *Current History* (September): 229–34.

24. Tax Reform: Not the Piketty Way

Jean-Philippe Delsol and Nicolas Lecaussin

The Rich: Taxes Paid and Jobs Created

In November 2013, the mayor of London, Boris Johnson, claimed to be very proud to lead the city with the largest number of millionaires, recalling that the rich are the ones who pay more taxes (2013). Yet, in 2009, the ex-chancellor, Gordon Brown, decided to adopt a tax for the "super rich" for ideological reasons and also in hope of reducing deficits. The top tax rate for the wealthiest (incomes of over £150,000 or €186,000 per annum) then went from 40 percent to 50 percent. The outcome was expected to be tax revenue of £7.2 billion. Two years later, the British Treasury published the results of the rise in taxes: taxes paid by the wealthiest had declined, falling from £116 billion to £87 billion, a loss of close to £30 billion (HM Revenue & Customs 2012)! Suddenly, David Cameron reduced the upper bracket to 45 percent and tax revenue increased. In 2013, the wealthiest 1 percent paid 29.8 percent of the total income tax, a higher portion than the 20 percent they had paid under Brown's regime. It seems the "Laffer effect" is not just theory.

In France, in the early 2010s, the wealthiest 10 percent were paying about 70 percent of the income tax, while about 50 percent of the population paid no income tax. In 2014, the government proposed removing the first income tax bracket, so that going forward about 53 percent of the French people would not pay income tax. First, the measure would create more inequality, it would aggravate the burden on the middle classes and the wealthy, and it would have no economic benefit. Second, economic studies generally show that the better move would be to lower taxes for the middle class and, above all, the wealthiest. As Boris Johnson noted, those are the people who already pay the most tax. They are also the ones who can create employment.

The 10 wealthiest French people (according to the ranking put together by *Challenges* magazine) alone are responsible for more than 700,000 jobs. But many have gone abroad. A survey by the Belgian financial newspaper *L'Echo* shows that the French hold around €17 billion in Belgium (Keszei 2014). That level of investment represents 124,000 jobs created, and that is a huge problem. In 2013, the Institute for Research in Economic and Fiscal Issues (IREF) sounded the alarm on the increasing number of French people leaving France and especially on their profile: younger, less wealthy, and more entrepreneurial (Delsol 2013). France is losing its entrepreneurial forces.

Thus, the government would have done better to propose a tax measure promoting the repatriation of those billions. IREF made a calculation based on multiple scenarios showing that once those billions were invested, they could create tens of thousands of jobs. A private-sector job costs on average €40,000. So the €17 billion "lost in Belgium" represents 425,000 jobs in the private sector. But of course money invested in the economy does not only translate into new jobs created. Using data from Agence Française des Investissements Internationaux (*French Agency for International Investments*) and Ernst & Young about foreign investment in France, IREF found that those €17 billion could create a minimum of 15,000 jobs and a maximum of 124,000 jobs. And in turn, the jobs created would mean more tax revenue and social security contributions.

The French talk a lot about reform. In terms of taxation, reform is more than necessary, given the aberrant piling up of taxes. The complexity of French tax law—coupled with incessant changes in the legislation, which generate uncertainty and insecurity—is a growth killer. In a way, France is the poster child of taxation madness.

The Piketty Way?

The reduction of inequality is at the heart of Piketty's theory, and his preferred tool is taxation. In a collective work in French, which translates to *For a Tax Revolution* (Landais et al. 2011), he proposed a tax of 60 percent on the first euro of all incomes above €100,000 per month. The idea certainly aroused François Hollande's ill-advised proposal to tax incomes above €1 million at a rate of 75 percent. And it has contributed to the climate of mistrust that, since 2012, has driven away foreign investors in France and weakened the French economy.

However, rather than using taxes to harass people, especially the richest contributors and the middle class, it would be better to reform taxation from the top down, simplify it, and make it bearable—in other words, make it favorable to the creation of business, employment, and growth. In France, the top marginal rates for the income tax (64.5 percent with the "generalized social tax"), corporate tax (38 percent with the extra corporate tax created by Nicolas Sarkozy and Hollande), and inheritance tax (45 percent) are amongst the highest rates in the world. Employees also support welfare taxes that are the highest of all developed countries, accounting for a staggering 80–100 percent of the average net wage. The middle classes are particularly affected by paying proportionally more welfare costs but not benefiting more from this "social insurance." Of course, it is not insurance but, in fact, a new progressive tax since the lowest wages are increasingly exempt.

The Prospects of a Flat Tax

A flat tax (or proportional tax) would be an acceptable solution. In France, the Generalized Social Contribution (CSG) is already a flat tax, and it generates higher revenues than the income tax: around €72 billion from income taxes and more than €90 billion from CSG in 2015. IREF has calculated that a "soft" flat tax, with two rates of 2 percent up to €8,000 per year and 15 percent above that, would be more productive than the current progressive tax.

A flat tax of that type could involve all the French in the payment of income taxes, which would be a lot more democratic than exonerating more than 50 percent of households, for whom public spending thus becomes "painless." Such a flat tax could make it possible to suppress all legal tax loopholes and would reduce tax fraud. The tax revenues produced directly and indirectly—through the economic growth it would generate—would make it possible to compensate the poor for cost of taxation.

Serious Reform

All taxes must be reduced, especially their top rate. But we should insist on the necessity of reforming the following:

- Taxes on capital. France cumulates high recording stamp duties (on transfers of real estate, shares in companies, or even non-physical assets such as reputation and customer base), gift or estate taxes (with only a modest exemption of €100,000) with rapid progressivity and high rates, and a wealth "solidarity" tax of 1.5 percent per year.
- Taxes on corporations. The tax on corporate profits is 50 percent higher than the average rate in Europe.
- Taxes on income. The income tax, in addition to social taxes, reaches such high levels that successive governments have had to create loopholes, which are dubious in general and always entail expensive justification.

Those taxes are the most sensitive. The tax on wealth, in particular, has become the phobia of taxpayers who are successful and feel they are being robbed of the capital they have accumulated—after having already paid many taxes and contributions. Its removal would be beneficial. That is to say, governments should stop creating new taxes and take the opportunity to remove a multitude of existing taxes that have marginal yield and yet harm those who pay them.

Generally, lower and more stable direct taxation would recreate trust and confidence, which are the foundation of any prosperous society. Indeed, people who have confidence in the future and in the stability of their social and economic environment can set up businesses, launch projects, invest, and hire. Tax reform must generate the incentives for private-sector growth and jobs.

References

Delsol, Jean-Philippe. 2013. "Les Raisons de l'Exil Fiscal." IREF, January 17. http://fr.irefeurope.org/Les-raisons-de-l-exil-fiscal,a2177.

HM Revenue & Customs. 2012. *The Exchequer Effect of the 50 Per Cent Additional Rate of Income Tax*. London: HM Revenue & Customs. webarchive.nationalarchives.gov.uk/20130129110402/http:/www.hmrc.gov.uk/budget2012/excheq-income-tax-2042.pdf.

Johnson, Boris. 2013. "We Should Be Humbly Thanking the Super-Rich, Not Bashing Them." *Telegraph*, November 17. http://www.telegraph.co.uk/comment/columnists/borisjohnson/10456202/We-should-be-humbly-thanking-the-super-rich-not-bashing-them.html.

Keszei, Nicolas. 2014. "Ces Riches Français de Belgique." *L'Écho*, September 13. http://www.lecho.be/actualite/economie_politique_belgique/Ces_riches_Francais_de_Belgique.9544615-3158.art.

Landais, Camille, Thomas Piketty, and Emmanuel Saez. 2011. *Pour une Révolution Fiscale*. Paris: Seuil/La République des idées.

Notes

Introduction

Jean-Philippe Delsol and Emmanuel Martin

[1]Amazon Kindle data showed people would read the book until page 26 or so, on average. As Deirdre McCloskey wrote in her review of Piketty's book: "The Kindle company from Amazon keeps track of the last page of your highlighting in a downloaded book (you didn't know that, did you?). Using the fact, the mathematician Jordan Ellenberg reckons that the average reader of the 655 pages of text and footnotes of *Capital in the Twenty-First Century* stops somewhere a little past page 26, where the highlighting stops, about the end of the Introduction"(McCloskey 2014).

1. The Great Process of Equalization of Conditions

Jean-Philippe Delsol

[1]Horwitz (2015, 16) notes that a color television in 2013 is worth 20 percent of what it was in 1973.

[2]Many goods can be expensive and at first accessible only to the rich, such as microwave ovens and videocassette recorders a generation ago. However, the cost and limited accessibility are preconditions that enable the launching of the products and their eventual price decrease, which in turn benefits a greater number, including the poor. The inequality in the beginning is thus crucial to the subsequent "equalization." See Horwitz (2015, 16).

[3]The increase in quality remains true even after taking into account the shorter lifespan of many products today. Some goods, such as cars, actually have a longer lifespan than in the past. See Horwitz (2015, 18).

[4]Saab uses the OECD (2013) data to show that the strongest increases in income for the 10 percent poorest are associated with the strongest increases in income for the richest.

[5]At the very least, Piketty dodges the issue by ignoring the lessons of the theory of incentives.

[6]Horwitz recalls that "between 1980 and 2006, the percentage of U.S. households making less than $75,000 fell from approximately 81% to 70%, while those making more than that increased from 19% to 30%, or

over a 50% increase in the percentage making more than $75,000.... *[M]ore households went from middle class to rich than went from poor to middle class"* (Horwitz 2015, 12).

[7]As Horwitz notes, mobility in the United States seems to have stagnated for the last 15 years. However, one needs to take into account the "optical illusion" of those quintiles or deciles: "As the total amount of income grows, the width of each quintile expands as well, requiring progressively more income each year to move up from one quintile to another" (Horwitz 2015, 10). The income of many households can improve within each quintile, without them moving up to the next quintile.

[8]Quoting a study by Michael Cox and Richard Alm, Horwitz notes that, "of the poor households in 1979, almost 86% were able to move up at least one quintile by 1988" (Horwitz 2015, 7). In the period 1975–1991, mobility was even more impressive "with almost 95% of poor families moving out of the lowest quintile ... and almost 60% of them ending up in one of the top two quintiles" (Horwitz 2015, 8).

2. Longevity, Education, and the Huge New Worldwide Increases in Equality

Nicholas Eberstadt

[1]This chapter is an extended and updated version of an Op-Ed piece titled "How the World Is Becoming More Equal" in the *Wall Street Journal*, August 26, 2014.

[2]Readers may note in Figure 3.2 that the trajectory of decline in lifespan inequality has slowed considerably in the United States since the start of the 21st century. Recent reports and research, furthermore, have pointed to slowdown or even reversal of health progress for significant portions of the American population during those same years and to a tendency of widening gaps in life expectancy at birth by income stratum (Arias 2016, Case and Deaton 2015). These are highly disturbing developments. Without in any way minimizing the significance of these worrisome American trends, however, we may observe that the "slope shift" we see for the United States since roughly the year 2000 is not a distinctive American phenomenon. Quite the contrary: a similar slowdown in lifespan inequality declines for each given year of increase in life expectancy can be seen in both Sweden and Italy. Interestingly enough, both Sweden's and Italy's slowdowns commenced once overall life expectation at birth had reached the mid-70s—just as was the case in the United States. All this warrants additional examination—but it suggests that the remarkably

linear historical relationship between life expectancy increases on the one hand and decreases in lifespan inequality on the other may tend to "bend" once very high levels of life expectancy are achieved, irrespective of local patterns of socioeconomic inequality.

3. Where Are the "Super Rich" of 1987?

Juan Ramón Rallo

[1]This article was translated from the French version published by *Contrepoints* as "Où Sont Passés les Super-Riches de 1987?" June 3, 2014, http://www.contrepoints.org/2014/06/03/167232-ou-sont-les-super-riches-de-1987.

4. Piketty on Management and Wealth

Henri Lepage

[1]This article is taken from a longer, 2014 study published as "The Specter of Inequality," *Inference—International Review of Science* 1 (1), http://inference-review.com/article/the-specter-of-inequality.

[2]The numbers are taken from the minutes of board meetings. They may differ from the amounts actually received. The numbers include salaries, bonuses, stock, and options.

5. The Sociology of Piketty's Anti-Rich Stance

Nicolas Lecaussin

[1]During the French Revolution, any organization between the citizen and the state was suspicious as it was seen as generating an *esprit de corps* and distracting individual citizens from the general interest. For example, guilds were banned by the Le Chapelier law in 1791 (and not repealed until 1884).

[2]"Let us concede that there were some rich jerks on the actual *Titanic*. So what? Many of the richest people on earth were passengers on the *Titanic*, including Isidor and Ida Strauss (owners of Macy's), mining heir Benjamin Guggenheim, and John Jacob Astor IV (the wealthiest man on the ship). They, and numerous others, refused to get in lifeboats until all the women and children, including the poor women and children, got on first (Ida Strauss refused to leave her husband, preferring to die in his arms). After helping other passengers escape, Guggenheim and his secretary changed into their evening wear, saying they were "prepared to go down like gentlemen." Meanwhile the most famous real-life cad on the ship was George Symons, a crewman who refused to let anyone else

on his lifeboat even though there were 28 empty seats. Money, it seems, doesn't tell you everything about a man." (Goldberg 2014)

[3]Hayek for instance saw intellectuals as "second-hand dealers in ideas" (Hayek [1949] 1990, 6).

[4]"Everyone is political in his or her own way. The world is not divided between a political elite on one side and, on the other, an army of commentators and spectators whose only responsibility is to drop a ballot in a ballot box once every four or five years. It is illusory, I believe, to think that the scholar and the citizen live in separate moral universes, the former concerned with means and the latter with ends. Although comprehensible, this view ultimately strikes me as dangerous" (Piketty 2014, 574).

[5]See also, "Here we have numbers; a well-defined group situation of proletarian hue; and a group interest shaping a group attitude that will much more realistically account for hostility to the capitalist order than could the theory—itself a rationalization in the psychological sense—according to which the intellectual's righteous indignation about the wrongs of capitalism simply represents the logical inference from outrageous facts" (Schumpeter [1942] 2003, 153).

[6]One could add that the theory was very convenient for the aid bureaucracies as it supplied their justification. See also Boudon (2004b, 779): "The fundamental process that can explain the rejection of liberalism by many intellectuals seems to be the following: at the starting point of this process, the economic situation and the socio-historical context reveal salient facts perceived by the collective sensitivity/ collective opinion. These circumstances create a demand that intellectuals following an 'ethics of conviction,' and particularly 'organic intellectuals' according to Gramsci, undertake to exploit. When these salient facts give the impression of some failures of liberal societies, they incite these same intellectuals to tap into the explanatory patterns placed on the market of ideas by the traditions of thought that oppose liberalism, in order to build their own diagnosis. If the denunciation of these failures displays 'good intentions,' and the explanation they offer seems 'simple,' it is likely to experience media success and not come up against criticism."

6. Piketty Gets It Wrong

Michael Tanner

[1]This article appeared in the *National Review (Online)* on April 23, 2014.

7. Thomas Piketty's Great Contradiction

Juan Ramón Rallo

[1]This article was translated from the French version published by *Contrepoints* as "La grande contradiction de Piketty," June 4, 2014, http://www.contrepoints.org/2014/06/04/167149-la-grande-contradiction-de-piketty.

8. Piketty and Emerging Markets

Álvaro Vargas Llosa

[1]This article was first published by *The Beacon*, the blog of the Independent Institute, June 14, 2014.

9. Piketty's Numbers Don't Add Up

Martin Feldstein

[1]This article was first published in *The Wall Street Journal*, March 14, 2014.

10. The Rich, and Everyone Else, Get Richer

Richard V. Burkhauser

[1]This article was first published in the *Orange County Register*, August 21, 2013.

11. Is Housing Capital?

Henri Lepage

[1]This article is taken from a longer, 2014 study published as "The Specter of Inequality," *Inference—International Review of Science* 1 (1), http://inference-review.com/article/the-specter-of-inequality.

[2]Piketty's figure 3.2 is recalculated here, showing with greater clarity the relative importance of housing in total national capital (Bonnet et al. 2014, 2).

14. Piketty Is Misleading about the Swedish Case

Malin Sahlén and Salim Furth

[1]This article was first published by www.timbro.se/en. © Timbro 2014. Reprinted with permission.

15. Challenging the Empirical Contribution of Thomas Piketty's *Capital in the 21st Century*

Phillip W. Magness and Robert P. Murphy

This article was first published in *The Journal of Private Enterprise*, 30(1): 1–34.

contribution was top-notch—at least until Chris Giles's 2014 bombshell report in the *Financial Times*, which was the first major piece to challenge this aspect of Piketty's work.

[2]See, for example, the Tax Policy Center's chart, "Historical Income TaxParameters,"http://www.taxpolicycenter.org/taxfacts/displayafact.cfm?Docid=543.

[3]We call attention to the recurring complexity of Piketty's error here as attesting to his ideological bias. If Piketty had only been wrong about 1932 versus 1933, and then 1936 versus 1937, we might attribute the errors to a misunderstanding of the tax year versus the filing year (or fiscal year versus calendar year, or even election year versus presidential inauguration year). But there is really no way to easily explain his mistake about the tax rate being reduced to 25 percent "in the late 1920s ... under Hoover's ... presidency" when in fact it happened *four years* earlier under Coolidge. Whatever the explanation, notice that Piketty's mistakes—which are so basic that they would discredit a high school history paper—serve to bolster his narrative of the low-tax, awful-economy Hoover versus the high-tax, economic-recovery Roosevelt. The odd inclusion of the word "again" in the quotation—when Piketty writes "and again under Hoover"—may refer back to page 473, where Piketty establishes that "the top rate under Hoover had been only 25 percent." Because the book was translated into English from French, the extremely generous reader could acquit Piketty of intentionally misleading the reader here, but translation difficulties cannot explain why he claims that a 1925 tax-rate reduction occurred "in the late 1920s" and consistently mentions Hoover but not Coolidge.

[4]Piketty's historical narrative for the United States may be said to exhibit the pattern described by Hayek wherein "historical beliefs which guide us in the present are not always in accord with the facts; sometimes they are even the effects rather than the cause of political beliefs" (1954, 3–4).

[5]The first person to our knowledge who caught Piketty's dubious minimum wage discussion was Furchtgott-Roth (2014). Historical minimum wage rates are readily available from the U.S. Department of Labor, Wage and Hour Division, "History of Federal Minimum Wage Rates under the Fair Labor Standards Act, 1938–2009."

[6]Piketty's (2014b) data table TS9.1 actually shows he had access to U.S. federal minimum wage data by year from the same U.S. Department of Labor source we used, although he adjusts the timeline of each hike to the beginning of the nearest calendar year. Not only does the adjustment add further confusion to his timeline, but the errors in both wage rates

and attributed presidential administrations persist even after we take it into account.

[7]The War Revenue Act of 1898 was repealed in 1902, although certain inheritance tax provisions from it did not expire until 1907, providing almost a decade of operations that go unnoticed by Piketty (2014b, 338), who traces the first American estate tax to 1916.

[8]Annual U.S. federal tax revenue is easily attainable in a standardized form going back to 1821, and state revenues may be reliably ascertained or estimated throughout the 19th century. Several widely available estimates have been made for U.S. national income in the 19th century as well. Piketty simply did not incorporate them into his source material.

[9]See in particular McCloskey (2014).

[10]The SCF-based estimate in Wolff (1994) does not contain a data point for the 1970s.

[11]Giles (2014) first drew attention to the hard-coding of this 36 percentage point adjustment into Piketty's estimates for the top 10 percent from 1910 to 1950. We acknowledge that this number may derive from another unnamed source or method, but Piketty (2014a, 7–8) did not clarify its origin when specifically pressed by Giles to do so.

[12]Auerbach and Hassett (2015, 5–6) reach similar conclusions of Piketty's figure 10.5, focusing on his use of the SCF-derived sources. When stripped of Piketty's unconventional smoothing techniques, they note, the SCF data become "noisy" and the trend line "no longer rises without interruption in an apparently deterministic trend from 1970 onward."

[13]We call the reader's attention to the stark explanatory reversal by coauthor Saez between these two papers. In 2004, Saez interpreted his findings by noting "we tentatively suggest (but do not prove) that steep progressive income and estate taxation, by reducing the rate of wealth accumulation of the rich, may have been the most important factor preventing large fortunes to be reconstituted after the shocks of the 1929–1945 period (Kopczuk and Saez 2004, p. 3)." The then-observed flat trend line was "consistent with the decreased importance of capital incomes at the top of the income distribution documented by Piketty and Saez (2003), and suggest[s] that the rentier class of the early century is not yet reconstituted (Kopczuk and Saez 2004, p. 1)." In an accompanying policy brief for their 2014 paper, Saez, along with Zucman, asserts, "Wealth inequality, it turns out, has followed a spectacular U-shape[d] evolution over the past 100 years. From the Great Depression in the 1930s through the late 1970s there was a substantial democratization of wealth.

democratization of wealth. The trend then inverted, with the share of total household wealth owned by the top 0.1 percent increasing to 22 percent in 2012 from 7 percent in the late 1970s (Saez and Zucman 2014b)." Offering their own suggestions to avoid what they dub "this dystopian future," they call for a resumption of "progressive estate and income taxation" measures, which—they say—"were the key tools that reduced the concentration of wealth after the Great Depression." Also note that the one constant in Saez's work between these two otherwise divergent interpretations of conflicting data results for the same time period is a strong prescriptive endorsement of progressive income and estate taxation.

[14]In a later chapter of his book, Piketty describes the Soviet experiment thusly, possibly hinting at the basis of his underlying assumption: "By abolishing private ownership of the means of production, including land and buildings as well as industrial, financial, and business capital (other than a few individual plots of land and small cooperatives), the Soviet experiment simultaneously eliminated all private returns on capital" (2014b, 531). Although that is perhaps an accurate expression of Soviet ideological claims, it is inexcusably naïve if not outright misleading to incorporate such claims into the construction of a historical time series purporting to illustrate operational characteristics of global capitalism. It is also negligent by its omission of the simultaneous economic effects of a state-driven collectivization of the capital stock, including pervasive economic inequality under the historical Soviet system. For a detailed discussion of this issue see Henderson, McNab, and Rózsás (2005).

16. The Rise and Decline of the General Laws of Capitalism

Daron Acemoglu and James A. Robinson

[1]This article was first published in the *Journal of Economic Perspectives* 29 (1): 3–28. We thank David Autor, Amy Finkelstein, Johan Fourie, Bengt Holmstrom, Chang Tai Hsieh, Chad Jones, Matthew Kustenbauder, Naomi Lamoureux, Ulrike Malmendier, Kalle Moene, Joel Mokyr, Suresh Naidu, Jim Poterba, Matthew Rognlie, Timothy Taylor, Ragnar Torvik, Laurence Wilse-Samson, and Francis Wilson for their comments and Pascual Restrepo for extensive discussions, comments, and superb research assistance. To access the Online Appendix and Data Set, visit http://dx.doi.org/10.1257/jep.29.1.3.

[2]There is no consensus on Marx's exact formulation of the relationship between the "substructure," comprising productive forces and sometimes the relations of production, and the "superstructure" which includes what

we call political institutions and most aspects of economic institutions. In Chapter I of the *Communist Manifesto*, Marx and Friedrich Engels wrote, "The history of all hitherto existing society is the history of class struggles" (Marx and Engels [1848] (2007), p. 8). But the idea here, so far as we understand, is not that "class struggle" represents some autonomous historical dynamic, but rather that it is an outcome of the contradictions between the forces of production and the ownership of the means of production. In some writings, such as *The Eighteenth Brumaire of Louis Napoleon*, Marx also allowed for feedback from politics and other aspects of society to the forces of production (Marx [1883] 2016). But it is clear from his work that he regarded this as second order (see Singer 2000, chapter 7, for a discussion of this point). Marx never formulated an approach in which institutions play the central role and themselves change endogenously.

[3]However, the interest rate and the growth rate are linked from both the household side and the production side. For example, with a representative household, we have $r = \theta g + \rho$, where θ is the inverse of the intertemporal elasticity of substitution and ρ is the discount rate. The fact that the representative household assumption may not be a good approximation to reality does not imply that r is independent of g. On the production side, g affects r through its impact on the capital stock, and it is the second channel that depends on the elasticity of substitution between capital and labor.

[4]It is unclear whether $r > g$ is a force toward divergence of incomes across the distribution of income or toward convergence to a new and more unequal distribution of income. In many places, including those we have already quoted, Piketty talks of divergence. But elsewhere, the prediction is formulated differently. For example, he writes: "With the aid of a fairly simple mathematical model, one can show that for a given structure of... [economic and demographic shocks]..., the distribution of wealth tends towards a long-run equilibrium and that the equilibrium level of inequality is an increasing function of the gap $r - g$ between the rate of return on capital and the growth rate" (2014, 364). In our Online Appendix, we discuss a variety of economic models linking $r - g$ to inequality.

[5]The number of countries varies depending on the measure of the interest rate used and specification. In columns 1–3 panel A, we have 27 countries: Argentina, Australia, Canada, China, Colombia, Denmark, Finland, France, Germany, India, Indonesia, Ireland, Italy, Japan, Malaysia, Mauritius, Netherlands, New Zealand, Norway,

Portugal, Singapore, South Africa, Spain, Sweden, Switzerland, United Kingdom, and United States. In column 2 panel B, we lose China and Colombia, and additionally Portugal in column 3. In column 4 panel A, we lose the non-OECD countries, China, Colombia, India, Indonesia, Malaysia, Mauritius, and Singapore relative to columns 1–3, and additionally Germany in columns 5 and 6. In panel B, we additionally lose Portugal in columns 4 and 5, and Portugal and Germany in column 6. In column 7 panel B, we have Uruguay in addition to the 27 countries in column 1. In columns 8 and 9, we lose Germany and Uruguay. In panel B, we lose Uruguay in column 7 relative to panel A; China and Colombia in column 8; and Argentina, China, Colombia, Indonesia, and Portugal in column 9.

[6]With returns to capital determined in the global economy, that is, $rit = rt$ (where i refers to country and t is the time period), variation in rt is fully absorbed by the time effects in these regression models, making the $r = 0$ normalization without any loss of generality. Note, however, that what determines the dynamics of inequality in a country, according to Piketty's general law, is that country's growth rate, supporting the methodology here, which exploits country-specific variation in growth rates (conditional on country and year fixed effects).

[7]To avoid the mechanical serial correlation that would arise from averaging the dependent variable, we take the top 1 percent share observations every 10 or 20 years. If an observation is missing at those dates and an observation exists within plus or minus two years, we use those neighboring observations. The results are very similar with averaging.

[8]This table uses two alternative measures of the capital share of national income, from the Penn World Tables and from the OECD. We do not present regressions using the marginal product of capital from Caselli and Feyrer (2007) because that measure is computed using the capital share of national income, making it mechanically correlated with the dependent variable in this table.

17. Get Real: A Review of Thomas Piketty's *Capital in the 21st Century*
Donald J. Boudreaux

[1]Commendably, he expresses concern about the potential for his tax regime to expand the size of government: "Before we can learn to efficiently organize public financing equivalent to two-thirds to three-quarters of national income," he cautions, "it would be good to improve

the organization and operation of the existing public sector" (Piketty 2014, 483). It would indeed be "good" to make such improvements.

20. Piketty's World Formula

Hans-Werner Sinn

[1]This article was first published in German under the title "Thomas Piketty's Weltformel," *Frankfurter Allgemeine Sonntagszeitung* no. 19, May 11, 2014, and made available in English as "Piketty's World Formula," *Ifo Viewpoint* no. 158, Munich, May 14, 2014.

21. A Controversial Assumption

Henri Lepage

[1]This article is taken from a longer, 2014 study published as "The Specter of Inequality" *Inference—International Review of Science* 1 (1), http://inference-review.com/article/the-specter-of-inequality.

Index

Note: Information in figures and tables is indicated by *f* and *t*; *n* designates a numbered note.

Contributors

Daron Acemoglu is professor of economics at the Massachusetts Institute of Technology. He is the author of several books, including *Introduction to Modern Economic Growth* (Princeton University Press, 2009), and with James Robinson, *Why Nations Fail: Origins of Power, Poverty and Prosperity* (Crown Publishers, 2012). He is the author or coauthor of more than a hundred articles in academic journals and 40 chapters in collective works.

Donald J. Boudreaux is a professor of economics at George Mason University and a member of its Mercatus research center. Former president of the Foundation for Economic Education, he is the author of numerous academic articles but has also published articles for newspapers such as the *Wall Street Journal*. He is the author of the book *Globalization* (Greenwood Press, 2007). He is an expert in globalization and the theory of public choice.

Richard V. Burkhauser is the Sarah Gibson Blanding Professor of Policy Analysis at the Cornell University College of Ecology. His research focuses on the impact of public policies on the economic behavior and well-being of vulnerable populations. He has published widely on those topics in journals of demography, economics, gerontology, and public policy.

Jean-Philippe Delsol is a tax lawyer, doctor of law, and president of the Institute for Research in Economic and Fiscal Issues. He regularly publishes articles in the French economic press. He is the author of *Pourquoi Je Vais Quitter la France* (Tatamis, 2013) and, with Nicolas Lecaussin, *À Quoi Servent les Riches* (JC Lattès, 2012, "What's the Use of the Rich").

James A. Dorn is a senior fellow at the Cato Institute in Washington and editor in chief of the *Cato Journal*. He has headed more than 10 collective works, notably about the Chinese economy and monetary economics. He regularly publishes articles in the *Wall Street Journal*, the *Financial Times*, and *Forbes*.

Nicholas Eberstadt is an economist at the American Enterprise Institute in Washington. He is also an adviser to the National Bureau of Asian Research and a member of the Global Leadership Forum at the World Economic Forum. His publications notably cover development, exterior aid, world health, demographics, and poverty. He is the author of numerous case studies and articles about North Korea, South Korea, Asia and the East, and the former Soviet Union. He is the author of *The Poverty of the Poverty Rate* (AEI Press, 2008).

Martin Feldstein is a professor of economics at Harvard University and president emeritus of the National Bureau of Economic Research. He presided over the Council of Economic Advisers from 1982 to 1984 and was an economic adviser to President Ronald Reagan. He has authored more than 300 articles and books. As a specialist in macroeconomics and public finance, he was a pioneer in pension reforms research. He is considered one of the most influential economists, not only at Harvard, where some of his students have also become famous economists, but also in the United States and around the world.

Salim Furth is a doctor of economics and a public policy analyst at the Heritage Foundation in Washington, D.C., in particular, the Center for Data Analysis. His research in public policy focuses on the role of the entrepreneur and entrepreneurial incentives in the United States. His academic research focuses on volatility in developing countries.

Chris Giles is a columnist at the *Financial Times* and has been its economics editor since 2004. Based in London, he has a particular focus on trends in the world economy and in the UK. Previously at the *Financial Times*, he was the economics editorial writer. He won the prestigious Wincott Award for journalism in 2014 and the British Journalism Award's business journalist of the year prize in the 2012. He has also won the Royal Statistical Society prize for excellence in journalism in both 2008 and 2012. Before joining the *FT* in 2000, Chris was an economics correspondent at the BBC. He started his career in research, spending seven years as an economist for the Institute for Fiscal Studies.

Randall Holcombe is a professor of economics at Florida State University and past president of the Public Choice Society. He is the author of 12 books, including *The Economic Foundations of Government* (New York University Press, 1993) and *Entrepreneurship and Economic Progress* (Routledge, 2006). He has published hundreds of articles in academic and professional reviews. He is a specialist in the analysis of public finances and public policy.

Nicolas Lecaussin is director of the Institute for Research in Economic and Fiscal Issues (IREF), a graduate of the Paris Institute of Political Studies (Sciences Po), founder of Entrepreneur Junior, and author of multiple books. Those include *Cet État Qui Tue la France* (Plon, 2005, *"This State which Kills France"*), *L'Absolutisme Efficace* (Plon, 2008, *"Effective Absolutism"*), *Au Secours, Ils Veulent la Peau du Capitalisme* (First Editions, 2009, *"Help, They Want the Skin of Capitalism"*), and *L'Obsession Antilibérale Française* (Libréchange, 2014, *"The French Antiliberal Obsession"*). He is also coauthor, with Jean-Philippe Delsol, of the book *À Quoi Servent les Riches* (JC Lattès, 2012, *"What's the Use of the Rich"*).

Henri Lepage is a French economist, director of the Turgot Institute, and former associate professor at Paris-Dauphine University. He has popularized in France the renewal of American economic thought, notably on the theory of public choice, supply side economics, competition theory, and institutional analysis. He was part of the French "new economists." He has written numerous books, including *Demain le Capitalisme* (Open Court, 1978, *Tomorrow, Capitalism*).

Álvaro Vargas Llosa is a Spanish-Peruvian writer and commentator on political life, notably Latin America. He is the author of a famous documentary for National Geographic about contemporary Latin America. He is a senior fellow at the Independent Institute, for which he writes regular columns and is the author of *Liberty for Latin America* (Farrar, Straus and Giroux, 2005).

Phillip W. Magness is a historian and director of academic programs at the Institute for Humane Studies at George Mason University. He is the author of *Colonization after Emancipation: Lincoln and the Movement for Black Resettlement* (University of Missouri Press, 2011). He has published in the *Constitutional Political Economy* and the *Journal of the Early Republic* and also in mainstream newspapers such as the *New York Times* and the *Daily Caller*. His research has also covered federal income tax in the United States. He received his doctorate from George Mason University.

Emmanuel Martin is an economist. He writes on current affairs and public policy for Geopolitical Intelligence Services and IREF, and in Francophone and international newspapers and magazines. He is the former director of the Institute for Economic Studies – Europe, an educational think tank based in Paris. He was the founder of LibreAfrique.org, a project of the Cato Institute and Atlas Network. He recently published *L'Argent des Autres* (Les Belles Lettres, 2014, *"Other People's Money"*).

Jeffrey Miron is a senior lecturer and the director of undergraduate studies in the Department of Economics at Harvard University. He is also the director of economic policy studies at the Cato Institute. Dr. Miron has previously served on the faculties of the

University of Michigan and Boston University; at the latter, he was department chairman for six years. He has been the recipient of an Olin fellowship from the National Bureau of Economic Research, an Earhart Foundation fellowship, and a Sloan Foundation faculty research fellowship. Dr. Miron holds a BA in economics from Swarthmore College and a PhD in economics from the Massachusetts Institute of Technology. Dr. Miron's area of expertise is the economics of libertarianism. He has written extensively on the economic case against drug prohibition.

Robert P. Murphy is an American economist at the Institute for Energy Research. His academic research has been published in the *American Journal of Economics and Sociology*, the *Review of Austrian Economics*, and the *Journal of Private Enterprise.* He has also been published in the *Washington Times*, *Forbes*, and *Barron's*. He is the author of the book *The Politically Incorrect Guide to the Great Depression and the New Deal* (Regnery Publishing, 2009).

Juan Ramón Rallo is a Spanish economist and director of the Juan de Mariana Institute. He is a professor and the director of the masters' economics program at the Centro de Estudios Superiores Online de Madrid Manuel Ayau. He received his doctorate at the Rey Juan Carlos University in Madrid. He is a prolific commentator on economic life and author of several books about the financial crisis.

James A. Robinson is a professor at Harris School of Public Policy at the University of Chicago. He is a specialist in comparative economic and political analysis and is particularly interested in the development of Latin America and Sub-Saharan Africa. He is the author of around 60 academic articles, notably with his coauthor Daron Acemoglu with whom he wrote the book *Why Nations Fail: Origins of Power, Poverty and Prosperity* (Crown Publishers, 2012).

Malin Sahlén is a Swedish economist and is responsible for the analysis of political economy for the Swedish think tank Timbro. She has worked for the Confederation of Swedish Businesses, where she played an active role in the debate over reforming the job market. She has published a book on youth unemployment.

Hans-Werner Sinn is a German economist and professor of economics and public finance at Munich University. He is president of the Institute for Economic Research and an adviser to the German minister of the economy. He has published tens of academic articles. Many of his works are famous, such as *Casino Capitalism* (Oxford University Press, 2010), in which he gave his interpretation of the financial crisis, and *The Euro Trap* (Oxford University Press, 2014). His contributions to the discipline of economics are numerous.

Michael Tanner is a senior fellow at the Cato Institute in Washington, D.C. His tribunes are regularly republished in *The Wall Street Journal*, the *Washington Post*, and the *New York Times*. He recently coedited *Replacing Obamacare* (Cato Institute, 2012) and is the author of multiple works such as *Leviathan on the Right: How Big Government Conservatism Brought Down the Republican Revolution* (Cato Institute, 2007). He is a specialist in pension reforms and is considered one of the architects of the movement in favor of individual retirement accounts.

Institute for Research in Economic and Fiscal Issues

www.irefeurope.org

***IREF** is a European think tank founded in 2002 by members of civil society from academic and professional backgrounds with the aim of developing independent research in economic and fiscal subjects. The institute is independent of any party or political organization. It also refuses government funding.*

IREF publishes studies, reports, books, and a weekly newsletter. Its publications deal with various themes such as French and worldwide taxation, property rights, globalization and the free market, public policy, pensions, health, and ecology.

The IREF team investigates fiscal and taxation questions from a free market perspective. IREF is working toward efficient, noninvasive, and small government that is able to partner with the private sector. Originally from different countries, the IREF team members use a comparative scientific approach and recognize the globalization process and its consequences for tax competition.

Contact: Nicolas Lecaussin
Director of IREF – Institute for Research in Economic and Fiscal Issues (*www.irefeurope.org*)

Cato Institute

Founded in 1977, the Cato Institute is a public policy research foundation dedicated to broadening the parameters of policy debate to allow consideration of more options that are consistent with the principles of limited government, individual liberty, and peace. To that end, the Institute strives to achieve greater involvement of the intelligent, concerned lay public in questions of policy and the proper role of government.

The Institute is named for *Cato's Letters*, libertarian pamphlets that were widely read in the American Colonies in the early 18th century and played a major role in laying the philosophical foundation for the American Revolution.

Despite the achievement of the nation's Founders, today virtually no aspect of life is free from government encroachment. A pervasive intolerance for individual rights is shown by government's arbitrary intrusions into private economic transactions and its disregard for civil liberties. And while freedom around the globe has notably increased in the past several decades, many countries have moved in the opposite direction, and most governments still do not respect or safeguard the wide range of civil and economic liberties.

To address those issues, the Cato Institute undertakes an extensive publications program on the complete spectrum of policy issues. Books, monographs, and shorter studies are commissioned to examine the federal budget, Social Security, regulation, military spending, international trade, and myriad other issues. Major policy conferences are held throughout the year, from which papers are published thrice yearly in the *Cato Journal*. The Institute also publishes the quarterly magazine *Regulation*.

In order to maintain its independence, the Cato Institute accepts no government funding. Contributions are received from foundations, corporations, and individuals, and other revenue is generated from the sale of publications. The Institute is a nonprofit, tax-exempt, educational foundation under Section 501(c)3 of the Internal Revenue Code.

Cato Institute
1000 Massachusetts Ave., N.W.
Washington, D.C. 20001
www.cato.org